Intersex and Identity

Intersex and Identity

The Contested Self

SHARON E. PREVES

RUTGERS UNIVERSITY PRESS

New Brunswick, New Jersey, and London

Library of Congress Cataloging-in-Publication Data

Preves, Sharon E., 1968–
    Intersex and identity : the contested self / Sharon E. Preves.
      p. cm.
    ISBN 0–8135–3228–0 (cloth) — ISBN 0–8135–3229–9 (pbk.)
    1. Hermaphroditism—Psychological aspects. 2. Hermaphroditism—Social aspects.
    3. Gender identity—Social aspects. I. Title.

    RC883 .P74 2003
    616.6'94—dc21

                          2002012493

British Cataloging-in-Publication information is available from the British Library.

Manufactured in the United States of America

For those with the wisdom and courage to forge a new path

Contents

Illustrations

Acknowledgments

I BEGAN THIS PROJECT as a young graduate student perplexed and troubled by the medical sex assignment of intersexed children. After my initial introduction to the subject in a course on gender and science, I wanted to know more. I wanted to know how people experience and cope with sexual difference in a culture that demands sexual conformity. So, I set out in search of answers. I had no idea that during the process of my research, I would encounter the beginnings of a social movement and witness firsthand the impact of this movement on the treatment and perception of intersexed children and adults. I also didn't know that I would meet so many incredible people along the way, some of whom have profoundly changed my life. The people who generously consented to share their most private and emotional life stories with me amazed and touched me time and again. Many shared a spirit of courage, tenacity, and creativity that is testimony to the resilience of the human spirit. I am privileged to have been enlightened by their experiences.

The interest that was piqued ten years ago in that gender and science course evolved to become my dissertation research and culminated in the writing of this book. While these pages may reflect a solo endeavor, my work would not have been possible without the sage guidance and support of many people, first and foremost my dissertation committee at the University of Minnesota: Jeylan Mortimer, Walter Bockting, Elizabeth Heger Boyle, Amy Kaminsky, Douglas Hartmann, and Jacquelyn Zita. Their commitment to me and to my research has been unwavering. The timeliness and thoroughness of their feedback is second to none and they have gone to exceptional lengths to mentor me in the fields of sociology, social psychology, sexology, and feminist studies. I have benefited profoundly from their direction, and I am honored to count them among my mentors, colleagues, and friends.

Several others have given generously of their time, providing comments throughout my research and writing, and on earlier chapters and drafts. For this I thank Nico Taranovsky, Kristin Mapel Bloomberg, Alice Preves, Navid Mohseni, Laura Preves Helgeson, Jane Neroni, Jane McLeod, Jennifer Pierce, Ira Reiss, Lorie Schabo Grabowski, Amy Kaler, Pamela Aronson, Sylvia Tamale, Debbie Engelen-Eigles, Marit Berntson, Perry Seymour, Britt Abel, Nathan Stormer, Gail Lippincott, Greg Preves, Alice Dreger, Cheryl Chase, Martha Coventry, Eric Mein, and the editorial staff at the University Publishing Group, *Current Sociology*, and *Signs: Journal of Women in Culture and History*.

David Myers is an exceptionally enthusiastic and dedicated editor. His encouragement, timely feedback, insightful comments, and reviewer's suggestions helped give this book its shape. I also thank the production staff at Rutgers, including my production coordinator, Alison Hack, and copyeditor, Debbie Self, for their invaluable assistance during the publication process.

Family and friends provided me with much-needed love and support throughout this work. For the walks, laughter, food, and song, I thank Nico Taranovsky; Marty, Colfax, Vladimir, and Alexei Preves-Taranovsky; Laura, Scott, Mariah, Hannah, and Faith Helgeson; Alice Preves; Judith and David Anderson; Jane, Del, and Hilary Neroni; Todd McGowen; Jen Gehrig; Lorie Schabo Grabowski; Deb, Jon, Ellen, and Aaron Halvorson; Barbara Bedney; Susan Rothbaum and Kathie Bailey; Jo Devlin and Linda Crawford; Jane Levin and Judy Reisman; Pat Levine; Hannah Dunevitz; Barbara Block; Carole Evenchik; David Harris; Annabelle Crips; Greg Preves; Paulette Krebill; and Jan Sajwaj. Your presence in my life brings me balance, depth of meaning, and an abundance of joy.

This was an expensive project because I traveled throughout North America to complete it. Doing so would not have been possible without the generous financial support of many sources, including a Hanna Grant from Hamline University and several grants from the University of Minnesota's Graduate School and Department of Sociology. My family generously provided me additional subsidies throughout the research. For this I thank my mother, Alice Preves, and my aunt and uncle, Judith and David Anderson.

My colleagues and students at Hamline University and Grand Valley State University were wonderfully inspirational and supportive during my writing of this book. From Hamline, I thank my mentors and colleagues Kristin Mapel Bloomberg, Navid Mohseni, Melissa Embser-Herbert, Martin Markowitz, and Maggie Jensen for their support of and interest in my work throughout this project, from beginning to end. From Grand Valley, I thank my colleagues Mary deYoung and Fran McCrea for their guidance, humor, and unwavering support. I am also indebted to Christine Mack and Lisa Mallon for their help in transcribing the interviews, and to Leslie Zavadil and Tana Adams for their invaluable editorial and organizational assistance.

Most importantly, this book would have been little more than a dream if it were not for those of you who so graciously shared your stories with me. I thank you for giving of yourselves so willingly and so freely. I thank you for supporting my research and I commend you for your courage in speaking out.

Intersex and Identity

Chapter 1   Beyond Pink and Blue

If doctors really want to do something for their intersexed patients, I would say the first thing is [to] put the intersex person in touch with other people who are intersexed. Number two is see number one. And number three is see number one. That's it. Doctors think that you're going to kill yourself if you find out the truth. People kill themselves because they feel alone and isolated and helpless; that's why they kill themselves. When doctors don't tell their patients the truth, they're cutting them off from the opportunity of incredible support.

——Excerpt from interview with Sherri

Recently I participated in a cultural diversity fieldtrip with twenty-two second graders in St. Paul, Minnesota. When I arrived at their school, the kids were squirrelly with anticipation. They were a colorful and varied bunch—some were tall and thin, others short and stout. Moreover, they were from a variety of racial and ethnic backgrounds and spoke nearly a half dozen native languages. When it was time to begin our community walking tour, the teachers attempted to bring the busy group to order quickly. How did they go about doing so? They told the children to form two lines: one for girls and the other for boys. The children did so seamlessly because they had been asked to line up in this manner countless number of times before. Within moments, the children were quiet and attentive. I was struck then, as I had been many times before, by how often and in the most basic ways societies are organized by a distinction between sexes. Even with children of every shape and color, the gender divide worked as a sure way to bring order to chaos. "Girls in one line, boys in the other." But sometimes the choice between the lines—and sexes—isn't so easy.

Which line would you join? Think about it seriously for a minute. How do you know whether to line up with the girls or the boys? For that matter, what sex or gender *are* you and how did you *become* the gender you are? Moreover, how do you *know* what sex and gender you are? Who decides? These questions may seem ridiculous. You may be saying to yourself, "Of course I know what gender I am; forget this book." But really stop to think about how you know what sex you are and how you acquired your gender. Most of us have been taught that sex is anatomical and gender is social. What's more, many of us have never had the occasion to explore our gender or sexual identities, because neither has given us cause for reflection. Much like Caucasians who say they "have none" when asked to explore their racial identity, many women and men find it difficult to be reflective about how they know and "do" gender.[1]

This book explores what happens to people who, from the time of their birth or early adolescence, inhabit bodies whose very anatomy does not afford them an easy choice between the gender lines.[2] Every day babies are born with bodies that are deemed sexually ambiguous, and with regularity they are surgically altered to reflect the sexual anatomy associated with "standard" female or male sex assignment. There are numerous ways to respond to this plurality of physical type, including no response at all. Because sex and gender operate as inflexible and central organizing principles of daily existence in this culture, such indifference is rare if not nonexistent. Instead, interference with sex and gender norms are cast as a major disturbance to social order, and people go to remarkable lengths to eradicate threats to the norm, even though they occur with great regularity.

Recent estimates indicate that approximately one or two in every two thousand infants are born with anatomy that some people regard as sexually ambiguous. These frequency estimates vary widely and are, at best, inconclusive. Those I provide here are based on an exhaustive review of recent medical literature.[3] This review suggests that approximately one or two per two thousand children are born with bodies considered appropriate for genital reconstruction surgery because they do not conform to socially accepted norms of sexual anatomy. Moreover, nearly 2 percent are born with chromosome, gonad, genital, or hormone features that could be considered "intersexed"; that is, children born with ambiguous genitalia, sexual organs, or sex chromosomes. Additional estimates report the frequency of this sexual variance as comprising approximately 1 to 4 percent of all births.[4]

These estimates differ so much because definitions of sexual ambiguity vary tremendously.[5] This is largely because distinctions between female and male bodies are actually on more of a continuum rather than a dichotomy. The criteria for what counts as female or male, or sexually ambiguous for that matter, are human standards. That is, bodies that are considered normal or abnormal are not inherently that way. They are, rather, classified as aberrant or customary by social agreement.[6] We have, as humans, created categories for bodies that fit the norm and those that don't, as well as a systematic method of surgically attempting to correct or erase sexual variation. That we have done so is evidence of the regularity with which sexual variation occurs.

Melanie Blackless and colleagues suggest that the total frequency of nongenital sexual variation (cases of intersexed chromosomes or internal sexual organs) is much higher than one in two thousand.[7] They conclude that using a more inclusive definition of sexual ambiguity would yield frequency estimates closer to one or two per one hundred births, bringing us back to the 1 to 2 percent range.

To put these numbers in perspective, although its occurrence has only recently begun to be openly discussed, physical sexual ambiguity occurs about as often as the well-known conditions of cystic fibrosis and Down syndrome.[8] Since there are approximately four million babies born annually in the United States, a conservative estimate is that about two to four thousand babies are born per year in this country with features of their anatomy that vary from the physical characteristics typically associated with females and males.[9] Some are born with genitalia that are difficult to characterize as clearly female or male. Others have sex chromosomes that are neither XX nor XY, but some other combination, such as X, XXY, or chromosomes that vary throughout the cells of their bodies, changing from XX to XY from cell to cell. Still others experience unexpected physical changes at puberty, when their bodies exhibit secondary sex characteristics that are surprisingly "opposite" their sex of assignment. Some forms of sexual ambiguity are inherited genetically, while others are brought on by hormonal activity during gestation, or by prescription medication women take during pregnancy. Regardless of its particular manifestation or cause, most forms of physical sexual anatomy that vary from the norm are medically classified and treated as forms of intersexuality, or hermaphroditism.

Take Claire's experience as an example.[10] Claire is a middle-class white woman and mother of two teenage daughters who works as a writer and editor. She was forty-four years old when she conveyed the following story to me during a four-hour interview that took place in her home. Claire underwent a clitorectomy when she was six years old at her parents' insistence, after clinicians agreed that her clitoris was just "too large" and they had to intervene. The size of her clitoris seemed to cause problems not for young Claire, but for the adults around her. Indeed, there was nothing ambiguous about Claire's sex before the surgery. She has XX chromosomes, has functioning female reproductive organs, and later in life went through a physically uneventful female puberty. Claire's experience illustrates that having a large clitoris is perceived as a physical trait dangerous to existing notions of gender and sexuality, despite the sexual pleasure it could have given Claire and her future sexual partners. In fact, doctors classify a large clitoris as a medical condition referred to as "clitoral megaly" or "clitoral hypertrophy." Conversely, small penises for anatomical boys, are classified as a medical problem called "micropenis." These are topics that I will discuss further in chapter 2.

Reflecting on the reasons for the clitorectomy she underwent at the age of six, Claire said, "I don't feel that my sex was ambiguous at all. There was never that question. But I'm sure that [clitorectomies] have been done forever because parents just [don't] like big clitorises because they look too much like a penis." Even more alarming are the physical and emotional outcomes of genital surgery that might be experienced by the patient. About the after effects of her surgery, Claire said,

> They just took the clitoris out and then whip stitched the hood
> together, so it's sort of an odd-looking thing. I don't know what they
> were hoping to preserve, although I remember my father thinking that
> if someone saw me, it would look normal because there's just a little
> skin poking out between my lips so it wouldn't look strange. I
> remember I was in the hospital for five days. And then it just got
> better and everything was forgotten, until I finally asked about it
> when I was twelve. [There was] total and complete silence. You know,
> it was never, never mentioned. I know you know what that does. I was
> just in agony trying to figure out who I was. And, you know,
> why . . . what sex I was. And feeling like a freak, which is a very
> common story. And then when I was twelve, I asked my father what
> had been done to me. And his answer was, "Don't be so self-examin-
> ing." And that was it. I never asked again [until I was thirty-five].

During the course of my research I spoke with many other adults across North America who had childhood experiences remarkably similar to Claire's. Their stories are laden with family and medical secrecy, shame, and social isolation, as well as perseverance and strength of spirit, and eventual pride in their unique bodies and perspectives.

Personal Narratives

Being labeled as a misfit, by peers, by family members, or by medical diagnosis and treatment, is no doubt a challenge to one's identity development and stability. This is especially true for children whose bodies render traditional gender classification ineffective, for there is seemingly no place to belong without being gendered, especially during childhood. Negotiating identity, one's basic sense of place and self, is a challenge for many of us, and is potentially far more challenging for people whose sex is called into question. The social expectation for gender stability and conformity is prevalent across social spheres. Nearly every aspect of social life is organized by one's sex assignment—from schooling and relationships, to employment and religion, sports and entertainment, medicine and law. Because North American cultures are structured by gender, successful participation in society's organizations and personal relationships requires gender categorization. Many of us negotiate questions of sex and gender with little effort. Others, however, do not have the luxury or ease of fitting neatly into a dual-gendered culture.

In an attempt to understand how intersexuals experience and cope with their marginality in a society that demands sexual conformity, I turned to them directly for answers. In the end, I interviewed thirty-seven individuals throughout North America whose bodies have been characterized by others as intersexed.

Previous research on this topic has explored the history, procedures, and clinical success of medical sex assignment, but has rarely focused on questions addressing quality of life for patients who undergo medical intervention. In addition, most research in this area has been either case study research or quantitative in nature. These studies are valuable and have contributed significantly to the fields of gender identity research and medical sex assignment. Despite these notable contributions, the scope of this research has been limited. Moreover, it is difficult to gain a deep and broad understanding of people's experiences using either quantitative or case study research because quantitative measures typically limit answers to closed-ended responses and case studies often focus on only one or two people's experiences.

In turning directly to people characterized as intersexed for answers, I attempted to bridge this gap when I conducted in-depth life history interviews with more than three dozen people who were born sexually ambiguous. My research methods were geared toward gleaning a deep understanding of these individuals' experiences and lives. Such depth of understanding is commonly achieved through qualitative life history research. Given that there has been very little follow-up research with adults born intersexed, and the success and value of medical sex assignment has recently been called into question, such in-depth exploration of their experiences and perspectives is crucial to a more nuanced understanding of the implications of living with bodies characterized as sexually ambiguous and the long-term impact of medical sex assignment procedures.

The heart of this book is built upon the personal narratives intersex activists and support group members relayed to me during these in-depth face-to-face interviews. Focusing on the stories told to me during these life history interviews is particularly important in the study of intersexuality because most research in this area has centered upon physiological and biomedical concerns related to intersexuality, rather than on the experiences of intersexuals themselves.

HOW I BECAME INTERESTED IN THE PROJECT

I began this research in 1993, when I was a first-year doctoral student in medical sociology at the University of California, San Francisco.[11] I was enrolled in a class on medicine and the family and was given an assignment to conduct research on some aspect of medicine as it relates to families. My interest in intersexuality was sparked earlier that spring when I read Anne Fausto-Sterling's article "The Five Sexes: Why Male and Female Are Not Enough."[12] After reading this article, I was compelled to address several questions that remained unanswered, the foremost of which was, "What is the experience for individuals who were born sexually ambiguous and medically assigned to a category of female or male?"[13] As I began to formulate a topic for my class research assignment, I focused first on families' involvement with sex assignment decisions. For this task I looked for research on parents' experiences with sexually ambiguous children, and found nothing. I examined research literature in social work, psychology, and sociology and found neither information about families and intersex, nor information about intersex as a social category. Then I went in search of former patient narratives and came up dry. When I finally turned to the medical literature, I hit the proverbial jackpot. What I found was a plethora of clinical articles detailing the diagnosis and treatment of sexual ambiguity.

While completing this early project, I was astonished to find that so little research had been conducted with former patients or families about the social experiences and outcomes of these medical procedures. However, around that same time, the publication of Fausto-Sterling's "Five Sexes" article acted as a catalyst for some adult intersexuals to come forward and tell their stories. From this point, they began to form intersex support and advocacy groups, spurring the beginnings of a burgeoning intersex social movement. Due to the fact that these events coincided with my own research on intersex, I became aware of the important opportunity to speak with intersexuals about their experiences and perspectives firsthand.

INTERVIEWING MEMBERS OF AN INVISIBLE POPULATION

Initially, recruiting willing interviewees for my study was a challenge because sexual ambiguity is generally not visible, and members of this population typically don't self-identify as intersexed and therefore are generally not mobilized. During the course of my research, however, several intersex support and advocacy groups either emerged or came to my attention. Because they are a self-selected group, members of these organizations cannot be expected to represent the diversity of experience within the intersex population. In fact, given the difficulty of identifying members of this population, it is not possible to get a truly representative sample. Rather, these organizations served as a strategic and theoretically promising sampling base, given the social context of an emerging intersex social movement and my interest in the experience and process of social marginalization.

I began to recruit subjects for my study by mailing information packets to the sixteen currently established intersex support organizations in the United States and Canada. I was amazed at how quickly people responded to my initial study announcement when I heard back from four different support group leaders within two weeks. I felt the need for this study was validated when the first person responded by calling within three days of my initial mailing. I assume she called the day she received my packet, as she lived several states away.

In contrast with prior research in this area, which is primarily medical and quantitative in nature, my approach is sociological and qualitative, with in-depth interviews with adult intersexuals serving as the primary data source. I conducted intensive interviews with adult intersexuals to address their subjective experiences with intersexuality. The interviews concentrated on participants' life histories with specific attention to how they learned of their intersexuality, their experiences with medical intervention, as well as how they dealt with issues of identity development, and what significance they placed on social support. In addition, the interviews explored participants' sexual identities, their experience of gender and sexual identity development, challenges associated with being intersexed, and how they respond to those challenges. (See chapter 7: Methodological Appendix for further information on how I conducted the research.)

In conducting this research I attempt to inform and reshape existing theory on intersex clinical management, using the technique of the extended case method suggested by Michael Burawoy.[14] In the traditional use of this method, I reevaluate an existing theory via the analysis of an anomalous case. I use Erving Goffman's theory of stigmatized identity, which articulates how people who are socially outcast internalize feelings of self-despair. In particular,

I focus on Goffman's expectation that deviant individuals will attempt to conform or pass as normal. I evaluate Goffman's work on identity management as it relates to the negotiation of the self, with special regard for potentially stigmatized individuals.[15] In the interview guide, I also incorporate the theories outlined by Candace West and Don Zimmerman, and later by Judith Butler, to explore these individuals' responses to anatomical disruptions of gender binarism.[16]

Allowing individual voices to be heard through the use of life history interviews is particularly important in the study of intersexuality because most research in this area has been centered only on physiological and biomedical concerns related to intersexuality. I employed the method of phenomenological interviewing, which is "an interviewee-guided investigation of a lived experience."[17] In using this technique, I asked intersexuals to relay the most central elements of their life histories related to intersex, within a thematic framework I created through extensive literature review.

While my primary method of data collection was in-depth interviewing, I employed additional methods, as is common in fieldwork. In this regard, I supplemented intersexuals' narratives with my own field notes on the process of conducting the research, detailing my interactions with participants, my own feelings throughout the project, and key themes as they emerged during analysis. In addition, I used two self-administered instruments that I created for this project: a life course gender identity time line and a sexual identity questionnaire (see chapter 7: Methodological Appendix).

In the end, I interviewed thirty-seven intersexed adults from March of 1997 to September of 1998. Research participants ranged in age from twenty to sixty-five with a mean age of forty, and lived in nineteen different states and Canadian provinces. At the time of interview, 24 percent of interviewees were living as a gender different from their sex of assignment and rearing; six were transitioning or had transitioned from male to female, and three from female to male. In 51 percent of the sample, intersexuality was apparent at birth or in infancy due to genital ambiguity; for 49 percent intersexuality was not apparent until puberty.

The sample was exceedingly well educated, in that all are high school graduates and 96 percent have at least some college education. Seventy-eight percent are college graduates, 43 percent have at least some graduate education, and 27 percent have graduate degrees. Thirty-eight percent were living with a spouse or domestic partner, and 27 percent were single and not dating. The other 35 percent were engaged in some form of dating or monogamous relationship. Sixteen percent reported that they were not sexually active. Of those who were, 46 percent engaged in sexual activity with partners living in the same gender role. That is, 46 percent engaged in sexual relations that are "homosexual" in outward appearance. Twenty-seven percent of the sample elected to use their real first names in the study instead of a pseudonym. Interestingly, 24 percent had also changed their legal names, taking on and using new names in their daily lives rather than the ones they were given at birth. Despite my attempts to talk with a diversity of people, 89 percent of the sample is Caucasian, and 11 percent is Latino/a, Asian/Pacific Islander, Native American, or biracial. Forty percent were employed in medical fields or in social services, 14 percent as teachers and writers, and 14 percent were unemployed.

I conducted the interviews in a private, face-to-face format, primarily in participants' homes.[18] Privacy was essential for these meetings because the interview guide covered many sensitive topics. Face-to-face encounters were important for this reason as well. Building a feeling of rapport with interviewees was particularly significant given the sensitivity of the subject matter. Face-to-face meetings also provided ample contextual data and opportunities to glean more from people's lives than their spoken words provided. Finally, based on recurrent feedback I received from participants, meeting face to face allowed for a valuable interview experience.

Organization of the Book

Throughout my research, I have heard stories of powerlessness, violation, reclamation, and personal empowerment. Interview after interview, participants shared stories of feeling scrutinized and sexualized by medical professionals, of being treated as oddities and freaks, of lacking control over their own bodies, and of the resulting shame and secrecy of such experiences. They also spoke of arduous battles to gain accurate information about their bodies and attempts to find other intersexuals—aiming to piece together a puzzle whose solution was sure to hold the key to identity. In spite of these difficulties, participants were largely capable of overcoming this sense of despair and were able to claim the power of their difference.

In order to make sense of medical sex assignment and the stories and activism of intersexed adults, I weave several bodies of literature and theoretical perspectives into the pages of this book. I begin by exploring the importance of gender to social structure and social order. This context is vital to understanding the experiences of those who are labeled as sexually ambiguous, as well as the objectives of medical sex assignment. In doing so, I draw on the work of several symbolic interactionists and gender theorists to explore gender as a social process and social structure that is central to identity formation, social relations, and the ability to function in society.

In chapter 2, I examine the social context within which the current medical paradigm originally took hold and the tenets of medical sex assignment, with special attention to the historical development of medicine as an institutional authority on gender and sexuality. I provide this history to illustrate that there have been institutional shifts in responding not only to intersexual "deviance," but to other types of nonconformity as well. In this chapter, I incorporate the work of several medical sociologists, as well as the work of historians of medicine and sexuality.

In chapter 3, I explore how interviewees experienced medical sex "normalizing" procedures. I turn to participants' narratives and experiences to explore the impact of medical sex assignment on the formation of identity. Participants spoke repeatedly of sex assignment procedures as compounding feelings of alienation and shame, rather than alleviating the feelings of social isolation and exclusion as they were intended to do. Here I again incorporate the work of several symbolic interactionists and social psychologists to explore the impact of stigmatization on identity formation and social interaction.

I explore in chapter 4 the major social changes, such as the gay pride movement, that set the groundwork for the current mobilization and activism of intersexuals who are critical of surgical sex assignment of sexually ambiguous children. I provide this context as a backdrop to participants' stories of coming to terms with their intersexuality and their stories of seeking others like them who have been similarly outcast. This chapter is the foundation for understanding the intersex social movement and a reworking of intersexed identity from one of stigma and shame, to that of pride and potential activism.

In chapter 5, I once again turn to the narratives of former patients for further insight into intersex mobilization, empowerment, and pride. As in the previous two chapters, I apply models of coming out and community empowerment and note a similar process of coming to terms with difference that has been identified in other marginal groups, such as people with disabilities or those who identify as gay, lesbian, bisexual, or transgender (GLBT).

Identity-based social movements are powerful to behold. They teach volumes about the power and efficacy of individual or small group action on making social change. In the case of redefining sexual ambiguity in a more positive and empowering light, individual and collective action has had a tremendous impact in a very short period of time. I conclude the book, in chapter 6, with a discussion of the impact of such change, and suggest direction for future action and research with parents and doctors of intersex children. Chapter 7 is a methodological appendix, where I provide more detail about the research I conducted that serves as the backbone of this book.

Before discussing interviewees' personal narratives in more depth, I will first set the context for their experiences by exploring the predominant cultural agreements and understandings about gender and medicine that shape all of our lives so profoundly.

Intersex is a Social, Not Medical, Problem

The occurrence of physical sexual variation is a given. How to respond to that variation is not. In fact, there is tremendous disagreement about what that response ought to be. This book went to press during a long and heated debate between intersex activists, scholars, and clinicians all seemingly dedicated to a similar goal: destigmatizing people who are born with sexual ambiguity. Primary points of contention between these groups are whether or not most medical intervention on intersex children is necessary for their physiological or mental health, or whether these procedures are primarily cosmetic or potentially physiologically and psychologically harmful and alienating.

The jury is still out on this issue, and has been for a long time. Many people say there isn't valid evidence to support continued medical attempts to efface sexual variation. Others dismiss the critiques of intersex activists as representative of only an unhappy minority. What is clear is that a considerable number of former patients have recently come forward to speak out against procedures they consider harmful not only to their lives, but also to the lives of their families and culture at large. I explore their stories and what they teach us at length in the pages of this book. Furthermore, I frame their stories with a sociological discussion of gender, the history of intersex medicalization, recent mobilization of intersexed adults, and the implications of their activism on identity negotiation, medical practice, academe, and cultural norms.

While being born with indeterminate sexual organs indeed problematizes a binary understanding of sex and gender, several studies show—and there seems to be general consensus (even among the doctors performing the "normalizing" operations)—that most children with ambiguous sexual anatomy do not require medical intervention for their physiological health.[19] Nevertheless, the majority of sexually ambiguous infants are medically assigned a definitive sex, often undergoing repeated genital surgeries and ongoing hormone treatments, to "correct" their variation from the norm.

It is my argument that medical treatments to create genitally *unambiguous* children are not performed entirely or even predominantly for the sake of preventing stigmatization and trauma to the child. Rather, these elaborate, expensive, and risky procedures are performed to maintain social order for the institutions and adults that surround that child. Newborns are completely oblivious to the rigid social conventions to which their families and caregivers adhere. Threats to the duality of sex and gender undermine inflexibly gendered occupational, education, and family structures, as well as heterosexuality itself. After all, if one's sex is in doubt, how would they identify their sexual orientation, given that heterosexuality, homosexuality, and even bisexuality are all based on a sexual binary? So, when adults encounter a healthy baby with a body that is not easily "sexed," they may understandably experience an inability to imagine a happy and successful future for that child. They may wonder how the child will fit in at school and with its peers, and how the child will negotiate dating and sexuality, as well as family and a career. But most parents don't find a real need to address these questions until years after a child's birth. Furthermore, it is my contention that parents and caregivers of intersexed children don't need to be so concerned about addressing the "personal troubles" of their children either. Rather, we should all turn our attention to the "public issues" and problems wrought by unwavering, merciless adherence to sex and gender binarism.[20]

That medical sex assignment procedures could be considered cosmetic raises several important questions, including the human influences in constructing definitions of health and pathology. Bodies are classified as healthy or pathological (or as normal and abnormal) through social expectations, human discourse, and human interaction. As a result, what is seen as normal or standard in one culture and time is seen as aberrant and strange in another. Indeed, deviance itself is created socially through human actions, beliefs, and judgments.[21] Consider Gilbert Herdt's anthropological research in Papua New Guinea. The Sambia males of Papua New Guinea believe that they become masculine by ingesting the semen of adult men. In order to become virile, therefore, Sambian boys perform oral sex on and ingest the semen of adult men.[22] According to Herdt, such activity is considered a standard rite of passage to manhood among the Sambia in Papua New Guinea, much like a bar or bat mitzvah is seen as a customary ritual of young adulthood among Jews.

I offer the above example to illustrate that definitions of normal and abnormal vary tremendously by culture. That said, there is no reason to consider intersex as necessarily problematic in itself. In fact, since physical sexual ambiguity has been shown to be a cause of health problems in only very rare cases, sexual ambiguity could be considered a *social* problem, rather than a physical problem. Rare physical problems do occur in cases where eliminating bodily waste, such as urine and feces, is difficult because of internal physiological complications or infrequent cases of salt-wasting congenital adrenal hyperplasia, which is a condition where children have hyperactive adrenal glands and hormone therapy is required to regulate the endocrine system.[23] Because Western cultures place such strong emphasis on sexual (and other forms of) categorization, intersex ambiguity causes major social disruption and discomfort. If there were less concern about gender, there would be less concern about gender variation. Because intersex is often identified in a medical setting by physicians during childbirth or during a pediatric appointment in later childhood, the social response to intersex "deviance" is largely medical.

The Salience of Gender

There is tremendous emphasis on sexual categorization in this culture and in many others. As a matter of illustration, try—for just one hour—to stop yourself from classifying others' gender as you encounter them. Doing so is nearly impossible and will most likely heighten your awareness of the gender attribution process we go through every day to sort people into one category or another.[24] Of course we go through this classification process with other visible characteristics as well, such as race, ethnicity, body type, age, and attractiveness, but the importance of gender attribution to basic social interaction may outweigh the others. For example, we may be familiar (and therefore more comfortable) with people who are of mixed race, in contrast with people who are intersexed. While there is still a tendency to simplify the complexities of racial heritage by classifying people into one category or another, racial ambiguity does not cause the level of discomfort that sexual ambiguity does—in large part because of our familiarity with persons of mixed race.

Gender or sexual ambiguity is less integrated into the cultural mainstream and is therefore experienced as more disruptive. Consider the popularity of the "It's Pat" skit from the *Saturday Night Live* television program. The subject of this long-lived skit, and subsequent movie, was the troubling ambiguity of Pat's sex. Pat's androgyny caused such a stir, and was such a familiar quandary for TV and studio audiences, that the popularity of this skit endured endless attempts by its characters to unravel the mystery of Pat's sex. If gender attribution were less important to social interaction and belonging, the skit would have been a flop because audiences wouldn't have found it meaningful or interesting.

Why is gender attribution so meaningful to social order and why does the inability to classify someone's sex cause such a major disruption? In an effort to answer this question, I turn to the symbolic interactionist tradition of sociology. Symbolic interactionists study how people present and perceive themselves and one another in social interaction. More specifically, interactionist sociologists explore the tools or props people use, such as costumes and official titles, to designate their status, power, and role in relation to one another for the sake of making social interaction more coherent and predictable. An interesting aspect of this framework is its contribution to understanding how people create meaning, agreement, categorization, and stratification through human interaction. Working from this interactionist tradition, sociologists such as Erving Goffman and Eviatar Zerubavel claim that being able to classify ourselves and others into distinct categories is essential to smooth and meaningful social interaction.[25]

In his study of interaction rituals, Goffman concluded that we seek information about others, such as their gender or racial identification, in an attempt to define the rules and parameters for a given social exchange.[26] According to Goffman, people engage in this process of classifying others in order to make sense of the world around them so that they know what to expect from social encounters and how to act appropriately. Those not familiar with Goffman's theory might be saying, "I don't need to categorize someone in order to know how to act with them. I'm just myself, no matter the situation." Such confidence is important, but most likely exists alongside an unconscious process of sorting people into familiar categories to make interaction go more smoothly. Take e-mail or Internet chat rooms as an example. Unless you actually know the person beyond the electronic medium, you have no way to verify people's claims to identity online. Have you ever thought you were e-mailing a woman or man, and discovered your "gender sensor" was off? I recently had an experience like this of my own. A journal editor whom I knew only by name e-mailed to ask if I was willing to write a book review for a journal. I was delighted to be invited to do so, and e-mailed this person several times during the process of writing the piece, all the while thinking I was interacting with a man. Months later I discovered my mistake, and wondered if I would have presented myself differently or interacted in a different manner had I known the editor was female. Why on earth would I have considered altering my behavior based on someone else's gender?

According to Michael Schwalbe and Douglas Mason-Schrock doing so would be not only sensible, but also predictable. They argue that by attaining information about others, we begin to formulate social expectations, allowing us to prepare for and predict the tone or projected outcome of subsequent social encounters.[27] This ability to classify allows for some comfort in being able to predict, certainly with some inaccuracy, what to expect from people with whom we interact in daily social life. Given this line of thinking, when one is unable, for whatever reason, to assess a person's gender, the rules for social negotiation with that person are suddenly made unclear simply because the attempts to classify her/his gender fail. Relating this failure directly to the development of self, John Hewitt says that when an ascribed characteristic, such as sex, receives a negative evaluation from others, low self-esteem may result, for we base our own self-concept, in part, on others' evaluations. In fact, Hewitt argues that individuals' claims about identity are meaningful only when validated by others.[28] In this sense, one's gender identity or presentation of gender (or any other type of identity) requires reinforcement and acceptance from others in order for the identity claim to be successfully maintained.

Gender Socialization, Norms, and Attribution throughout the Life Course

Whether we are conscious of it or not, gender structures our most basic sense of self as well as our primary social institutions. From issues of identity development and everyday social interaction, to the structure of family, economic, political, religious, and educational relations, gender is one of the primary organizing principles of society and daily living.[29] Indeed, it is difficult to conceive of a world where distinctions based on gender do not exist because our experiences are so rooted in a society structured by gender.

At a very young age, children learn that gender is a central principle by which their lives are shaped. They also learn to expect clear distinctions between genders because, from the very moment of birth, girls and boys are socialized to inhabit and experience very different social worlds.[30] How and why do we teach our children that gender is so important?

Gender classification begins at birth (and sometimes well before via neonatal technology, such as ultrasound). Attaching a sex label (female or male) to newborns is one of the most basic elements of early socialization. Once a child's sex is assigned, typically based on its genital appearance at birth, gender-specific socialization may begin. Immediately thereafter parents often give their children gender-specific names, swaddle them in pink or blue blankets and clothing, and send out "It's a Girl!" or "It's a Boy!" birth announcement cards to family and friends in celebration. In fact, with ultrasound technology, many expectant parents are choosing to identify their child's sex even before it is born. One of the primary reasons they do so, no doubt, is the reality that social life is organized by gender. Many parents find it difficult to prepare for or even imagine a child's life without first knowing its sex.

Adults often interact with children in ways that reinforce the importance of gender and the expected distinction between gender roles. This includes family members surrounding children with "girl" and "boy" toys and teachers using gender as a way to separate children into competitive teams or lunch-room lines. Some parents are so concerned that people might mistake their baby for the wrong sex, that they tape pink bows to their bald heads, have their ears pierced in infancy, or dress them in gender-specific primary- or pastel-colored clothing.

Most children first learn about such cultural norms from their parents and other family members. Other important agents of (gender) socialization are teachers, literature, peers, media, religion, and even toys. Lawrence Kohlberg demonstrated in his research forty years ago that children are able to identify themselves as female or male by the age of three. By the age of five, Kohlberg argues, children adhere closely to traditional gender-typed behavior that is taught and reinforced by the society in which they live.[31] Likewise, children learn at an early age to interact with one another in ways that reinforce the importance of gender by playing gender-segregated games on the playground, such as jump rope for girls and baseball for boys. Children strengthen the sup-posed gender divide by playing games that create and reinforce gender bound-aries, such as pretending to pollute one another with the germs or "cooties" that are imagined to be associated with one gender or the other.[32] Toys such as Easy Bake Ovens and G.I. Joe prepare children to inhabit vastly different worlds in child- and adulthood, replete with emotions, occupations, economic standing, personal tastes, and even physical stature that all become laden with gendered meaning. Certainly gender roles are more flexible now than they were even twenty years ago, and there is significantly more crossover between genders. Even so, toys that are deemed "gender neutral," such as Big Wheels, boast gendered accessories, such as pastel or primary color schemes and frilly or angular edging, so that a distinction between genders is reinforced.

After early childhood, the significance of gender increases substantially when young adults consider and seek out dating and romantic endeavors. In fact, the very ability to identify one's sexual orientation as lesbian or gay, bi-sexual, or straight is dependent on one's identity as female or male and the social distinctions between those categories. From early high school romances to lifelong partnerships and parenting relationships, gender plays a central role. Gender continues to shape social life in education and career choices and in the division of parenting and housekeeping duties at home.

GENDER BINARISM AND THE HETEROSEXUAL MATRIX

It nearly goes without saying that a predominant expectation about gender is that there are only two "flavors," female or male, and that initial sex assign-ment is based on genital appearance at birth.[33] Social expectations about gen-der, however, do not stop there. In fact, they are much more complex. In their study of gender expectations and nonconformity based on the work of Harold Garfinkel, Suzanne Kessler and Wendy McKenna make several of these nuances clear. They summarize these expectations as follows:

1. There are two, and only two, genders.
2. One's gender is invariant.
3. Genitals are the essential sign of gender.
4. Any exceptions to the two genders are not to be taken seriously.
5. There are no transfers from one gender to another except ceremonial ones.
6. Everyone must be classified as a member of one gender or the other.
7. The female/male dichotomy is a natural one.
8. Membership in one gender or the other is natural.[34]

So, not only are the options for gender limited to two categories, membership in a gender category is also seen as natural and permanent.

The concept of gender becomes even more complicated when we consider the commonplace distinction between one's anatomy and one's identity, in that *sex* is considered by many to be anatomical and gender is considered a social category. That is, there is a tendency to differentiate sex from gender by defining sex as physiological (that is, genitals, gonads, chromosomes, and hormones) and gender as social (that is, the subsequently developing sense and presentation of self as a sexed individual).[35] More explicitly, we tend to infer children's gender from their genital sex in infancy and subsequently interpret their behaviors as "feminine" or "masculine." As children age, the reverse process occurs. Because we are typically unfamiliar with a child's genital makeup, we infer a child's sex from its behavior and other outward cues, such as clothing, name, and body type. In a culture that is heteronormative, there is often the presumption that girls and boys will grow up to desire each other.

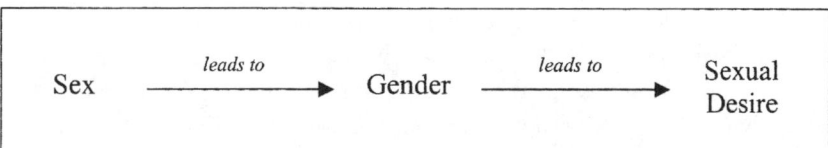

Figure 1. Butler's Heterosexual Matrix. Butler put her finger on the causal and linear assumptions most Westerners believe exist between the three components of sexual identity: anatomical sex, gender identity and presentation, and sexual desire. Here I provide a diagram of Butler's theory to visually characterize the widely presumed connections between these concepts. To my knowledge, Butler has no graphic depiction of the heterosexual matrix.

It is this complex set of linear and causal assumptions of sexual identity development which Judith Butler calls the heterosexual matrix.[36]

In her discussion of the heterosexual matrix, Butler demonstrates that normative Western assumptions about sexual identity are based on a belief that anatomical sex causes gender development which, in turn, causes sexual desire. In this sense, one is assumed to be anatomically "hard wired" to develop a gender identity (one's gendered sense of self) and gender role (one's gendered presentation of self) that correlate with one's birth genitalia. In addition, this model assumes heterosexuality, that is, that one will naturally be attracted to individuals whose genitals are different from their own. However, as Butler and others note, this model has many limitations, because gender identity and gender role do not always coincide with genitalia or result in heterosexual attraction.[37]

Given the tendency to conflate the categories of sex and gender, Kessler and McKenna, Butler, and others see no meaningful distinction between the two terms and, therefore, primarily use the term *gender* to refer to either anatomy *or* identity throughout their work. In the same fashion, I use the terms sex and gender interchangeably throughout this book, except in rare cases when distinction between the two terms is useful for clarity. The conflation of the terms sex and gender is particularly evident and apt when considering intersexuality, because physicians typically weigh quite heavily the success of a child's imagined future gender identity and presentation when making sex assignment decisions about newborns.[38]

Gender Nonconformity

Even though gender roles are far more flexible than they once were in our culture's recent history, gender continues to structure and shape all of our lives day in and day out from birth until death, and perhaps even before birth and after death as well; for example, when decorating an unborn child's nursery or planning a deceased love one's memorial service. Sexual ambiguity is disruptive precisely *because* of the emphasis we place on gender. If gender classification were socially less important, or if criteria for membership in one gender category or another were more flexible, variation in sexual anatomy would be of much less concern.

Despite their significance, our expectations for sex and gender categorization most often go unnoticed, until we are presented with a deviation from the norm.[39] Babies born with bodies that vary from traditional appearance, or children who undergo pubescent changes later in life that vary from the norm, challenge the most basic of social expectations. The belief that there are only two sexes, and that sex is defined by a specific genital appearance, creates a significant problem in that some people, with considerable frequency and regularity, have bodies that don't fit the norm. In a world where only two sexes are thought to exist, a person must be, or must present oneself as, one sex or the other in order to gain valid membership and recognition in that society's predominant culture. In this rigid belief system—if someone's identity or anatomy is not consistent with dualistic expectations—some people may take drastic measures to make others (or themselves) comply with the norm because it is considerably problematic to (involuntarily) challenge the norm when dealing with something as central to social identity and belonging as gender categorization.

The case of an intersex birth, a birth where one's sex cannot readily be ascertained, announced, and counted upon, provides a poignant example of normative expectations remaining unfulfilled. According to sociologist Harold Garfinkel, one is most able to ascertain the strength and specific nature of social norms by deviating from them and then closely gauging the response.[40] Garfinkel's theory, known as ethnomethodology, stems from an understanding of the three basic elements of social deviance. These elements are (1) the existence of a shared social expectation, or social norm; (2) a marked violation or deviation from the norm; and (3) the social response to such a deviation. Gauging the social response to normative violations is key to understanding the salience of the initial social expectation. That is, when there is very little response to a norm violation (say, for example, jaywalking), the indifferent response itself indicates that the expectation isn't all that important to maintaining social order. To further illustrate what may be learned about social expectations by breaching the norm, I'll provide a personal example. When I was eleven years old, I went to horse camp in rural northern Minnesota with my twelve-year-old girlfriend Gaelle, who was from Paris and was visiting the United States for the very first time. Gaelle and I decided to go swimming at the camp's beach. When we arrived at the beach, we both proceeded to take off our shorts and T-shirts in the same manner, with one major exception. I was wearing my swimsuit underneath my shorts and T-shirt; Gaelle was wearing nothing. Despite the stares, she proceeded to undress, take her bathing suit out of her beach bag, and change into her suit in broad daylight. Based on Gaelle's French upbringing, doing so was within the realm of beach etiquette. The gawks and stares she received from fellow campers and counselors at Little Elk Ranch quickly informed her that Americans aren't so free with public nudity, and served to reinforce the norm of public decorum.

In applying this model of social deviance to intersex, the shared social expectation is that babies are born in one of two clearly delineated anatomical types—female or male—as ascertained by genital presentation at birth. In the case of intersexuality, normative violation occurs when genitalia and/or later pubescent development are not congruent with this two-sex model. The social reaction to this form of deviance is primarily medical, due to the medicalization of childbirth and the medicalization of normality in this culture—a point I develop further in chapter 2. The social response to intersexual "deviance" is so strong that we have developed institutional means of covering up or erasing the violation, so that the initial social expectation of sex binarism may be upheld. More specifically, we have developed medical means of surgically and hormonally engineering bodies that adhere to a two-sex social system, thereby reinforcing and maintaining sex binarism and genital signification of sex as necessary and natural.

Recall that the process of being labeled as deviant is a social one. Being characterized as deviant is the result of people perceiving, naming, and treating one as an outsider. Therefore, qualities that are considered deviant, such as atypical genitalia, aren't fundamentally distinct from those that are considered normal. The difference lies in the act of successfully labeling and treating one physical type as deviant and the other as customary.[41]

LABELING, STIGMA, AND THE SELF

Why would a culture go to such great lengths to uphold a two-sex system when there are clearly consistent exceptions to this norm? One reason is because intersex is incongruent with the predominant, binary understanding of sex and gender, and this gender system provides the foundation for even the most basic social interaction and organization. Thus, any exception to gender norms generates the potential for social stigma and alienation. According to Goffman, such difference is often perceived as "Other," immoral, and odd. Being labeled as different often prevents a person or group from achieving total social acceptance, and that alienation may in turn cause a person to have difficulty accepting her- or himself.[42] Prevailing medical and psychological theories suggest the psychological necessity of surgically altering intersexed bodies to preclude such social stigma.[43] These theories are based on a fundamental assumption that without medical "clarification" of their sexual anatomy, intersexuals will lead a life of isolation and despair. The underlying thought here is that if intersexuals' bodies are altered so that they don't appear unusual, people who are intersexed won't come to see themselves or be seen by others as abnormal. This theory illustrates the centrality of sex binarism to Western cultural belief systems. It also highlights both the importance of self-evaluation and the impact that others' perceptions may have on the development of identity.

DEVELOPMENT OF THE SELF

In their brilliant contributions to the field of social psychology, Charles Horton Cooley and George Herbert Mead theorized the interplay between self-assessment and reflected appraisal in the development of the self.[44] Their theories are pertinent to the discussion of stigma, labeling, and identity, in that they discuss the development of the self in relation to the impact of others' perceptions of one's identity. Cooley uses the clever metaphor of the "looking-glass" to discuss his concept of the self.[45] According to the theory of the looking-glass, the self operates in the imagination and is based on what we think others think of us, whether their judgment is real or not. In Cooley's words,

> A self-idea of this sort seems to have three principle elements: the imagination of our appearance to the other person, the imagination of his [sic] judgement of that appearance, and some sort of self-feeling, such as pride or mortification.[46]

In short, Cooley's looking-glass self can be summarized by the saying, "I am not what I think I am. I am not what you think I am. I am what I think you think I am." The concept of the looking-glass self is especially pertinent to the discussion of social stigma and development of psychosocial identity because one's self-concept is thought to develop in line with others' reflected appraisals.

Like Cooley, Mead saw the self as a social object. In his own words,

> The individual experiences himself [sic] . . . indirectly, from the particular standpoints of other individual members of the same social group, or from the generalized standpoint of the social group as a whole to which he belongs. For he enters his own experience as a self or individual, not directly or immediately, not by becoming a subject to himself, but only in so far as he first becomes an *object* to himself . . . and he becomes an object to himself only by taking the attitudes of other individuals toward himself within a social environment or context of experience and behavior in which both he and they are involved [emphasis added].[47]

Mead's theory, like Cooley's, is relevant to understanding the impact of social stigma on the development of identity.[48] If others identify and react to us as aberrant and strange, we may in turn come to see ourselves in a similar fashion.

MEDICAL RESPONSE

Given that gender is so important to social organization and interaction, and that genitals are regarded as an essential sign of gender, the attempt to conform "deviant" genitalia to the norm makes some sense and may even be a relief to some. Indeed, some adults surrounding an intersexed child are likely to have great difficulty interacting with the child socially until its sex is somehow normalized or made to appear clear. In a culture where so much emphasis is placed on the appearance of genitalia in initial sex categorization, clarity of genitalia literally grants an individual "personhood"; that is, being clearly sexed gives a person the capacity to be socially understood and accepted.[49]

Because of an inflexible social expectation for anatomical and sexual conformity, variations from the norm are covered up, erased, and hidden away in the hopes of precluding intense social stigma that may await a child who is identified and labeled as sexually deviant from the start.[50] Not surprisingly, in a culture where childbirth, sexuality, and normalcy are within medical purview, the social response to sexual ambiguity is primarily medical. Despite the typically medically benign occurrence of intersexuality, the social problem of physical sexual variation and the medicalization of childbirth lead to the social definition of intersexed bodies as diseased, unruly, and in need of medical attention or cures.

Surgery is just one of many possible responses to sexual variation and medical sex assignment is a product of specific cultural and historical factors. In setting the context for intersexuals' experiences, I turn next to an exploration of the conditions within which medical sex assignment became a viable response to sexual variation.

Chapter 2 — Medical Sex Assignment

"Oh my god. Your child is a monster that we have to fix."

—Excerpt from interview with Suegee

Intersex 101

There are many causes, forms, and interpretations of sexual ambiguity. I interviewed people who had a variety of anatomical presentations in an attempt to ascertain commonalties and dissimilarities across intersex diagnoses. Because I discuss medical treatments specific to intersex diagnoses throughout the book, I include here a brief section on the causes and forms of sexual ambiguity, as well as participants' experiences with diagnosis-specific issues.

In typical sexual development, children are born with forty-six paired chromosomes, twenty-three from their mothers and twenty-three from their fathers. Twenty-two of these chromosome pairs are identical to each other, while the twenty-third pair, known as the "sex chromosomes" are typically either XX or XY. This typical genetic development results in a 46,XX girl or a 46,XY boy.[1]

When explaining the sexually ambiguous anatomy of their children to parents, doctors commonly discuss neonatal physiological development, stressing that girls' and boys' reproductive organs and genitalia form from the same basic structures. That is, in neonatal development, zygotes remain sexually undifferentiated until six to eight weeks of gestation. Both XX and XY zygotes have Mullerian ducts (which form into ovaries, fallopian tubes, and uterus) and Wolffian ducts (which form into testicles). The structure that becomes a clitoris or penis, known medically as the genital tubercle, is sexually bipotential at this early stage of neonatal development, meaning that it could

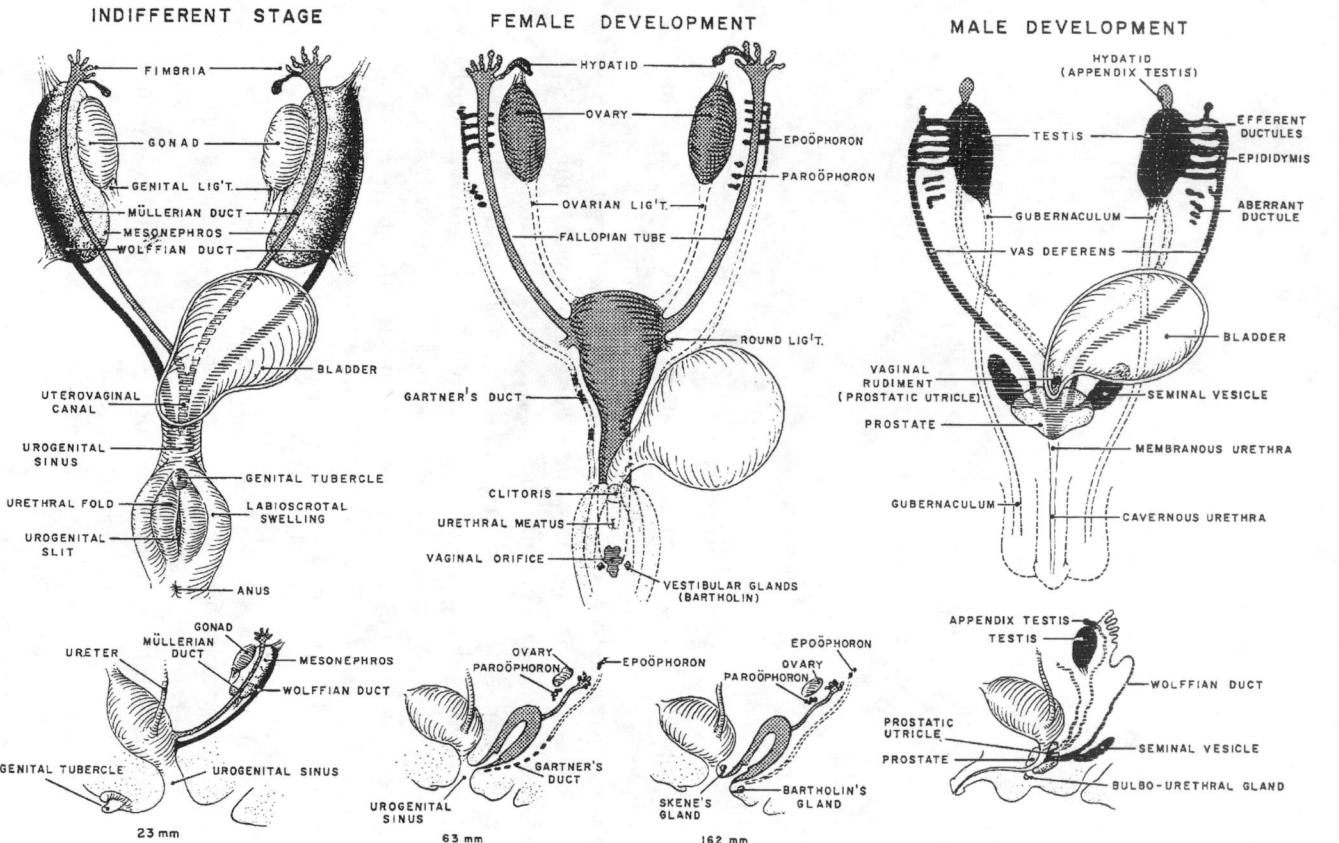

INDIFFERENT STAGE

FIMBRIA
GONAD
GENITAL LIG'T.
MÜLLERIAN DUCT
MESONEPHROS
WOLFFIAN DUCT
BLADDER
UTEROVAGINAL CANAL
UROGENITAL SINUS
URETHRAL FOLD
UROGENITAL SLIT
GENITAL TUBERCLE
LABIOSCROTAL SWELLING
ANUS

FEMALE DEVELOPMENT

HYDATID
OVARY
EPOÖPHORON
PAROÖPHORON
OVARIAN LIG'T.
FALLOPIAN TUBE
ROUND LIG'T.
GARTNER'S DUCT
CLITORIS
URETHRAL MEATUS
VAGINAL ORIFICE
VESTIBULAR GLANDS (BARTHOLIN)

MALE DEVELOPMENT

HYDATID (APPENDIX TESTIS)
TESTIS
EFFERENT DUCTULES
EPIDIDYMIS
ABERRANT DUCTULE
GUBERNACULUM
VAS DEFERENS
BLADDER
VAGINAL RUDIMENT (PROSTATIC UTRICLE)
PROSTATE
SEMINAL VESICLE
GUBERNACULUM
MEMBRANOUS URETHRA
CAVERNOUS URETHRA

URETER
GONAD
MÜLLERIAN DUCT
MESONEPHROS
WOLFFIAN DUCT
GENITAL TUBERCLE
UROGENITAL SINUS
23 mm

OVARY
PAROÖPHORON
EPOÖPHORON
GARTNER'S DUCT
UROGENITAL SINUS
63 mm

EPOÖPHORON
OVARY
PAROÖPHORON
SKENE'S GLAND
BARTHOLIN'S GLAND
162 mm

APPENDIX TESTIS
TESTIS
WOLFFIAN DUCT
PROSTATIC UTRICLE
PROSTATE
SEMINAL VESICLE
BULBO-URETHRAL GLAND

Figure 2. Typical sexual differentiation of the internal organs. Grumbach and Conte 1998: 1323. *Reprinted with permission of W. B. Saunders Company.*

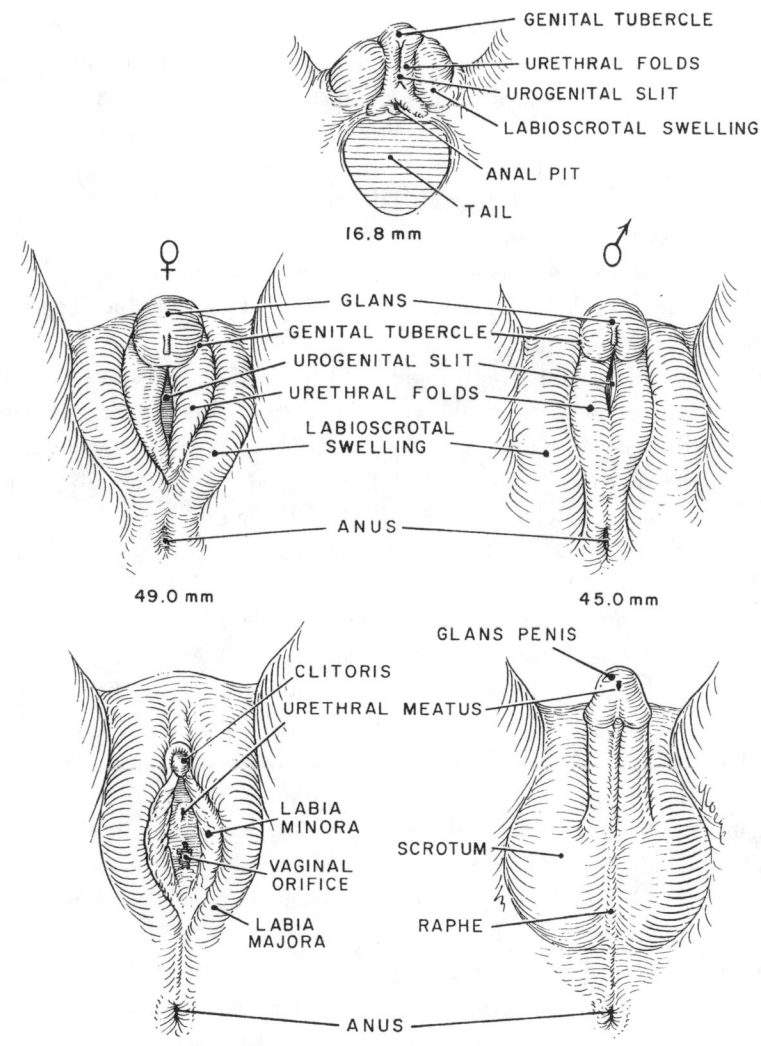

Figure 3. Typical sexual differentiation of the external organs. Grumbach and Conte 1998: 1325. *Reprinted with permission of W. B. Saunders Company.*

become either a clitoris or a penis. By twelve weeks of gestation, the end of the first trimester of pregnancy, most fetuses are sexually differentiated both internally in their reproductive organs and externally in their genitalia.[2]

For typical XY neonates, internal reproductive structures develop before external genital structures do. Usually Y chromosomes carry a gene known as the sex-determining region of the Y chromosome, or the SRY. The SRY region of the Y chromosome leads to male sexual differentiation via the introduction of androgens ("male" hormones) to the neonate. For example, the presence of Mullerian inhibiting substance (MIS) leads to the degeneration of the Mullerian ducts and prevents the development of these ducts into the fallopian tubes, uterus, and upper vagina of typical females. Furthermore, testosterone, one form of androgen, leads to the development of the Wolffian ducts at six weeks of gestation, and allows their differentiation into the epididymis, vas deferens, and seminal vesicle of typical males. Dihydrotestosterone (DHT) leads to the development of male external genitals, a process which begins at the eighth week of gestation.[3]

Far less is understood about XX (female) sexual differentiation, although for typical XX neonates, external genitalia develop before the internal Mullerian structures do. Certainly XX typical fetuses are exposed to more estrogens and progestins than androgens. Without the presence of substances such as MIS, the Mullerian ducts develop into the fallopian tubes, uterus, and upper vagina of typical females. Likewise, internal and external male organs do not develop without the presence of testosterone and DHT.[4] Thus, as many have noted, the "fundamental genital type is female. Masculinization of the external genitalia is the result of androgen action."[5] It is easy to see how with even a small change in chromosome or hormone structures, internal reproductive or external genital features could be changed as well.

Much more could be learned about typical XX (female) neonatal development. Scientists have studied and therefore have come to understand far more about the structure and development of male bodies. The current medical model of neonatal sex differentiation reflects a larger cultural notion of male action and female inaction and results in a "female by default" understanding of neonatal development.

Using a system first introduced by Theodore Klebs in 1876, intersex is medically classified in three primary categories: true hermaphroditism, female pseudohermaphroditism, and male pseudohermaphroditism.[6] Klebs identified people as true hermaphrodites only if they had the very rare combination of ovarian and testicular tissue in the same body. This simultaneous overlap of gonadal tissues may be present in one gonad (e.g., one gonad with both testicular and ovarian cells) or may present itself separately in each gonad (e.g., one gonad is a testicle, the other is an ovary). True hermaphrodites more commonly have a 46,XX karyotype than 46,XY, but may have either karyotype. The external genitalia of true hermaphrodites are typically ambiguous. In Klebs's system, all other forms of intersex, for example people with ambiguous genitalia but no combination of gonadal tissue, are identified as pseudohermaphrodites.

Female pseudohermaphrodites have a female-typical 46,XX karyotype, but have genital and other organ variations caused by hormonal influences that may distinguish them from others. The most common type of female pseudohermaphroditism is congenital adrenal hyperplasia (CAH), where the body's endocrine system produces an excess amount of androgens (male hormones) due to an enlargement of the adrenal gland.[7] Girls with CAH typically have an enlarged clitoris, with the possibility of nearly complete virilization (masculinization) of the external genitals. In contrast, the internal organs, such as the fallopian tubes, uterus, and upper vagina, develop in typical fashion and reproductive capacity is present.[8]

Eleven percent of the people I interviewed had a diagnosis of CAH. They spoke of issues particular to living with CAH, such as taking medication since infancy and throughout their lives to balance their hormones and to suppress the development of male secondary sex characteristics. Some things that could happen if someone with CAH didn't take this medicine include the development of secondary sex characteristics typically associated with men. Some of these characteristics are male-pattern balding, facial hair, increased muscle mass, and masculinized genitalia. Here one study participant, known as Chimera, describes the traumatic masculinization of her body when she stopped taking her hormone pills in adolescence:

> [I wanted to] look like a girl. To be able to tell, at a glance, that you were dealing with a woman. If I could do a body transplant, I'd do it in a heartbeat. This is not the sort of life I would choose for myself. If they had told me at the time they started telling me, "If you ever stop taking these medications, you're going to die," if they had told me . . . "If you ever stop taking these medications, you're going to be a freak caught somewhere between male and female and nobody is ever going to believe you that you're a girl." Man, I'd have never quit taking those medications for anything in the world. But nobody ever said that to me. They always figured that death ought to be enough to scare anybody away from anything. Death was not such a scary prospect at that particular point in time. There are worse things in life than death and one of them is looking like this.

People classified as male pseudohermaphrodites have a male-typical 46,XY karyotype, but have atypical genital and other organ characteristics caused by unusual genetic or endocrine features. The most common type of male pseudohermaphroditism is androgen insensitivity syndrome (AIS), known historically as testicular feminization. Individuals with AIS are chromosomally and gonadally male (that is, XY with testicles), but lack a key androgen receptor that facilitates the ability, fetally and onward, to respond to the androgens (male hormones) produced in normal amounts by the testes. That is, people with AIS are unresponsive to the androgens that are required for the development of male genitalia and male secondary sex characteristics. This insensitivity to androgens results in a feminization of the external genitalia and testicles that typically remain undescended. Some individuals with AIS are completely insensitive or unresponsive to androgens (CAIS), and some only partially (PAIS). Most people with AIS are sexed as female, unless masculinization is only slightly affected by insensitivity to androgen, in which case male sex assignment would prevail.[9] Most humans have a combination of androgens and estrogens in their bodies. For example, it is the presence of androgens that leads to the development of acne and underarm and pubic hair in women as well as in men. Likewise, estrogens are present in most men and women. Because of this, at puberty, individuals with AIS respond to the normal levels of estrogen produced by their bodies and develop breasts. AIS individuals typically develop very little, if any, body hair, and are tall and lean. It is indeed paradoxical that many children with complete AIS develop anatomy consistent with contemporary Western ideals of female beauty. All people with AIS are sterile, but many do adopt children.[10]

Twenty-seven percent of interviewees had complete androgen insensitivity syndrome, and 14 percent had partial androgen insensitivity syndrome. CAIS and PAIS certainly have similar physical manifestations, but the dissimilarities are perhaps even greater. Those who have a complete inability to respond to androgens have bodies that, regardless of how much and how consistently they are given testosterone injections, will not masculinize. Because girls with CAIS look no different than girls who don't have AIS, their sex often doesn't come into question until puberty when they don't menstruate or develop pubic or underarm hair. Because many live unquestionably as female for so much of their lives, discovering their male anatomy can be disruptive, especially if it had been hidden from them as a secret by family and doctors. Like many who were desperate for accurate information about their bodies, Flora, a forty-five-year-old editor, searched for information on her own when she was twenty-four years old. She was stunned to learn that her body had mixed sexual anatomy. In her words,

> I came across [the words] "testicular feminization." It never occurred to me that there would be anything testicular in my body. I suffered horrible anxiety. I thought, "I'm going to die young. I'm gonna get cancer. I'm going to become hairy. I'm going to masculinize." I imagined this array of terrible possibilities.

Had Flora been given age-appropriate information about AIS throughout her life, this alienating discovery in the stacks of her local university's medical library could have been prevented.

Because partial androgen insensitivity does allow for some masculinization to occur, people with PAIS usually live with contested sex throughout their lives. Peggy was forty-four years old when I interviewed her. Her anatomy had caused such confusion to the adults around her when she was born, that she was initially given a female sex assignment and was reassigned as male at three months of age. She had been living as a woman for twenty-three years when we met. Peggy, like many who have various types of intersex, underwent exploratory surgery on her reproductive organs in infancy. Here she describes how her father explained her abdominal scar when she got older.

> I had exploratory surgery when I was about two months old [and] I have a scar across [my stomach]. My father told me when I was a little kid that [the scar] was from an appendectomy I had as a child. I remember as a child being curious about other people's appendix scars and even going to the Museum of Science in Boston where they had wax figures that show how an appendectomy is done and I really wondered why my appendectomy scar was shaped completely differently from anyone else's appendectomy scar. And I remember once asking my father if the appendectomy was the cause of my physical condition. I had the idea that somehow having had the appendectomy caused me to be anatomically different.

Regardless of intersex etiology, interviewees' lives were permeated with the disastrous consequences of secrecy and lies.

Another common form of male pseudohermaphroditism is 5-alpha-reductase deficiency (5-ARD). People with 5-ARD are also chromosomally and gonadally male, but have genitals that may be ambiguous or more female than male in appearance until puberty. Due to a lack of the enzyme 5-alpha-reductase, these children cannot convert their body's normal production of testosterone into dihydrotestosterone (DHT), a process which is necessary for the development of male genitalia. Unlike people with CAIS who are incapable of responding to male hormones, with the production of more testosterone at puberty, children with 5-ARD will develop secondary sex characteristics standard for men, including facial hair, muscularization of the body, and deepening of the voice, despite the continued low levels of DHT. That is, they go from looking outwardly female to looking outwardly male. Often, their testicles will voluntarily descend and the small phallus will increase in size enough to be considered a small penis.[11] No one I spoke with had a diagnosis of 5-alpha-reductase deficiency, although 22 percent did not know of the origin of their intersexuality.

Sometimes sexual variation is apparent in the chromosomes (e.g., XO or XXY) rather than the genitalia or reproductive anatomy. One type of chromosomal variation is known as Klinefelter's Syndrome, where a child has one Y chromosome and more than one X chromosome, such as a 47,XXY (or 48,XXXY, or 49,XXXXY). Genital ambiguity is not typically present in Klinefelter's Syndrome, but testes may be small and firm, and partial breast development (gynecomastia) is common at puberty. Secondary sex characteristic development is limited, and men with Klinefelter's are almost always sterile.[12] Three percent of those I interviewed had Klinefelter's Syndrome. To help enhance male secondary sex characteristic development, many men with Klinefelter's take testosterone. Jana was sixty-two years old when I interviewed him, and he started taking testosterone when he was sixty years old. The physical changes he experienced after doing so were dramatic.

> Well, I never could shave, I never had to shave. If I tried to grow a
> mustache I could go for about four months and somebody would say,
> "Oh are you trying to grow a mustache?" At one point when the town
> we were in had its bicentennial, everybody grew a beard, except me,
> of course. It was not physically possible to produce anything. Now I
> have a full mustache and after our anniversary I'm gonna see what
> happens with a beard. Just to see if I can. Now I *have* to shave every
> day.

Three percent of the people I interviewed also had Turner's Syndrome. Turner's Syndrome is another form of chromosomal variation, resulting in one X chromosome, one missing sex chromosome, and a 45,XO karyotype.[13] Children with Turner's Syndrome will develop unambiguous female genitalia, yet will have underdeveloped breasts, uterus, and vagina. Some will have testicular tissue and primitive gonadal "streak" tissue. They commonly do not develop secondary sex characteristics and are very short. Some may have a webbed neck, a "shield chest," and short fingers and toes.[14] Meta was forty-four years old when we spoke. She talked about the difficulty of being short and doctors' concern with giving her growth hormones.

> I was always very short. The shortness really set me apart. I was about
> sixteen and then they were concerned about sexual development and
> they did some tests—started me on hormones when I was between
> seventeen and eighteen. They started me on steroids because they
> didn't want to give me the estrogens right at first. They wanted to see
> if they could get me to grow and then they do the x-rays of your wrists
> and you can actually see the fact that I did grow a little bit. They were

very proud of that. I mean that doesn't seem that much, but just that half an inch gave me a little bit more height.

In addition to the etiologies discussed above, 5 percent of participants had enlarged clitorises, like Claire, and were diagnosed as having progestin-affected clitoral megaly (enlargement of the clitoris) due to exposure to excess progestin during gestation. The remaining 15 percent of people I interviewed had diagnoses of gonadal dysgenesis (atypical gonadal structure), micropenis, true hermaphroditism, or hypospadias.

Tiger is a forty-year-old psychologist who was born with hypospadias where the urethral opening is somewhere along the shaft or base of the penis rather than at the tip. He spoke of the dire consequences of social conformity he was subjected to because of repeated genital surgeries:

> I've had sixteen [genital] surgeries total in my lifetime. The first surgery was at age three months, so this was the story of my childhood. Every summer other kids went on vacation. I went to the hospital. I was always between surgeries and always managing the last surgery and always "looking forward" to the next one. And sixteen surgeries later and *several* skin grafts later I have a structure that I can use for insertion.[15] I've got scars all over my body from places they've taken skin to plant into my penis. [It] is something that looks like a bunch of skin sewn together with scars all over it that doesn't feel like much and doesn't really work very well . . . 'cause that's the nature of plastic surgery, even now. And, from the point of view of the physicians, I am a competent male. From my point of view, I wish they would have left me alone.

Tiger's story of repeated unsuccessful genital surgery is shocking, but not rare. Surgery to reroute the urethral opening to the traditional position at the tip of the penis is commonly performed on children who have hypospadias, primarily to allow them to urinate while standing. (Yet another consequence of rigid expectations for gender conformity. Do boys really have to stand to urinate in order to "make it" successfully as boys or men?) Many patients experience chronic urinary tract problems following surgery, including recurring urinary tract infections and urethral strictures (narrowing) caused by scar tissue or inflammation, making urination painful if not altogether impossible. Chronic complications resulting from surgeries to "correct" the position of the urethra are so common, in fact, that doctors coined the term "hypospadias cripples" to describe patients who experience ongoing and debilitating iatrogenic, or medically induced, complications as a result of surgery on the urinary tract.[16]

I return to participants' narratives in far more detail in the next chapters. Before doing so, though, I will explore medicine's control of sexual variation and how doctors make and carry out decisions and treatment in medical sex assignment.

A Brief History of Sexual Ambiguity in Medicine, Religion, and Law

In this contemporary era of patients' rights and advocacy, it may be difficult to understand surgery as a viable response to sexual variation, let alone grasp how it became the primary response. Here I explore the historical and social context within which medical sex assignment was developed.

Before the medicalization of human sexuality in the nineteenth century,[17] sexual ambiguity was "treated" within the realm of family, legal, or religious institutions. Rather than relying on surgical intervention, parents gendered their children by social means (through naming, clothing, etc.). This approach is still plausible today, despite the availability of surgical and hormonal techniques of clarifying ambiguous sex because the appearance of genitalia (or other potentially ambiguous features such as gonads, hormones, and chromosomes) is relatively unimportant and invisible on a day-to-day basis. Most of us don't even rely on genitalia as signifiers of gender in daily interaction. Instead, we look for gender cues in the very public indicators of first names, style of dress, hair and makeup, mannerisms, general body shape, career and hobby involvement, and partner choice. How is it, then, that the irregular appearance of one's genitalia has become a social and medical emergency?

In an attempt to answer this question, I turn briefly to the historical literature on early medical involvement in sexual regulation and childbirth. Then I explore more fully the rather recent yet strong presence of surgery as a response to sexual variation.

HERMAPHRODITES IN HISTORY

There are historic precursors to the current trend of early infant sex assignment that are important to consider in trying to understand the current debate over genital surgery. Here I provide a brief history of pre–twentieth-century conceptions of intersex to historicize and contextualize the dominant contemporary paradigm of intersex medical sex assignment. During the early years of the Enlightenment, in the late eighteenth century, medical doctors began to gain authority over the body. This was, in large part, related to the developing science of taxonomy.[18] This newly emerging scientific focus on classifying, documenting, and cataloging every species and its parts had a major impact on how clinicians viewed and treated human bodies, especially when bodies or body parts seemed to defy standard categorization. As regulators of the human body and human sexuality, doctors took on the role of controlling various physical or social deviations from the norm, including intersex.

Like many other issues that are commonly treated as medical problems today, sexual variation has not always been within the purview of medicine. As the medical sociologists Peter Conrad and Joseph Schneider illustrate, the institutional authority to regulate deviance has markedly shifted hands over the course of time. Deviance has shifted from being cast as sin, to crime, to sickness.[19] When deviance was socially considered a sin or a moral blemish, the institutional response to regulating or controlling deviants was primarily religious. For example, someone who was perpetually adulterous was expected to atone for their sin by asking for absolution from a religious figure, rather than by spending time in a treatment center for sexual addiction, which they might do today. When deviance came to be seen as a crime, institutional regulation was predominantly legal. For example, someone who was chronically alcoholic commonly did time in a criminal institution, rather than in a treatment center or twelve-step program of contemporary times. As medicine gained authority over the dealings of the mind and body, the institutional response has increasingly shifted to medicine. With this transition, the medical industry and related fields have expanded tremendously in the twentieth century.[20] According to Conrad and Schneider, medicine is the second largest industry in the United States.[21] As the realm of medical expertise has expanded, so have the number and types of conditions considered for treatment by physicians. Similar historical shifts in institutional responses to intersex are evident in the following historical review.[22]

Social expectations for gender roles and conceptions of hermaphroditism change significantly over time and vary tremendously by culture. For example, Cary Nederman and Jacqui True review twelfth-century theological and medical writings that characterize sex in a way quite different from our current binary understanding.[23] Unlike later twentieth- and twenty-first-century claims that "true" hermaphrodites are extraordinarily rare, if not entirely mythological, hermaphrodites were regarded as a discrete third sex during the twelfth century in Western Europe. Rather than regarding people with sexually ambiguous genitalia as "pseudohermaphrodites" whose ambiguity is seen as obscuring an underlying "true sex" of female or male, as contemporary medicine would, sexual ambiguity in the twelfth century seemed to signal a third option for sex categorization.[24] The concept that hermaphroditism was a third sex was based on Galen's second-century theory, which claimed that there were gender differences in body temperature, especially in the reproductive and sexual organs.[25] According to this theory, sex distinctions were based on a continuum of heat, with males' bodies being internally hotter than females', thus creating the impetus for external male reproductive organs and colder, internal female organs.[26] In Thomas Laqueur's analysis, this differential temperature theory actually provided the basis for a one-sex conceptual model, with females being seen as the inverse of males.[27] (That is, female and male anatomy was viewed as identical, although the vagina was viewed as an inverted penis, the uterus as an internalized scrotum, the fallopian tubes as seminal vesicles, the ovaries as internal testicles, and so on).

In the early seventeenth century, scientific thought about girls who developed male secondary sex characteristics at puberty was also associated with Galen's temperature model. The esteemed seventeenth-century surgeon Ambroise Pare viewed an excessive amount of internal heat (typically associated with males) as the cause of this female pubescent virilization. According to Pare, this heat was typically brought on by the activities of children themselves, such as jumping and playing roughly, which then led to the "pushing out" and transition of internal female organs into external male organs.[28] This notion of female physical activity having disastrous consequences is no doubt linked to later medical claims that girls and women shouldn't exert themselves too extensively, or they may risk not only their femininity, but reproductive capacity as well.

These early theories of sexual differentiation seem to be based on Hippocrates' humoral theory of the body's fluids and temperature, which governed medical practice and belief until at least the middle of the nineteenth century.[29] Consider the widely read and highly acclaimed pseudo-Galenic text *De Spermate*, which further defined sex differentiation in reproduction. According to *De Spermate*, both the male "seed" and the female uterus played active roles in determining the sex of the offspring. The uterus and testicles were thought to be divided into distinct sections or chambers that varied in temperature, and these differences in temperature were believed to be responsible for generating the sex of the child. For example, when male seed was planted in the warmer, right section of the uterus, it was believed that the baby would be male. A female baby would be conceived when the male seed was implanted in the colder, left section of the uterus. If the seed planted itself in the midsection, a hermaphroditic baby was produced.[30] In this model hermaphroditism was conceptualized as a natural, if not expected, state given that the uterus was thought to have a separate chamber for nurturing hermaphroditic, as well as female and male fetuses.[31] Further evidence of three distinct sex categories comes from the late-twelfth-century Italian civil jurist Portius Azo, who wrote in his *Summa Institutionum*, "There is another division between human beings, namely that some are male, others are female, others are hermaphrodites."[32] Although attitudes toward hermaphroditism varied widely in twelfth-century Europe, from viewing hermaphrodites as monsters to seeing hermaphroditism as natural, the above evidence demonstrates that hermaphroditism was seen as a separate, third sex category. This acceptance of hermaphroditism as a sex distinct from female or male is remarkably different from a later Western medical model of viewing hermphroditism as obscuring an underlying true sex of female or male, which is made clear through surgical and hormonal "clarification."[33]

In their historical review of medical literature, Myra Hird and Jenz Germon demonstrate that based on this humoral theory, sixteenth-century philosophers and physicians regarded hermaphroditism as evidence of two sexes existing in one body.[34] With the invention of microscopy and surgery on *living* patients at the beginning of the twentieth century (rather than upon autopsy after death), the notion of anatomical hermaphroditism was transformed. Hird and Germon argue that the newer concept of one "true sex" being hidden by sexually ambiguous anatomy didn't enter the fray until Klebs's classification system. Recall that in this model, Klebs identified five categories of sexual classification: female, male, female pseudohermaphrodite, male pseudohermaphrodite, and true hermaphrodite. Klebs identified people as true hermaphrodites only if they had the very rare combination of ovarian and testicular tissue in the same body. All other cases of hermaphroditism, for example people who had ambiguous genitalia but no combination of gonadal tissue, were identified as pseudohermaphrodites. Klebs's classification system served to drastically decrease the number of people who were defined as hermaphrodites, and thus reinforced the newly popular thought that there were two and only two sexes: female and male, with a very rare and unusual exception in the case of true hermaphroditism.

Early surgical attempts to regulate the appearance of sexual anatomy, such as lowering abdominal testicles, appeared in the beginning of the nineteenth century.[35] A primary motive for the social insistence upon outward displays of gender clarity was an underlying fear of homosexuality, or "hermaphroditism of the soul," a threat that was present in the sexually ambiguous (or, quite literally, *bisexual*) body of the hermaphrodite. By appearing, outwardly, to be of the "other" sex, it was feared hermaphrodites would tempt heterosexual partners into "homosexual" relations.[36]

As Alice Dreger, Myra Hird and Jenz Germon, and others point out, medical methods of response to physical sexual ambiguity have changed yet again in more recent times.[37] Unlike eighteenth- and nineteenth-century medical attempts to reveal a "true sex" that is disguised by pseudohermaphroditic (or false) sexual ambiguity, the current medical model relies on making a sex assignment that is most appropriate for heterosexual capacity. Hird and Germon refer to this as the "best sex" mentality in medical sex assignment. I explore this paradigm more fully below, in a detailed discussion of contemporary medical responses to sexual ambiguity.

HERMAPHRODITES IN THEOLOGY

Historically, theologians had great influence over the perception and treatment of hermaphrodites, especially preceding the eighteenth-century separation of church and state. Throughout early theological texts, the fear of hermaphrodites posing a threat to heterosexuality is apparent. For instance, regarding the moral regulations applied to hermaphrodites of the twelfth century, the Parisian Peter the Chanter wrote,

> The church allows a hermaphrodite—that is, someone with the organs of both sexes, capable of either active or passive functions—to use the organ by which (s)he is most aroused or the one to which (s)he is most susceptible. If (s)he is more active, (s)he may wed as a man, but if (s)he is more passive, (s)he may marry as a woman. If, however, (s)he should fail with one organ, the use of the other can never be permitted, but (s)he must be perpetually celibate to avoid any similarity to the role inversion of sodomy, which is detested by God.[38]

This widely accepted twelfth-century religious tolerance of hermaphroditic choice in her/his sex/gender/sexuality stands in striking contrast to the twenty-first-century medical authority in sex assignment decisions that is standard in contemporary sex assignment.[39] However, it appears that although physiological ambiguity was allowed to persist in premedicalized times, there was a strong cultural mandate for hermaphrodites to live as clearly sexed (and heterosexual) women or men.

LEGAL MATTERS: SEX CLASSIFICATION IN LAW

In contemporary and historic times, legal concerns related to sexual ambiguity are located within a system of gendered rights and obligations. Through their physical deviation from the norm, "Hermaphrodites highlight the privilege differential between male and female precisely because they cannot participate neatly in it."[40] Throughout history, the family, church, and state have exercised control over overt expressions of gender such as one's choice of occupation, the gender of one's marital/sexual partner, and the style of one's clothing as a means to distinguish between women and men and to decrease the sex/gender/sexual ambiguity presented by hermaphrodites.[41] For example, in the mid-twelfth century, a person's ability to serve as a legal witness depended on her or his gender. Because women were excluded from providing court testimony, and from voting privileges and property rights, hermaphrodites who presented themselves as more feminine than masculine were also precluded from exercising the legal rights accorded to males at that time.[42]

The legal motivation for making precise sex distinctions was, and is, grounded in a morally based attempt to preserve heterosexuality and the institution of marriage, which are both predicated on the existence of two and only two sexes.[43] By the end of the eighteenth century, "The sex of husband and wife was beset by rules and recommendations. The marriage relation was the most intense focus of constraints; it was spoken of more than anything else."[44]

Throughout history, demarcations for lawful marital unions are precise even when legal definitions of sex are lacking. According to Roger Ormrod, "To constitute a valid marriage the parties must be of different sexes, for the simple reason that is what the word [marriage] means."[45] This discussion is, of course, relevant to current legislative discourse regarding the legalization of homosexual marriage and the 1996 Defense of Marriage Act.[46] (Take, for example, the recent Vermont Supreme Court ruling requiring the state of Vermont to provide the benefits of marriage to same-sex couples.)

While the Defense of Marriage Act effectively defined marriage as a legal relationship between a woman and a man, it failed to define what criteria were necessary to claim woman- or manhood. Similar to battles of inclusion in woman- or man-only space, such as the now infamous Camp Trans established outside the gates of the Michigan Womyn's Music Festival (when transsexual women and men were banned admission and now continue to challenge definitions of gender), transsexuals are highlighting problems with the 1996 federal marriage law. Take the case of J'Noel Gardiner, a male-to-female transsexual whose access to her deceased husband's estate was denied when their marriage was invalidated after the Topeka, Kansas, state courts discovered Gardiner's sex at birth. In March of 2002, the Kansas Supreme Court upheld the lower court ruling that one's sex is based on one's chromosomes. Despite Gardiner's sex reassignment surgery and legal documentation as female, the courts ruled that her XY chromosomes make her a man.[47]

The recent court ruling in Kansas is based on an earlier precedent set in San Antonio, Texas, in 1999. In the San Antonio case a male-to-female transsexual widow was pursuing a wrongful death suit after her husband's death. Upon learning of Christie Lee Littleton's transsexuality, the court refused to hear the case, ruling that she had no right to pursue a medical malpractice suit because her marriage was null and void due to the fact that both she and her deceased husband had XY chromosomes.[48]

Upon learning about the newly established legal definition of sex in their state, a Texas lesbian couple, Jessica Wicks and Robin Manhart Wicks, decided to give legal marriage a try because Manhart Wicks is a male-to-female transsexual like Littleton and Gardiner. Since Texas had defined legal sex on a chromosomal basis, the two women figured their XX and XY status would give them a shot at legal marriage in the state. After being refused a marriage license in their home county of Harris, they traveled to Bexar County, Texas, where the Littleton case was heard. On September 16, 2000, the two women legally married.[49]

Clearly the attempt to regulate marriage as a heterosexual institution is failing. Gardiner is pursuing a U.S. Supreme Court appeal. If the Court agrees to hear her case, we could wind up with a chromosomally based federal definition of sex. Such a step could be the beginning of a bureaucratic nightmare for transsexuals and intersexuals whose chromosomes and genders don't match, but who are nonetheless involved in loving monogamous partnerships.

Although overt legal discourse surrounding the validity of marital unions concentrates on sex (as in genitals, gonads, and chromosomes), the underlying motive for the insistence upon "opposite" sex wedlock appears to be social insurance against sodomy. This is evidenced by legal clauses relating to the traditional penile-vaginal heterosexual consummation of marriage vows. Roger Ormrod and Donna Hawley note that an inability to consummate a marriage in this manner provides legal grounds for annulment.[50]

Additional reasons for requiring legal registration and classification of sex at birth include the prevention of fraud; restriction for the carrying out of sex-specific rights, duties, and obligations; and the preservation of morality and family life (otherwise known as the prevention of homosexual relations).[51] In Alexander Capron and Richard D'Avino's words, "To enforce the prohibition (and, incidentally, public sexual displays) between members of the same sex, society needs a legal means of classifying all individuals by sex."[52] In the same article, the authors reiterate the importance of maintaining a stable sex once it is proclaimed: "The state's insistence on a dual classification [of sex] is usually accompanied by a requirement of *permanency* in the designation."[53] In fact, transgressions of sex/gender stability have been met historically by punishments as severe as death. Such transgressions are often met with extreme levels of hostility, as seen in ongoing violence against people who are transgender, transsexual, lesbian, bisexual, or gay.

In early seventeenth-century France, hermaphrodites were allowed to marry a person "opposite" their gender role. Once a hermaphrodite made such a visible commitment to living in one gender role, through marriage, they were morally and legally expected to adhere to that decision. Similar to Peter the

Chanter's statement above, if a hermaphrodite turned against the commitment to living as one gender by participating in a sexual relationship with a person of the same gender, they were charged with sodomy, publicly whipped, hanged, and/or burned.[54] In contrast with twelfth-century allowance of social gender choice, in eighteenth- and nineteenth-century Western Europe, female pseudohermaphrodites who gained access to male privilege through outward male displays such as marriage to women and working in "male" occupations, were often charged with fraud or usurping male privilege, and subjected to public punishment such as whipping, hanging, and burning.[55]

A shift in the power of sexing from the more intimate setting of the family and the intersexed individual to that of impersonal medical committees on gender ambiguity is evident in the history of hermaphroditic treatment.[56] In Dreger's words, "By consulting with medical men, hermaphrodites supplied an acknowledgement of the medical men's authority, confirmation that the medical men were indeed the just and trustworthy arbiters of pathology and identity."[57] Certainly the medical establishment has become an obvious and powerful force in defining deviance in the United States as disease-like. As Goffman and others have demonstrated, the meaning of sexual ambiguity, or other conditions regarded as deviant, is created collectively by humans through social interaction and discourse.[58] But it is certainly not just "medical men" who desire the simplicity of gender binarism. People who are sexually ambiguous and their families (may) also desire some semblance of normalcy in relation to social expectations of sex and gender. In fact, prior to the medicalization of hermaphroditism in the West, some intersexuals attempted to pass as "normal" through the use of observable signifiers of gender such as clothing and accessories, type of occupation, and sex/gender of partner. In fact, most intersexuals continue to use socially recognized gender signifiers as a means of identity expression in contemporary times, and most intersexed activists argue in favor of nonsurgical sex assignment.[59]

CROSS-CULTURAL RESPONSES TO SEX/GENDER VARIATION

In an attempt to make the social components of intersex medicalization clearer, I provide a brief discussion on cross-cultural responses to sex/gender ambiguity. The value of doing so is outlined nicely by Kessler and McKenna:

> Just as [the study of] transsexualism [or intersexuality] in our society is informative because it raises the possibility that gender is an accomplishment, studying gender categories in other cultures also makes gender problematic, that is, [it] uncovers our taken-for-granted belief in the facticity of gender which prevents us from seeing gender as a social accomplishment.[60]

I begin with Gilbert Herdt and Julianne Imperato-McGinley et al.'s work on cases of people with 5-alpha-reductase deficiency in Papau New Guinea and the Dominican Republic.[61]

Recall that 5-alpha-reductase deficiency is a type of male pseudohermaphroditism in which boys appear externally female in several respects until they reach puberty, at which point they virilize and become visibly male. Contrary to Western responses of sexing these babies as females at birth via castration to prevent a masculinizing puberty, in Papau New Guinea and the Dominican Republic these children are allowed to go through a natural sex change from female to male at puberty without medical intervention.

Outlined in Herdt's anthropological work on the Sambia in Papau New Guinea, these children are not sexed and gendered as female, as they would be in North America. Instead, they are assigned a sex/gender category specific to their particular anatomical presentation. Because the cultural framework in New Guinea allows for such variation from female and male categories, 5-alpha-reductase children are called "kwolu-aatmwol" or "changing/transforming from a female thing into a male thing."[62]

To ensure their virility, which is believed to reside in their semen, Sambia men of Papau New Guinea participate in homosexual oral sex as a part of pubertal passage rituals. Children identified as kwolu-aatmwol are allowed to participate in these rituals, but receive repeated "inseminations" (as givers of fellatio) over longer periods of time to "bring out their maleness." Five-alpha-reductase children who are incorrectly sexed/gendered as girls do not receive these inseminations and are never given male status and privilege, even following their postpubertal virilization. In an attempt to avoid such sexing mistakes, midwives and other women go to great lengths inspecting infants' genitalia to check for signs of kwolu-aatmwol ambiguity.

While the Sambia seem to have room for sexual variation in their worldview, infants sexed as kwolu-aatmwol are stigmatized nonetheless. Although they are given the designation of a third sex, kwolu-aatmwol are gendered in the direction of masculinity. That said, however, there is still a limit to male socialization in that kwolu-aatmwol children are not allowed to be socialized into latter-stage rituals of manhood.

Regarding gender identity, Herdt found that the kwolu-aatmwol did not clearly identify as either male or female. I suspect this is due to an exclusion from gendered coming of age rituals. Herdt argues that while the kwolu-aatmwol appear to exist as a third sex, they do not have their own, separate, third-gender rituals. I contend that their exclusion from these adult male rituals and their extended period of fellatio insemination contact appears to approximate a separate and distinctive gender pattern.

In critiquing the biologically based work of Imperato-McGinley and colleagues in the Dominican Republic, Herdt also found a third sex category for 5-alpha-reductase individuals.[63] Here, these children are labeled as "guevedoche" or "balls at twelve." Imperato-McGinley et al.'s work on female-to-male gender shifts at puberty not only highlighted the potential biological aspects of gender identity, but also provided two direct challenges to John Money's theory of gender development. Money's theory characterizes children under two years of age as gender "bipotential," meaning their gender identities are pliable and largely based on socialization. Conversely, Imperato-McGinley argues that gender may appear to be more biologically determined than socially determined. In her research, Imperato-McGinley presented cases of nonproblematic gender identity transitions at puberty, directly contradicting Money's theory of gender stability after early childhood. Herdt offers yet another view, which again brings to the fore the importance of the social elements of gender identity development:

> Contrary to the biomedical explanation, then, my hunch is that the Dominican guevedoche does not experience postpubertal developmental change as being from female to male. Instead, the transformation may be from female—possibly ambiguously reared—to male-aspiring third sex, who is, in certain social scenes, categorized with adult males.[64]

Hijras of North India provide another challenge to contemporary Western gender binarism. In her anthropological work, Serena Nanda defines hijras as "a religious community of men who dress and act like women and whose culture centers on the worship of Bahuchara Mata, one of the many versions of the Mother Goddess worshipped throughout India."[65] Mythically, the hijras are believed to be born hermaphroditic, yet truly most are impotent men[66] who undergo an emasculation ritual involving the surgical removal of their genitals.[67] This surgery is conducted by hijras themselves for and on one another.[68] Although contemporary Western medical constructions of sex/gender emphasize the "realness" of genitals, the hijras do not undergo what we know in the West as male-to-female transsexual sex reassignment surgery, with the construction of a vagina.[69] Instead, hijras consider themselves to be "eunuchs" who are neither men nor women, but a distinctive third gender.

Through her fieldwork, Nanda discovered that most hijras join the community voluntarily, as young teenage boys. In addition to physical characteristics that set them apart from other genders, the hijras' occupation is distinctive. They perform ritual dances and blessings at childbirths, weddings, and temple festivals to confer fertility, prosperity, long life, and reproductive capacity. Hijras are also allowed to conduct careful inspection of children's genitals at birthing rituals. If they discover that a child has ambiguous genitalia during such inspections, they are permitted to take the child from its family and raise it in the hijra community. Many hijras also work as prostitutes with male clientele.

While they are accepted as a third sex/gender and are respected as performing needed spiritual and religious ceremonies, hijras live in a segregated form of housing known as hijra houses, which are similar to the drag houses of New York City.[70] In addition, they have their own temples, and their main temple is located in Bombay.[71] Such separation is perhaps evidence of both social stigma and social recognition of a distinctive third-gender category.

My final cross-cultural example of third gender stems from Will Roscoe and Walter Williams's studies of Native American berdaches, or two-spirits.[72] At the outset, it may appear that berdaches are similar to male-to-female transgenders, although they are better described as individuals who simultaneously encompass and express characteristics typically associated with both women and men. According to Williams, "a berdache can be defined as a [physiological] male who does not fill a society's standard man's role, who has a nonmasculine character"[73] and as someone who may do work traditionally associated with women of a given tribe.[74] "Male" berdaches have been documented in one hundred fifty North American societies and seem to be born into their berdache gender.[75] They appear to be socially accepted and integrated members of their various tribes, and are often granted special respect and social status. Berdaches are often economic and religious leaders of their tribes. As with the hijras, some berdaches have been feared by members of their communities because of the supernatural powers they are believed to possess.[76]

With regard to gender identity, gender display, and sexual orientation, berdaches appear to be quite flexible. Some crossdress and publicly present as "female" while others don't feel it necessary to take on "opposite" gender behavior or display. Some berdaches engage in sexual relations exclusively with males (non-berdaches), others are exclusively sexual with females (non-berdaches). Still others are bisexual with freedom to fluctuate in the gender of their sexual partners.[77] There seems to be not only great variation between individual expression of the berdache gender, but great tribal variety as well.[78]

Juxtaposing this third sex/gender discussion of the kwolu-aatmwol, guevedoche, hijras, and berdaches with Western ideas of gender binarism illuminates challenges to contemporary sexing protocol. Although the kwolu-aatmwol and guevedoche are the only physiologically intersexed illustrations provided in this cross-cultural comparison, each of these cases illustrates the culturally specific nature of social responses to third sexes/genders. In Kessler and McKenna's words,

> The kinds of questions that arise from studying gender in other cultures would be less likely to arise if we focused only on our own society, for membership in a culture blinds us to the constructed nature of that culture's reality.[79]

Challenges to gender binarism in many cultures are widely viewed as forms of deviance to be identified, regulated, and eradicated. But these examples show that other, less pathological views are viable as well.

Medicine as an Authority

Although medicine began to distinguish itself as a discipline separate from theology and philosophy in classical Greece, medical authority was not widely recognized until its initial European development during the Renaissance, and medicine became far more influential during and after the Enlightenment.[80] Prior to the development of the medical field and its authority, "disease was given supernatural explanations, and 'medicine' was the province of priests or shamans."[81]

The medical profession became more established during the nineteenth century by gaining the support of lawmakers. Through implementing a state licensing policy, physicians attempted to confine the practice of certain activities for the first time to licensed physicians. While their attempt to control medical practice was not successful at first, mostly due to the "poor image of medicine and lack of standards in medical training and practice," the founding of the American Medical Association in 1847 served to regulate and professionalize medical doctors and medical practice.[82] This professionalization was a major step in the process of the medical institution's rise to becoming the primary authority over the body and mind. When medical authority expanded rapidly during the late nineteenth and early twentieth centuries in Europe and North America, medicine's purview grew as well. Issues that were formerly considered the domain of theology (such as morality) or law (such as criminal activity) were quickly reconceptualized within the realm of medical theory and practice.

MEDICALIZATION

As the disciplines of both medicine and sociology expanded, medical sociologists began to study the scope and impact of medical authority over matters of the body and mind. Early medical sociologists were especially concerned with issues that were once considered natural human experiences but came to be viewed within a medical realm, such as childbirth or menopause. More specifically, "*Medicalization* describes a process by which nonmedical problems become defined and treated as medical problems, usually in terms of illnesses or disorders."[83] Certainly this process of medicalization is evident in the case of intersex. An issue that was once managed by families, religious doctrines, and courts of law is now primarily in the hands of medical doctors and staff.

A major consequence of both medicalization and criminalization is the individualizing, or depoliticizing, of social problems. For example, in order to survive in a very hectic postmodern society, an ever-growing number of children and adults find themselves taking mood-altering drugs. Rather than address the social problems created by living such a fast-paced and alienating lifestyle, people who have difficulty coping are labeled as sick and in need of chemical assistance to keep up. In the case of intersex, where questions of locker room confidence and comfort undoubtedly come up, rather than subjecting individual children to surgical procedures aimed at helping them look normal, we might instead assess the anxiety that mandatory public nudity in adolescence gives rise to. In Dreger's words, "When I talk about intersex, people ask me, 'But what about the locker room?' Yes, what about the locker room? If so many people feel trepidation around it, why don't we fix the locker room? There are ways to signal to children that they are not the problem, and normalization technologies are not the way."[84]

Not surprisingly, once a phenomenon comes to be seen through a medical lens, medical treatments may seem logical if not necessary. An example of the acceptance of medical management of intersex conditions was evident in an episode of the television hospital drama *Chicago Hope*.[85] In this episode, following the birth of a physically healthy intersexed infant, the delivering physician immediately consulted a pediatric endocrinologist and urologist to ascertain the baby's sex. The medical team treated the infant's sexual ambiguity as a medical emergency and, in the end, strongly recommended a female sex assignment and genital surgery due to the small size of the infant's phallus. The parents consented to the procedure without getting a second opinion or seeking additional information. Medical authority in regulating intersexed bodies is apparent in this hospital-based television drama, in that the necessity of surgical intervention was never questioned, it was simply presumed.

Medicalization increases the range of phenomena linked to medical treatment and fuels the widespread implementation of medical concepts and cures.[86] Irving Zola documented the mainstreaming of medical terminology and thinking beyond medical arenas. He identified this phenomenon in the use of medical language and perspectives by lay people.[87] For example, when referring to newborns that are intersexed, clinicians often describe an ambiguous penis/clitoris as an hypertrophied (enlarged) clitoris or a micropenis, and use scientific instruments to measure and classify the anatomy in question.[88] Widespread cultural adoption of a medical paradigm is especially notable when intersexuals talk about their own experiences using medical jargon, referring to their "conditions," "diagnoses," or "disorders." This use of medical jargon to describe oneself reflects a general cultural acceptance of medical paradigms and authority. Because language and cultural perception tend to reflect and reinforce one another, adoption of a medical perspective makes it difficult for lay people to question medical opinion or authority, or to seek alternative care.[89]

MEDICINE AS AN AUTHORITY IN MATTERS OF SEXUALITY AND GENDER

As medicine gained authority in matters of mind and body, and psychiatry was developed as a specialty within medicine, sexual activity and morality became one of its primary concerns. Medicine initially labeled same-sex sexual activity as homosexuality in the nineteenth century, when it created the term *homosexual* in 1869.[90] More recently, homosexuality was designated as a mental illness in the psychiatric *Diagnostic and Statistical Manual,* until its contested removal as a psychiatric disorder in 1973. For well over a century, sexual "perversion" and "inversion," as homosexuality was formerly called, has been in the hands of medicine.[91] As psychiatry developed its interest in sexual behavior in the late nineteenth century, it also developed classification systems and treatment models for sex and gender deviants, including transsexuality.

The medicalization of transsexualism has an interesting history that began with a prominent German writer, Karl Heinrich Ulrichs, and a prominent German physician, Magnus Hirschfeld. Both men were dedicated to the decriminalization of homosexuality, transvestism, and transsexuality in the latter half of the nineteenth century. They worked separately, as Ulrichs was Hirschfeld's predecessor, opposing the moral and legal condemnation of homosexuals, transvestites, and transsexuals, claiming that such "conditions" were inborn and, therefore, should be treated with compassion and understanding.[92] Their strides in the protection of transsexuals' civil rights paved the way for the gay liberation movement of the 1960s, the transgender pride movement of the 1990s, and perhaps the intersex rights movement we are currently witnessing.

Paradoxically, transsexuals' historical desires to achieve a physical body that "matches" their psyche reifies the stability of a sex/gender binary.[93]

Transsexuals have been historically characterized as having the correct gender and the incorrect sex (or genitals). According to Judith Lorber,

> bending gender rules and passing between genders does not erode but rather preserves gender boundaries. In societies with only two genders, the gender dichotomy is not disturbed by transvestites [or transsexuals], because others feel that a transvestite is only transitorily ambiguous [and]—is "really a man or woman underneath."[94]

Thus, the example of traditional transsexualism (that is, crossing from one sex to "the other" via sex reassignment surgery) is actually a reinforcement of gender binarism.[95] Like surgery on intersexed infants that "clarifies" sexual ambiguity, transsexual sex reassignment surgery is another example of the medical removal of sexual ambiguity. In Kessler and McKenna's words,

> Transsexualism, as a legitimate diagnostic category, exists largely because of advancements in medicine and cosmetology. It is a category constructed to alleviate ambiguity—to avoid the kinds of combinations (e.g., male genitals–female gender identity) that make people uncomfortable because they violate basic rules about gender.[96]

While the medical specialty of psychiatry was making inroads in the classification of sexual "ills," the development of obstetrics and gynecology standardized and medicalized human reproduction, pregnancy, and childbirth. Understanding medicine as an institution of social control in these seemingly disparate areas of life is paramount to comprehending how and why the treatment of physical sexual ambiguity is firmly entrenched within a medical realm today.

MEDICAL AUTHORITY IN CHILDBIRTH

Childbirth itself didn't fully enter a medical realm until roughly one hundred years ago. As a direct result of the continual expansion of the medical-industrial complex and the legitimation of medical authority in childbirth, medicine has gained control over birthing procedures and has, for the most part, successfully withstood challenges such as the 1970s natural/home birth movement.[97] Prior to the twentieth century, childbirth had a history of female lay control and was overseen by the women giving birth and their female assistants.[98] If an intersex birth occurred, it was most often handled privately, within the family, unless circumstances required medical intervention due to the rare cases of compromised health of an intersexed child.[99] This is no longer the case because the vast majority of U.S. births now occur in hospitals and there is significantly more medical intervention in situations where formerly there was none.[100]

Although physicians first began attending births in the early to mid–1700s, women retained control and authority in most birthing situations and made use of the doctors' expertise when there was some doubt of a safe delivery.[101] The decision to request a physician's attendance during childbirth depended largely on financial resources. Those women who could afford to pay doctor's fees ultimately opened up the intimate atmosphere of traditional childbirth to include a physician.[102]

Wealthy women initially called upon the physicians of the eighteenth century to provide relief from the painful or dangerous aspects of labor such as excessive bleeding, excruciating pain, or prolonged labor. Physicians took on this more active role in childbirth because of the development of new birthing technologies, such as the use of forceps and opium in the eighteenth century and anesthesia in the nineteenth.[103] Ironically, while the purpose of involving physicians in labor and delivery was to improve one's prospects for a safe delivery, doctors often aggravated nonproblematic situations by their lack of preparation. Throughout most of the 1800s, male physicians were instructed to deliver "without looking at women's genitals," and physicians commonly went straight from treating infectious patients to home birth sites without thoroughly washing their hands.[104] Once physicians gained entrance into the private world of childbirth, they gained a degree of control they were reluctant to relinquish. As a result, access to technologies and information necessary to care for oneself became limited. For example, the invention and use of new birthing technologies and drugs aided in the speed and ease of delivery, but were not made readily available to the lay public. More recent medical technologies used in birthing include fetal heart monitors and the use of intravenous fluids in standard hospital births.[105] While birthing was traditionally an all-woman, closed-door event to which no strangers were granted entry, contemporary childbirth is very often physician assisted.[106]

Zola's theory of medicalization readily applies to the case of childbirth.[107] Judith Leavitt's analysis further articulates the transition of power from the lay to the medical.[108] Leavitt details five factors which led to the current medical authority over childbirth: (1) The "shadow of maternity" or fears of death and illness that sometimes caused women tireless concern over the well-being of themselves and their fetuses before, during, and after birth. Knowledge of difficult and/or fatal deliveries prompted some (wealthier) women to seek medical assistance in order to decrease the likelihood of complications in their own deliveries; (2) The evolution of the germ theory by Louis Pasteur and others in the mid- to late 1880s led to an attempt to sterilize the home birth environment, based in the belief that germs were the primary agent of infection. Antiseptic techniques became commonplace in the home, and due to a

lack of ability to control the home environment entirely, physicians urged the
transfer of births from the home to the highly controlled hospital environment. The germ theory school of thought and its primary science—bacteriol-
ogy—exacerbated the already prominent use of medical terminology and
technology, which increased the risk of alienating women from their own delivery experiences; (3) Industrialization and urbanization prompted a breakdown of the tightly knit women's network that served home births effectively
for centuries. With an increase in physical mobility, women found themselves
in closer proximity to hospitals than to their families or friends who had traditionally been called upon to support the delivering mother; (4) The development of new technologies such as forceps and anesthesia expanded the
already growing reliance on medical protocol and knowledge in birthing situations. With the rise of acceptance surrounding these new technologies, the
transfer of decision-making authority moved from the birthing and attending
women to the male physician. It was through their successful interventions
in high-risk births that physicians found their entry into the authoritative position regarding childbirth; (5) Finally, hospitals began to proliferate when federal funds became available to support child and maternal health.

Relating the medicalization of childbirth to the medicalization of intersex, Kessler comments on the central location of medicine in current protocol associated with intersex births:

> In the literature of intersexuality, issues such as announcing a baby's
> gender at the time of delivery, postdelivery discussions with the
> parents, and consultation with patients in adolescence are considered
> only peripherally to the central medical issues—etiology, diagnosis,
> and surgical procedures.[109]

Here we see evidence of medicine's position of authority in the social response
to intersexual "deviance." In working with intersexed newborns, physicians
are in a position of power working with a very vulnerable population, allowing for the possibility of misusing, albeit unintentionally, that authority.

While there has been some success in a movement to demedicalize
lifecycle events such as childbirth,[110] it does not extend to intersex infants.
A critical examination of contemporary medical management techniques in
intersex births provides a wealth of information about the degree of social discomfort with sexless infants.[111]

The threat that intersex poses to gender binarism has given rise to discourse surrounding the potential elimination of intersex ambiguity. In fact,
with the rise in the authority of medicine in our culture and the advent of
potent genetic technologies, such as the late-twentieth-century Human Ge-

nome Project and its implications for genetic testing and prenatal screening, intersexuality may be in danger of technological extinction.[112] Explicity, relating intersex to this potential, physicians Patricia Donohoe and her colleagues declare:

> We envision early in utero detection in pregnancies of families at risk [for intersexuality] and possible correction of defects with transection techniques. Better still, detection of carriers [of potentially intersexed genetic material] may reduce the incidence of such anomalies, thus making obsolete these complex interventions, which is the ultimate goal of our intense research efforts.[113]

Are Donohoe and her colleagues suggesting genetic elimination of intersex or are they "merely" hoping for abortive (selective breeding) techniques to prevent or limit intersex births? Does the detection of intersex in prenatal screening lead to requests for or medical suggestions to proceed with abortion? How is an intersex diagnosis presented by clinicians and perceived differently by parents before rather than after a child's birth? Although the answers to these questions are unclear, we may better be able to predict the outcomes of future biomedical intervention in and on intersexed bodies by studying contemporary sexing procedures.

With the mapping of the human genome and rapid advancements in the field of genetics, there is certainly reason to consider the ethical implications of detection, diagnosis, and treatment of intersex. In fact, due to the growth of prenatal screening and fetal surgery, diagnosis and treatment may begin before a child is born.[114] As a result, significant research is being conducted on the impact and implications of prenatal screening and diagnosis of intersex conditions.

In order to reduce or avoid genital ambiguity in neonatal development, clinicians have been researching ways to treat intersex neonates during gestation. For example, Maria New, a nationally respected professor of pediatrics and research on congenital adrenal hyperplasia, has developed prenatal hormone therapy to reduce or eliminate the development of ambiguous genitalia in neonates with CAH.[115] Because it is one of the only forms of intersex that is life threatening, and because it does occur with significant frequency, many countries and states have implemented CAH screening programs for newborns. At the time of this writing, thirty-three states in the United States have newborn CAH screening programs in place.[116]

Neonates and newborns aren't the only people being screened for intersex. For example, in an attempt to level the playing field, the International Olympic Committee (IOC) has used various means of weeding out "sex imposters" among female athletes since 1966 to disqualify genetic males who may live and compete as women. The presumption behind the testing is clear: men are considered to be naturally, biologically, better athletes than women. Since Olympic competition is reserved to intra-sex competition, no "man" is allowed to enter the female playing field. According to this line of thinking, it wouldn't matter much if a genetic female were competing as a man, because, after all, women are slower and weaker than men. (Ironically, though, recent track performances predict women will outrun men in speed in the near future.) The IOC's techniques for sex verification have changed over the years, and have run the gamut from requiring female Olympians to parade naked in front of a panel of "sex verifying judges" to chromosome testing.[117] After nearly a decade of protest from athletes, the International Olympic Committee suspended sex verification for the 2000 Olympic Games on a provisional basis. The IOC made the decision to suspend genetic testing in 1999, but declared that it "reserve(d) the right to conduct such tests, if necessary." Presumably, this means that the IOC will invoke sex verification if they suspect "sex imposters" at some point in the future.[118]

The Emergence of a Contemporary Surgical Solution

Several factors converged in the middle of the twentieth century to bring about a new paradigm for the treatment of sexually ambiguous children. Medicine had achieved an authoritative stronghold by that time and had gained dominance over matters concerning sexuality and childbirth. Psychiatry had furthered the importance of gender binarism and the heterosexual matrix by problematizing people who did not neatly fit into gender and sexual norms. This is especially notable in the earlier medicalization of homosexuality and transsexuality at the end of the nineteenth century.

Technological developments such as plastic surgery allowed for the medical "correction" of sexual deviations in the form of transsexual sex reassignment surgery, intended to bring the components of Judith Butler's matrix (sex, gender, and sexual desire) back into alignment. The first sex reassignment surgeries on transsexuals were performed in Denmark in the 1920s.[119] The first American to undergo surgical sex reassignment was Christine Jorgensen. After her 1952 surgery in Copenhagen, Jorgensen's highly publicized return home to the United States made the general population aware of transsexuality and sex reassignment for the first time.[120] The print media popularized her story. Newspapers ran stories with headlines like "Ex G.I. George Jorgensen returns home as blond bombshell, Christine Jorgensen" so often that her sex reassignment became one of the most widely reported news events of 1952 and

1953.[121] Due to the news coverage of Jorgensen's successful sex reassignment and the public acknowledgment of transsexuality that followed, medicine and psychiatry gained even more authority and domination over the body, gender, and sexuality.

These early sex reassignment surgeries were aided by the development of nineteenth-century medical specialties such as pediatrics, and advancements in the 1920s and 1930s such as urology, endocrinology, and plastic surgery.[122] But following decades of overwhelming social instability during the Great Depression and the Second World War, 1950s America was characterized by political conservatism, sexual repression, authoritarianism, and rigid reinforcement of gender roles. These factors, combined with the oppressive cultural conservatism and homophobia of the 1950s McCarthy era, paved the way for the contemporary surgical and hormonal engineering of intersexed bodies common today.

Evidence of a late-twentieth-century cultural movement toward conformity is abundant in popular culture, politics, and medicine. During this period, television became an influential form of entertainment for those who could afford it. Shows such as *Leave It to Beaver, Father Knows Best,* and *The Dick Van Dyke Show* touted simple domesticity and marked difference in gender roles. Television couples portrayed the new American trend toward earlier and more widespread marriage. These fictional television families also reflected images of the "good life," where dad worked hard to earn the family's livelihood while mom was content to do unpaid domestic labor and service at home.[123] Indeed, popular portrayals of the genders painted women and men as so different from each other, it's amazing they had anything to say to one another at all. Show themes frequently revolved around the placid images of mom cooking or serving a meal, and dad coming home from or leaving for work. Absent were discussions of "sordid" topics such as sex and pregnancy. In fact, television couples were shown sleeping in separate twin beds with a shared nightstand between them. Also missing from these shows were alternate (and possibly more realistic) economic or family arrangements, such as women working outside the domestic sphere. In contrast to the idealized family picture shown on living room televisions, the reality was that across race and class divisions, droves of women entered the paid labor force during the military buildup of the Second World War.

As postwar television and film industries were busy creating images of a new "traditional" family, the U.S. government, under the leadership of Senator Joseph McCarthy, was in the process of sanitizing the U.S. Statehouse, the entertainment industry, and the country by eliminating suspected communists and homosexuals. McCarthy and others who were consumed by the nationalist

rhetoric of the Cold War served as self-appointed moral protectors of the country, and attempted to weed out persons whom they saw unfit to work for the
government or even be civilians of the nation. This relentless public attack
on suspected political or sexual deviants reinforced cultural disdain for political nonconformity and connected it to sexual difference in the minds of the
American people.

At the height of this 1950s conservatism, U.S. psychologists and psychiatrists developed recommendations for infant surgical and hormonal sex assignment.[124] These suggestions took hold because the social, political, and
technological atmosphere all served to uphold this radical new treatment. If
plastic surgery and hormone therapy could work for adults who were unhappy
in their assigned gender, why couldn't a similar solution be offered to prevent
potential problems for those born with sexually ambiguous bodies? Surgical
and hormonal solutions seemed to offer transsexuals so much relief for their
gender dysphoria, perhaps these methods could also help alleviate stigma for
intersexed children as well. As a result, psychologists who first recommended
surgery on intersexed infants and children in the 1950s had a similar goal in
mind: to prevent the social stigma and isolation that was thought to accom-
pany intersexual "difference."

The same year George Jorgensen became Christine, a young Harvard psychology student named John Money completed his Ph.D. at Harvard University. Money's 1952 thesis, "Hermaphroditism: An Inquiry into the Nature of
a Human Paradox," gained attention from clinicians at Johns Hopkins University in Baltimore, Maryland. Lawson Wilkins, the leading pediatric endocrinologist of the time, invited Money to join him and two psychiatrists to
oversee the world's first clinic dedicated to the study and treatment of
intersexed individuals.[125] Money accepted his offer, and for the next several
years, Money and the psychiatrists, Joan and John Hampson, studied over one
hundred intersexed children and adults. They found that most of their research
subjects seemed happy and successful in their gender roles. What was most
striking about these findings is that these children had similar physical conditions, but had received different sex assignments at birth. How could children with similar sexual anatomy be raised successfully as either girls or boys,
and mature to become successfully gendered women or men? From studying
these "matched pairs," Money and the Hampsons concluded that children are
born with gender bipotential and that environmental factors supersede any
gender-related biological predisposition. These studies concluded that a child
can be successful in either gender role, if the child received adequate socialization and information, and if the child had a body with genitals and secondary sex characteristics to reinforce that role.[126]

What Is the Current Medical Paradigm?

John Money's theory of gender identity development and suggested standards of care are at the center of late-twentieth-century debates on how to best respond to intersex. Money and others' research in this area emphasizes the psychological need to clarify the sex of intersexed infants at birth in order to alleviate the social stigma that could potentially arise from sexual ambiguity.[127] The objective of this treatment model is the normative psychosocial development of intersexed children as clearly sexed individuals. It is precisely "for the sake of the children" and their families—in the hope of preventing social isolation and stigma—that cosmetic and other alterations of intersexed bodies are performed. In this case, "for the sake of the child" requires erasure of difference. More specifically, this model requires that sexual ambiguity be eradicated or hidden from view in order for intersexuals and their families to be granted normative social space.

In a summary of the first twenty years of case-study research on intersex, John Money and Anke Ehrhardt conclude that prenatal hormones do not conclusively fix development; rather, infants develop their gender identities through a combination of gender identity socialization and physiological influences.[128] Furthermore, Money and Ehrhardt argue that if an intersex infant receives a clear sex assignment before eighteen months of age (or two years of age at the oldest) and is raised unambiguously according to that assignment, gender identity development will proceed normally and the potential for stigma will be reduced.[129] Recent psychological reports also conclude that if children do receive ambiguous rearing, gender identity disorder may result.[130]

Money's writings illuminate his view on the plasticity of gender in infancy as well as his belief that sexual ambiguity must be downplayed to the intersexual and her/his family. In response to cases of male pseudohermaphroditism (that is, someone who has male chromosomes and gonads, but genitalia that appear somewhat feminized), Money writes:

> The closer the resemblance of the external organs to the normal female, the less is the likelihood that anything can ever be done to permit a normal male sexual life. Therefore there are many male hermaphrodites who should be designated female at birth, with a program then, and again in teenage [sic], of appropriate surgical correction and hormonal treatment. So treated, and with the parents properly counseled, such individuals grow up and function very well as girls. They differentiate a feminine psychosexual identity.[131]

Parental cooperation is central to the success of sex assignment; therefore, their education is crucial.[132] Parents are easily the foremost social influence in an infant's life and thus have a great deal of impact on the healthy gender identity development of their child. According to Money's theory, it is imperative for the child's successful gender identity development that parents treat their child as definitively sexed, and in agreement with medical sex assignment.[133] Moreover, related to the sociological issues of stigma, secrecy, and taboo, Money writes about disclosure issues for girls with congenital adrenal hyperplasia, a form of female pseudohermaphroditism. Money explains:

> My recommendation is always to say nothing until wedding plans are under very serious consideration. Giving away one's secrets is giving away a part of oneself. They are not to be entrusted casually to a person who may take off with them and spread them around.[134]

Clearly, Money believes that "the most important thing is early diagnosis, ideally at the time of birth. Then the girl can grow up oblivious of ever having had a problem."[135]

"True Sex," Female by Default, and Other Curious Notions

The primary concern of intersex medicalization in modern medicine is the swift assignment of a "genitally appropriate" gender for the infant.[136] But typically, an infant's family remains a marginal part of the decision-making process regarding the evaluation and treatment of the baby, while the medical team retains nearly exclusive control over the situation.[137] For example, a common method of handling an ambiguous birth includes telling the parent(s) that their child's genitals are not yet "fully developed" before quickly whisking the infant away for myriad medical diagnostic procedures with which to ascertain the infant's "most appropriate" gender assignment.[138] Most urban hospitals consult with members of their gender ambiguity teams to inform their decisions. Typically these teams are comprised of urologists, pediatricians, pediatric endocrinologists, surgeons, and, at times, a social worker or a psychologist.[139] Most parents are not offered access to support groups or referral to parents of other intersexed children or intersexed adults. When referrals do occur, they are typically insulated within professional clinical networks.

Surgical "completion" of the developmentally "incomplete" child is made possible by physicians for parents. In these cases, "Genital ambiguity is presented as 'hiding' an underlying sex, yet to be 'discovered' by the physicians."[140] Yet, in Ormrod's words,

If doctors speak of "assigning" [sex] often there is a risk that they will come to believe that they have actually determined the sex of the patient whereas all that they have done in fact is to recommend a particular mode of living.[141]

What's more, because of the failure on the physicians' part to fully disclose the sexual ambiguity of the intersexed infant, serious ethical implications are raised.[142] Doctors do not often inform parents that the sex of their child is in question. Instead, they convey an understanding that they will uncover and reveal the infant's *"true sex,"* bringing it out for the world to behold. According to Ellen Hyun-Ju Lee,

The intention, presumably, is to normalize the condition of the children for the parents, but the nature of this representation is misleading. It leads parents to believe that the actual sex was always there, obscuring the fact that the physicians construct the sex of the child.[143]

As Money's work demonstrates, the task of treating a newborn as neuter is challenging, because English and other languages lack gender-neutral terminology.[144] Medical discussions about sex assignment revolve around infants' genitals, chromosomes, hormones, and gonads, with special emphasis given to the potential for the appearance of genital, gender, and heterosexual normalcy in adulthood. Speaking to the primary issues involved in sex assignment decision making, the physicians Cynthia Meyers-Seifer and Nancy Charest write:

Gender assignment requires consideration of the potential for (1) an unambiguous appearance of the genitalia before and after puberty, (2) adequate sexual functioning, and (3) fertility. In addition, the family's perceptions, expectations, and desires should be assessed and included in the decision regarding the sex of rearing.[145]

Normative ranges for infant clitoral and penile size have been codified. The range for medically acceptable clitoral size is between 0–0.9 centimeters, that is, 3/8 of an inch. Any phallus larger than 0.9 centimeters is considered too large and therefore unacceptable for Western clitoral standards. Thus, according to current North American medical standards, the overbearing clitoris must be "receded" or "trimmed back," despite potential loss of sexual function or other iatrogenic consequences from doing so. Conversely, to be considered a penis, an organ must be at least one inch long, that is, between 2.5–4.5 centimeters in length.[146]

Although modern medical technology allows for the acquisition of chromosomal sex, contemporary sexing decisions ultimately revolve around the size and capacity of an infant's penis/clitoris. As a result, the overwhelming majority of intersex children are sexed as female. According to Donohoe and colleagues, "the decision to raise the child with male pseudohermaphroditism (XY sex chromosomes with ambiguous or female genitalia) as male or female is dictated entirely by the size of the phallus."[147] In other words, if a child has a phallus deemed socially adequate as a penis, the child is given a male sex assignment. Conversely, if a child's phallus is deemed socially inadequate to be a penis, the child will be assigned as female, despite gonadal or chromosomal composition.[148] Moreover, there is great concern that a child with a male sex assignment be able to urinate from the tip of his penis while standing.[149] Thus, a child's physical makeup may be male, but unless the medical team deems the infant's phallus to be of adequate size, capable of "proper" urination while standing, and likely to pass as [hetero]sexually "normal," the child will be surgically and hormonally constructed as female.[150] According to a widely cited article from the *Johns Hopkins Magazine* that includes interviews with leading intersex specialists Gary Berkovitz, John Gearhart, and Claude Migeon,

> In truth, the choice of gender still often comes down to what the external genitals look like. Doctors who work with children with ambiguous genitalia sometimes put it this way, "You can make a hole [vagina] but you can't build a pole [penis]." Surgeons can decrease the size of a phallus and create a vagina, but constructing a penis that will grow as the child grows is another matter.[151]

Clinical measures of successful vaginal construction most often rely on the ability of a vagina to be a receptacle for a penis during intercourse. This perception of vaginal function was exceedingly clear in Greta's experience with her doctor. Greta, a thirty-four-year-old realtor who has AIS, requested a vaginoplasty (surgical construction of a vagina) when she was twenty-five. In her words:

> The doctor said, "Well, I really don't want to do this because you're not in a relationship." I looked at him and I said, "Did you ever think the reason why I'm not in a relationship is because I don't wanna put somebody through that? That's something that I need to deal with on my own." Don't put your crap of "I'm not gonna do this for you until you're in a relationship." Well, excuse me, you know, you don't live my life. You need to do this and right things so they can be moved forward.

Several other intersex women I interviewed relayed experiences of being denied treatment to enhance their sexual function unless they were legally married or involved in a monogamous heterosexual relationship.

In the end, a child must have a penis of adequate size and function to be assigned a male sex. Thus, this model, like models of fetal sexual development, is female by default. According to the philosopher Kenneth Kipnis, the "penis = boy, no penis (or inadequate penis) = girl" logic is nearly tangible during his ethical consultations with physicians. He writes of one such experience with a pediatric surgeon:

> [T]he surgeon was immediately concerned about the child's abnormally small penis; technically, a micropenis. Apprehensive about the possibility of the child being shamed in the boys' locker room—psychosocial distress as he matured—the pediatric surgeon was counseling immediate surgical reassignment as a girl. According to the surgeon's plan, the testes would be removed and the genitalia fashioned into a cosmetic vulva before the baby left the hospital. The parents would be instructed to raise the infant as an unambiguous girl. At about the age of 12, estrogens would be administered to stimulate the development of female secondary sex characteristics. Eventually doctors would create an artificial vagina. Although the resulting woman would be unable to bear children, the surgeon anticipated that prompt surgical attention would allow the infant to enjoy a better and more normal life as a female than would be possible for a male with a very small penis [152]

Thus, the penis makes the man, in childhood and adulthood. This is made crystal clear when one stops to reflect on the medical research dedicated to erectile function, impotence, and virility. Consider, for example, the development of Viagra, penis-enhancement pumps, and the public sympathy for and notoriety of men with "penis troubles," such as John Bobbit and Bob Dole. We are a culture obsessed with the worth and function of the phallus.

The emphasis on infant phallic size as a correlate of adult phallic capacity is questionable because the normative ranges of infant phallic and clitoral size have been shown to be unrelated to adult genital size.[153] In addition, initial studies on boys raised with micropenises show that if their small penises are left intact, these boys fare quite well socially and sexually—far better than if they had feminizing genitoplasty.[154]

Effacing physiological sexual ambiguity upholds the sex and gender binary by making a delineation between the sexes clear, even if it is technologically constructed. Even so, traditional conceptual categories of sexual identity don't make sense if ambiguously sexed bodies aren't originally part of a gender binary. For example, if physiological sex is ambiguous, discussion of sexual orientation seems impossible because traditional understandings of sexual orientation are rooted in a binary understanding of sex. Sexual ambiguity problematizes this binary thinking. Moreover, contemporary sexing procedures do not adequately address questions of sexual attraction and behavior. If we take the common scenario of surgically altering a child with XY (male typical) chromosomes into a genital female and socialize this child to be a girl/woman who sexually desires boys/men, what, indeed, do we have? A chromosomal male who has been surgically altered into a physiological female and is behaving socially as heterosexual? In this scenario, the heterosexual behavior of this "girl/woman" actually brings together two chromosomal XY individuals who appear to have sexually differentiated genitalia. This inherent contradiction of traditional heterosexuality is reminiscent of the recent Texas Supreme Court ruling that sex is chromosomally based, which allowed the legal marital union of a lesbian couple (Jessica Wicks and Robin Manhart Wicks).

Despite the fact that most cases of intersexuality are not harmful to the infant's physical health, the medical protocol for managing intersex births treats the incident as a medical emergency,[155] when the motives for surgical sexing are actually predominantly social in nature. That is, the motive for medical sex assignment is to reduce social discomfort and not physical danger. According to Kessler, "It's striking that in the medical literature, although ambiguous genitals, in and of themselves, rarely pose a threat to the child's life, the post-delivery situation is treated as life-threatening and the genital surgery is described as necessary."[156] In addition, the long-term outcome of such procedures is not known. According to the pediatric urologist Justine Schober,

> As surgeons, we have addressed the aesthetic appearance and functionality of the external genitalia with the belief that these physical changes we impose would help increase psychosocial and psychosexual comfort. Medical and surgical therapies have changed in both timing and refinement. Physical treatment has been offered in two categories: surgery and/or hormonal intervention. The immediate aesthetic results seem to continually improve. However, the long-term efficacy of the structural results of various surgeries and their impact on the individuals' psychological, social, and physical adjustment remains unknown.[157]

As Schober and others illustrate, there are little systematic data on gender identity development in intersexuals that extend beyond John Money's research.[158] Indeed, there is little comprehensive research on intersexuals' adjustment following sex assignment on the whole. Prior research has been largely biomedical, focusing on physiological rather than socio-psychological adjustment to medical interventions. Related to this concern is the empirical omission of parents' and other family members' experiences of and responses to their intersexed children or loved ones. Unfortunately, this dearth of follow-up research is consonant with Money's theory of successful gender assimilation: the less the child and family are reminded of the child's intersex status, the better the prognosis for trouble-free gender identity development and overall psychosexual adjustment.

In addition to these problems with the current state of research on intersexuality, intersexuals' critiques of medical sex assignment have been dismissed as complaints from an unhappy and vocal minority. For example, during a recent interview about intersexuals' dissatisfaction with surgery, Laurence Baskin, associate professor of Urology and Pediatrics at the University of California, San Francisco, said,

> I honestly feel sorry for those people who feel mutilated by their surgeries. They need counseling to get over their loss. Their surgeries were performed years ago, and the nerve supply wasn't understood. For [every] three [unhappy intersexuals], my guess is there are 97 who are happy. But they're not going to be out talking [about it].[159]

Baskin's sentiment is prevalent among adherents to intersex medicalization.

Intersexuals' critiques will continue to be dismissed until systematic research investigates their experiences and perspectives beyond the anecdotal. This book attempts to fill that void by focusing on adult intersexuals' stories as a means of gaining further insight into their experiences and perspectives. In an effort to better understand the burgeoning intersex social movement and criticism geared at intersex medical intervention, I explore how intersexuals experience both clinical and movement-based attempts at destigmatization. It is my intention that this research informs the current debate surrounding medical intervention and that it provides a solid foundation for the direction of ethical treatment and research in this field.

I now turn to the voices of those I interviewed to assess their experiences with medical sex assignment and its effects on their sense of identity and belonging.

Chapter 3

Stigma, Secrecy, and Shame

There's no separating the fact that I hate my body and that I hate my body because of the message I got that my body was completely unacceptable and that they had to cut into it and never talk about it.

> —Excerpt from interview with Ana

Life Histories: Under the Medical Gaze

I became interested in speaking with adult intersexuals when I learned that so little follow up had been conducted on their experiences with medical sex assignment and its impact on their overall quality of life and sense of self. Interestingly, the process of coming to terms with their unique bodies and experiences echo the experiences of others who have been similarly outcast and stigmatized.

I have organized participants' narratives in this book in an order that preserves the way they communicated their life histories to me during the interviews. When participants spoke of their experiences with medical sex assignment, they initially conveyed tales of pain, sorrow, bewilderment, and anger. During the second half of our interview conversations, however, they spoke of their association with intersex support groups, and their stories then encompassed accounts of empowerment, identification, and reappropriation of intersexuality as a positive aspect of self. I learned that it was through their association with various intersex support and advocacy organizations that my study participants were better able to cope with the stigma of difference through "coming out" rather than assimilating to the norm or hiding their difference.

Despite the humiliation and disgrace evident in participants' stories, each one of the individuals I interviewed persisted in gaining accurate and complete information about their bodies and their histories. In addition, each person was determined to find others who were like them because they were convinced that others did indeed exist despite medical tales of the rarity of intersexuality. Eventually they sought additional information relevant to their self-concept in an attempt to renounce their spoiled identities and redefine themselves as nonstigmatized. Their process of renegotiating the self is similar to the coping strategies of others that have been stigmatized for being different from the norm.

Several scholars have explored individuals' means of living with stigmatized characteristics, such as physical disability. Their work in this area details the ways individuals gain pride in their stigmatized identities through political activism, autonomy, and visibility.[1] What's more, identifying with others who have been similarly outcast increases one's sense of empowerment in creating one's own identity. Through their empowerment, individuals work to counteract Erving Goffman's notion that living with a stigmatized identity can lead to a permanent inability to overcome the stigma, or what Goffman called a "spoiled identity." The recent development of well over a dozen intersex support and advocacy groups in North America not only provides an opportunity to study the identity politics of a social movement, but also an opportunity to understand more clearly how some intersexuals experience and respond to rigid social expectations of sex and gender via coming out and community empowerment.

Models of coming out identify a multistage process of embracing one's identity. These stages include (1) recognition of one's nonconformity; (2) acknowledgment of one's difference to self and others; (3) seeking and socializing with others who are similarly outcast; (4) pride in one's marginal identity; and (5) integration of one's identity within a prevailing sociocultural context.[2] In relaying their life histories, intersexed adults reported a similar process of coping with difference, although it was specific to their experiences of medicalization. Research on how gays and lesbians and people with disabilities cope with such stigma has contributed to an understanding of this coming-out process.

Theorists and activists have also applied the coming-out model to transgender individuals. For example, Sandy Stone called for transgender people to come out and affirm their unique transsexual identities that transcend heterosexual imperatives.[3] Walter Bockting has also discussed the implications of coming out for the clinical management of gender dysphoria.[4] The work of Stone, Bockting, and others demonstrates that similar to people with disabilities, people who are GLBT-identified also seek empowerment and, by organizing themselves, transform a stigmatized identity into one of dignity and pride. We are witnessing a similar trend among intersexuals who are also renegotiating and transforming a formerly stigmatized identity into one of acceptance and pride.

Coming Out, Stage One: Recognizing One's Nonconformity

As is true in models of coming out and community empowerment, during early stages of identity negotiation, intersexuals focus on their feelings of nonconformity and difference from others. Participants' narratives conveyed an internalization of stigma derived from an ongoing and alienating medical focus on genital difference and "inadequacy." Their internalization of stigma is consistent with an interactive theory of identity formation, such as Charles Horton Cooley's notion of the looking-glass self and labeling theory.[5] Participants reported feeling that they were objects of medical research, once they had been labeled and treated as such. They also told of their attempts to both feel like and be perceived as "normal" females and males. This sense of being a medical curiosity led participants to feel freakish, to question the authenticity of their sex/gender assignment, and to engage in excessive self-monitoring in their attempts to be socially accepted in their assigned gender role. Moreover, participants reported that "corrective" medical procedures served to decrease their sense of autonomy as well as undermine the development of a solid notion of self. In addition, they reported that medical procedures damaged their ability to engage in healthy sexual relationships due to both physical and psychological trauma.

I found individuals' experiences with medical attempts to "normalize" their bodies amazingly consistent, despite the widespread variation of diagnoses among those I interviewed. For example, intersexuals who underwent medical sex assignment in childhood experienced consistently negative and confusing messages about their bodies and their identities. In sum, study participants reported that they received the following three messages about themselves through medical sex assignment: (1) that they were objects of medical interest and treatment; (2) that they were not to know what was wrong with them or why they were receiving medical treatment; and (3) that such procedures were in their best interest and should remain uncontested and undisclosed. This model led participants to lack information about their own bodies; open and honest communication within their familial, clinical, and friendship networks; and association with a potential peer group of intersexuals with whom to relate.

Recall that the objective of contemporary intersex medical treatment is to decrease social stigma and optimize the formation of a clear and uncomplicated gender identity. Research participants conveyed that because they were given false or incomplete information about their bodies and medical treatments, and because they were encouraged to keep silent about their differences and surgical alterations, they experienced feelings of isolation, stigma, and shame—the very feelings that such procedures attempt to alleviate. Participants spoke frequently of wanting autonomy over their bodies, of longing to talk with others who had similar anatomy, and of wanting to participate in decision making related to medical intervention. Feelings of shame were most intense in those who had recurring medical examinations or treatments to impose clarity on ambiguous sexual anatomy. These individuals spoke of feeling "monstrous, Other, and freakish." In stark contrast, when the very same people spoke of gaining accurate information about their bodies, telling others openly about their physical differences, and finding other intersexuals with whom to relate, they relayed feelings of "relief, acceptance and pride" about their difference and their identities.

BEING AN OBJECT OF STUDY

If identity formation is interactive, as symbolic interactionist social psychologists suggest, then receiving repeated messages that one's own body is socially unacceptable leads to a lasting and damaging impact on one's concept of self.[6] Such is the case for intersexuals who undergo repeated, group examinations and operations on their genitalia. Conversely, if individuals receive positive feedback about their health and adequacy from the reflection of self offered by others, they will develop a sense of self that reflects that input.[7] While I adhere to the notion that individuals actively construct a self-concept by evaluating the information they attain about themselves from experiences, I find it hard to argue for the centrality of critical reflection to identity formation when speaking of infants and young children. Childhood is clearly a time of considerably less autonomy and increased vulnerability. Because children are less discerning about the world, they are more passive in the socialization process during their early years. As George Herbert Mead, John Hewitt, and others have argued, a reflected appraisal of the self may carry considerably more weight in childhood than in other periods of the life course.[8]

Recall from chapter 1 that symbolic interactionists see social realities as dependent upon a shared definition of the situation. In this sense, both deviance and stigma are social products that emerge from social encounters and negotiations.[9] In other words, no one is inherently "normal" or "deviant"; such characteristics do not lie objectively within a person; instead what is considered normal or abnormal is culturally variable and dependent on human reactions.[10] When characteristics central to one's core concept of self, such as sex/gender, race, age, or overall physical appearance, become stigmatized, deemphasizing the importance of those characteristics becomes difficult. In these cases, damage to one's self-concept may be dramatic, leaving a mark or stigma associated with a predominant characteristic upon which the self-concept is based. Here, the stigmatized characteristic becomes so central to one's overall identity that a concept of self will be developed around it, leading to a pervasive self-stigmatization that is generalized and associated with other, seemingly unrelated, aspects of oneself. In this sense, the stigmatized characteristic may become a dominating aspect of self from which (all) other concepts of self take their meaning.[11] For example, an intersexed child whose sexual anatomy is repeatedly assessed as problematic may come to view her/himself as a misfit in other matters as well.

The contrast in self-concept between participants who did not undergo medical sex assignment and those who did is striking. Drew, who was thirty years old at the time of our interview, was one of only two people in my study who did not undergo surgical or hormonal sex assignment in childhood. Drew spoke of first encountering the notion that her body was somehow pathological when she went to see a gynecologist for a routine exam at the age of twenty:

> When I was twenty, I had my first medical experience as an intersexed
> person. [The gynecologist] said, "Has your clitoris always been this
> large? I'd like to do some tests, 'cause I think maybe something's not
> normal." And she used the word "normal" specifically like something
> was not normal. It was the first negative association I'd had, and [I]
> started [having] this feeling that I wasn't normal.

Until this interaction, Drew had received feedback from other medical professionals, her family, and peers that she was healthy, adequate, and normal, and her obvious physical differences were without negative association until that point. The gynecologist's negative assessment of her clitoris, compounded by the authority of the doctor's medical position, led Drew to question her former concept of self in light of this new and contrary information.[12]

Similarly, Suegee was raised without medical attempts to diminish her/his sexual ambiguity. Despite identifying her/his own gender as intersexed, Suegee was raised as female and when we met was living as a man, legally married to a woman with a young child. Here thirty-five-year-old Suegee describes how s/he experienced positive or indifferent reactions to her/his body:

> It was at some point in my youth when I was playing doctor with
> other kids, or playing take off your clothes and show and tell, and

realizing that I was different from anybody else there. And I also remember it wasn't a big deal at all. Everybody was like, "Wow! That's cool. Hey, you look like this, I look like this. Oh, yeah cool, fine, whatever." And that wasn't really a big deal at all.

Similar to Drew, Suegee didn't have negative associations with her/his genitalia until s/he went to see a gynecologist at the age of sixteen.

When I was sixteen and I went off to see a gynecologist for the first time, which I was so excited [about]; I was like, "Oh boy! I'll get a whole bunch of answers." And she could just stutter out that she could recommend a good surgeon. And that was about it. She decided to examine my genitals and she was way too interested in examining my genitals. She was like…got me up in the stirrups and she's going, "Wow. Wow, that's…that's big! That's, that's real big!" And she was totally insensitive and completely just mesmerized by what she found.

But unlike Suegee and Drew, 95 percent of the people I spoke with underwent repeated medical examinations and procedures to downplay their physiological differences. And because they received extensive and prolonged reflections of themselves as pathological, many had internalized feelings of inadequacy and shame. As I have shown earlier, the inability to deflect negative interpretations of self may be one of the most harmful and traumatizing aspects of being intersexed in a society that adheres to the medical "correction" of such variation. As a result, the attempt to develop a coherent and positive concept of self amid continuous attempts to "fix" or change one's sex might be a project doomed to failure. According to J8, who was a thirty-six-year-old graduate student when we spoke,[13]

The primary challenge [of being born intersexed] is childhood; parents and doctors thinking they should fix you. That can be devastating not just from the perspective of having involuntary surgery, but it's even more devastating to people's ability to develop a sense of self. I have heard from people that are really shattered selves, they don't have a concept of who they are. The core of their being is shame in their very existence. And that's what's been done to them by people thinking that intersexuality is a shameful secret that needs to be fixed. So I think for most people the biggest challenge is not the genital mutilation, but the psychic mutilation.

As a means of illustrating the extent to which medicine alienates and objectifies intersexuals in its effort to study and control intersex variation, I quote extensively from intersexuals' life histories below. Each of these individuals speaks directly to medicalization and its procedures, the consequences of receiving ongoing negative attention to their difference, and the process of becoming stigmatized.

According to Goffman, differences that become socially stigmatized are those that are easily seen, such as the differences found among wheelchair users, amputees, and people with obvious facial scarring. Because clothing typically covers genitalia, genital differences are not readily visible.[14] Thus, intersexuals' genitalia must be made visible in order to allow for stigmatization. Repeated genital exams are a part of medical protocol for assessing intersex patients' physiological development. Often, these examinations are performed with several doctors present, for the purpose of teaching medical residents, interns, and other clinicians about sexual ambiguity firsthand. Participants spoke frequently about the shame associated with this public display of their "private parts." As Goffman notes, lacking control over others' access to one's body leaves individuals feeling threatened and out of control, as though "the stigmatized individual is a person who can be approached by strangers at will."[15] Several participants' relayed stories about lacking autonomy during group medical examinations. Chimera, whom I mentioned in chapter 2, when discussing CAH, was forty-one years old and studying massage therapy at the time we spoke. In her experience,

> Because [the hospital I went to] is a teaching hospital, they would line up shoulder to shoulder all the way around from one side of the bed at the head, all the way across to the front and back up the other side. And everybody got a peek and a poke between my legs. And along about nine [years of age] that started getting real uncomfortable for me. But I was not allowed the power to say, "No, I don't want to play this game anymore." I'd see twenty or thirty people at one time.

Because these group examinations were a common element of participants' histories, several developed their own names for the alienating genital exam procedure to express their feelings of being put on display. Some of these labels reflect participants' feelings of being exhibited in a contemporary medical version of the freak show, such as "the dog and pony show" and "the parade." Carol, a thirty-eight-year-old social worker, wife, and mother, whose complete androgen insensitivity syndrome was not apparent until her teen years, was also the object of study at grand rounds when she was hospitalized for her upcoming orchiectomy, which is a procedure that removes abdominal testicles to ward off the possibility that they become cancerous—a common procedure for women with AIS. At the time, Carol didn't know she had AIS or testicles, or even the reason for her impending surgery—another common experience of women with AIS. Carol spoke candidly of the shame and humiliation of one of many "parades" to which she was subjected during a hospitalization at the age of nineteen:

> A few hours after I [checked in] the parade started. I stopped counting after one hundred. But I'm guessing about one hundred and twenty-five physicians, interns, [and] residents paraded by my bed over those five days that I was admitted to the hospital. I counted literally one hundred and then quit counting because I didn't want to know. They came in groups. They just stood around my bed in a semicircle and talked. The doctor would give a little bit of a case history. He just said things like, "One hundred twenty-four pounds...five foot eleven and three quarters"...and things like that. I got so numb to it that I was eating and a parade of about ten came in at once and I kept eating. I just lifted my gown and kept eating. And they all touched, poked, looked, mumbled, and then they left. And I don't even remember looking at them. [I] put [my gown] down [and] kept eating.

Gaby, a thirty-eight-year-old graduate student with congenital adrenal hyperplasia, also spoke of the trauma of medical scrutiny she was subjected to as a child:

> They started pressuring me to have surgery around the age of eight. Since my parents were poor, I had the *lovely* experience of going in through free clinics and being seen by whoever was wandering around. So I was the local dog and pony show. "Come here. You wanna see something interesting?" Yeah, definitely medical traumatization. I probably went about once every three months up 'til a certain age. Then I went twice a year. The worst thing [about] being in a clinic is the dog and pony show. The worst thing is being put in a prone position, half-naked, [and] told to spread your legs while five or six other people look in your crotch and probe. That definitely had a direct effect on my sexuality. It is embarrassing. It is shameful. It's painful. It's really painful.

Greta also experienced shameful medical checkups recalled from her earliest childhood, "When I was probably three, four, five, you know." The medical examinations continued throughout her childhood and young adulthood. Like Gaby and Carol, Greta was subjected to group genital exams and naked picture taking. In her words,

> They were going in for taking x-rays; bone development. I remember going down to the bowels of the hospital and having some photographer take photos. And, you know this is the thing that was just unbelievable, is that I have such a hard time these days still, not so much anymore, setting boundaries. It's because my mother was

condoning this. This was happening in front of me. These were naked pictures. It was just ridiculous. It's unbelievable actually. I remember being on [an] examining table, and having medical students parade in and out, you know, and I was by myself. My mother was not in the room. I had to be like probably six, seven, [or] eight [years old]. [I] don't recall.

Lacking information—about one's physiology, the motive for, and means of medical examination and treatment—is a common experience that often leads intersexuals to question their health and potential diagnoses when they search for meaning in these alienating procedures. What makes Carol's experience with hospitalization at the age of nineteen even more alarming is that when she went to the hospital, she thought she was simply there for a checkup and had no idea that surgery to remove her abdominal testicles was impending. After she overheard hospital staff discussing her surgery, she inquired as to its purpose and was given little to no information. In her own words,

[I said to the doctor] as he was leaving, "Excuse me, the nurse said I'm having surgery." And he said, "Yes it'll be first thing in the morning." And I said, "For what?" And he said, "Don't worry, everything will be fine." And I said, "Why? Fine from what? Why am I having surgery?" And he said, "Well your condition has gonads that could have abnormal cell growth and we must remove them before it gets out of hand." And I said, "I have cancer, don't I?" And he said, "Oh, don't worry about it. Don't worry about it, you're just fine. No, no, no, don't be silly. No, you don't have cancer. Don't worry." I said, "Well, then why do I have…?" "Don't worry about it, you're just fine." And I thought, "He's lying. He is lying; I have cancer." 'Cause that was the best diagnosis I'd come up with yet.

As study participants' experience shows, in addition to conducting group genital examinations, clinicians make intersexuals' difference visible by documenting their genitals through photography. Each person I interviewed expressed that this scrutiny only served to exacerbate feelings of oddity and alienation already generated from ongoing medical curiosity. Because they were marked as different, they came to view themselves as deviant and therefore odd or unusual.[16] Melody, a fifty-five-year-old married homemaker, had the following experience at age twenty-two:

I remember [the doctor] telling me how rare this [condition] was, which didn't please me at all. I didn't like being "rare." And he asked if he could take pictures. He wanted measurements of my arms outstretched. My face was covered, so I posed for these pictures, which was humiliating only in that the curiosity was so bizarre. I didn't like being *that* different.

During a similar picture-taking session with her doctor, Peggy expressed that she felt like an object of medical research and fascination. Recall that Peggy has partial androgen insensitivity syndrome and was originally sexed as female at birth and reassigned as male at age three months. At the age of fourteen, Peggy underwent a double mastectomy in an attempt to uphold a male sex assignment. But at the time of our interview, forty-four-year-old Peggy had been living as a woman for over twenty years. At puberty, Peggy's doctor prescribed testosterone to assist her masculinization. Here she gives her perspective on her physician's attempts to chart the progress of her virilization at age thirteen:

> [The] doctor took another set of pictures of me. He took pictures of my nipples, he took pictures of my armpit, of my upper lip. I guess anything that would have shown the effect of masculinizing hormones. And looking back I can just see him, like figuratively rubbing his hands together because I'd be coming back in a few months with more hair, and this change and that change, and he'd take another set of pictures and be publishing another article [on me] and all that.

From the start of my project I worked with the medical literature on intersex, for it was truly the only source of information about intersex readily available at that time. Reading medical research on intersex caused me to become familiar with photographs like the ones Melody and Peggy posed for. The medical journals I consulted frequently contained articles with photographic documentation of the various conditions discussed. Standard medical articles about intersex contain black and white closeup photographs of children's genitals or full body shots of naked children standing next to a ruler on a wall (to show their height), with their arms held slightly outstretched and their identities obscured by a single black line concealing their eyes. According to Cheryl Chase and Alice Dreger, blocking out the eyes does nothing to obscure the subject's identity. Rather, Dreger says the experience of posing for her own version of such a photo for the cover of *Intersex in the Age of Ethics* showed that her identity was still discernable:

> I learned from contriving this "medical" photo of myself that the intersex activist Cheryl Chase was absolutely right when she told me the only thing the black band over the eyes accomplishes is saving the viewer from having the subject stare back. Even with my blackened eyes and [my "naughty bits"] blurred [out], those who know me can recognize me in that picture.[17]

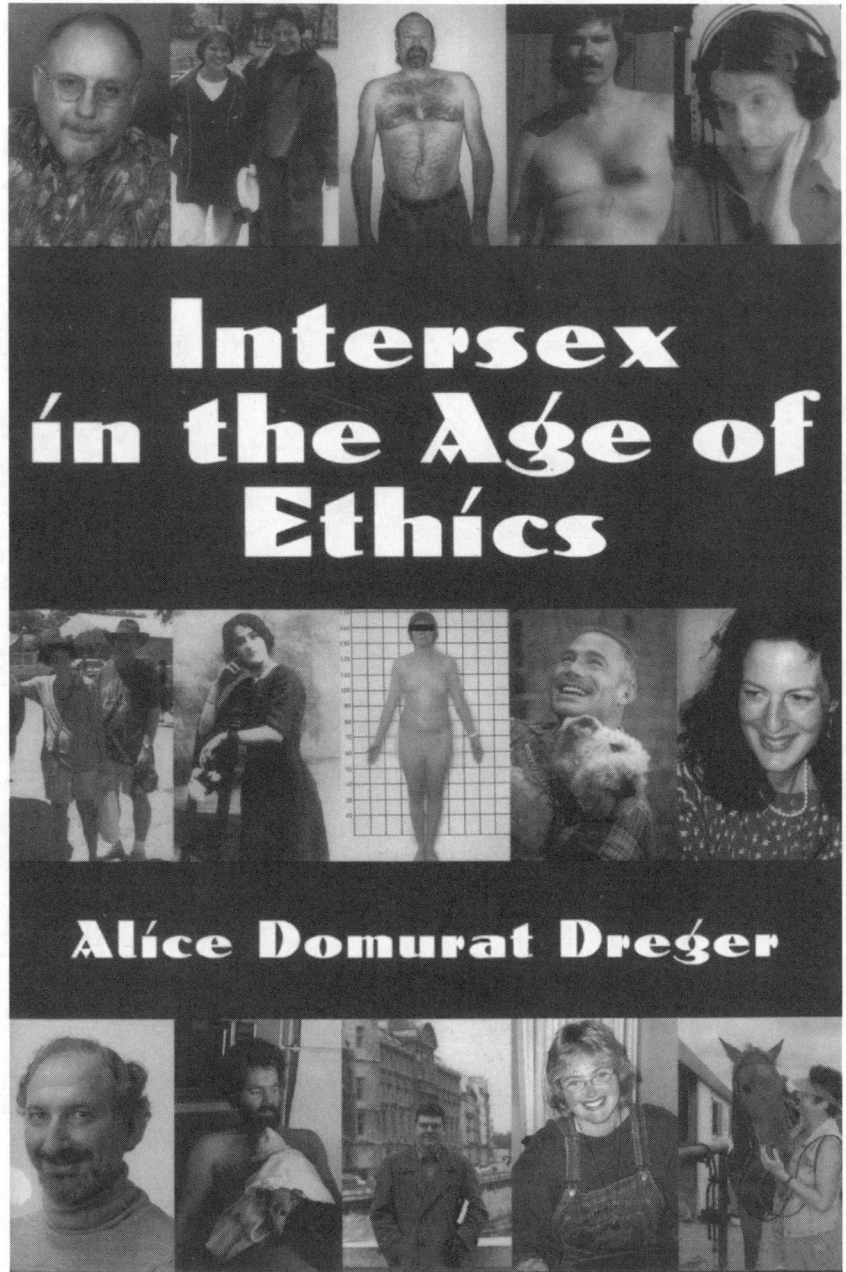

Figure 4. Book cover. *Intersex in the Age of Ethics,* 1999. *Reprinted with permission of the University Publishing Group.*

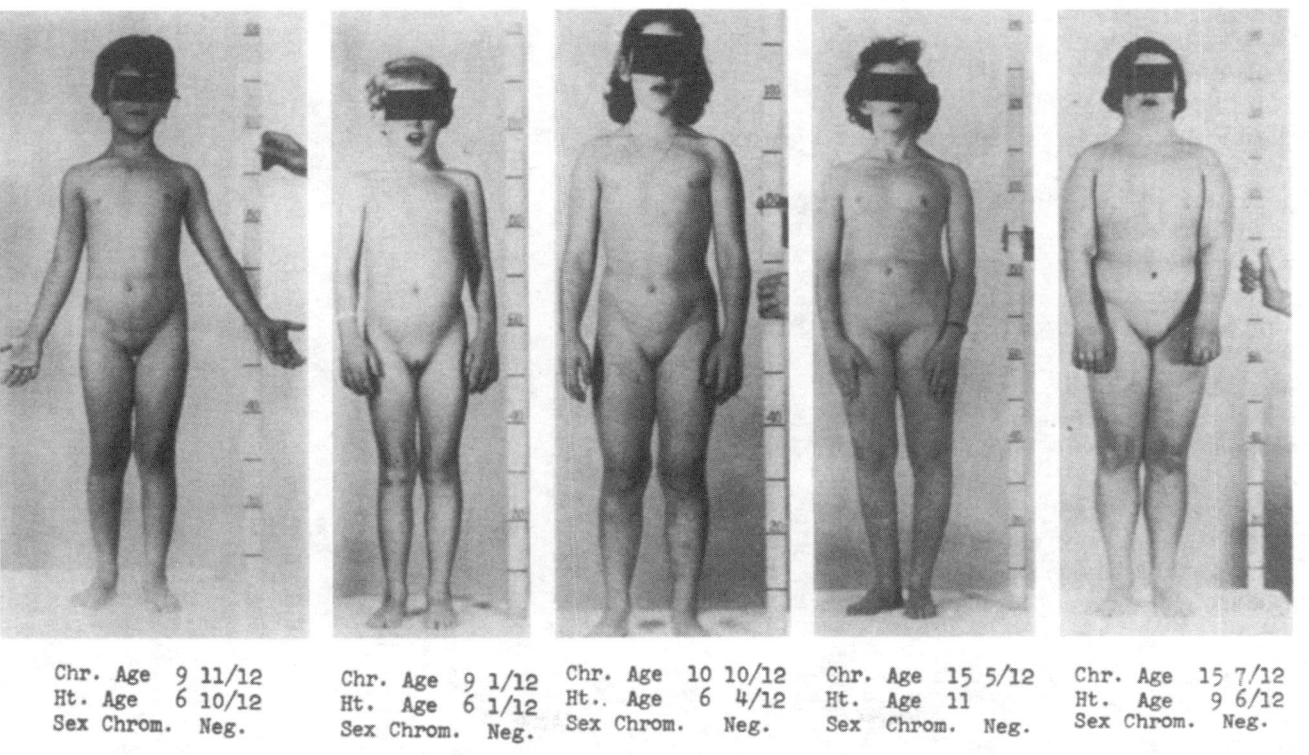

Chr. Age 9 11/12	Chr. Age 9 1/12	Chr. Age 10 10/12	Chr. Age 15 5/12	Chr. Age 15 7/12
Ht. Age 6 10/12	Ht. Age 6 1/12	Ht. Age 6 4/12	Ht. Age 11	Ht. Age 9 6/12
Sex Chrom. Neg.	Sex Chrom. Neg.	Sex Chrom. Neg.	Sex Chrom. Neg.	Sex Chrom. Neg.

Figure 5. These photographs are used to depict variation of physical appearance of five patients with Turner's Syndrome. Melvin M. Grumbach and Felix A. Conte's, "Disorders of Sex Differentiation." From *Williams Textbook of Endocrinology,* ed. Jean D. Wilson and Daniel W. Foster. 1998:1337. *Reprinted with permission of W. B. Saunders Company.*

My own experience with viewing these photos is often quite self-conscious as I sit in a library's medical stacks, flipping through articles with photographs that seem oddly reminiscent of child pornography. In an eerie way, these pictures also remind me of criminal mug shots. While the people in these pictures were posing for purposes of documentation, it is important to remember that they were in a vulnerable state that might not have allowed for their refusal of being photographed.

All children lack autonomy simply because they are children and are often unable to make decisions and implement them independently. An intersexual child's lack of autonomy is more evident than that of most children's, however, and this can impact the development and maintenance of a coherent self-concept. Intersex children not only experience a discrediting mark or stigma associated with their bodies, but also feel that they lack control over their bodies due to involuntary exposure to ongoing examinations and other medical procedures. As a means of illustrating the impact of this powerlessness on the development of the self, I turn to the metaphors used by my study participants to describe their medical examinations as a form of sexual violation. As I discussed earlier, many participants I spoke with viewed their medical exams and treatments as instances of sexual abuse. While I found this association startling at first, upon further reflection, it is not at all surprising. Recall that 95 percent of the sample encountered some form of medicalization, ranging from repeated genital exams to genital surgeries performed without their consent. Most of these procedures were carried out during the formative years of infancy and early childhood. A survivor of childhood sexual assault is perhaps more cognizant of any similarity between the two experiences. In Chimera's own words,

> After I got to be a teenager, I could see a very clear parallel [between the consequences of sexual abuse and medical treatment of intersex] because you have somebody who is able to examine your body, and you don't have the right to say, "No, you can't do this." Even though you're fairly certain that the doctors don't have any sort of sexual interest or intent towards you, it is still a thing that is done to your body, without your consent. And it amounts to the same thing, because you know while you're laying there that you don't have the right to say, "No. Stop. I don't want you to do this."

Like Chimera, many others described the medical exams or procedures they were subjected to as sexual abuse. In referring to the vaginoplasty (the surgical creation of a vagina from skin or colon grafts) she underwent in adolescence, Gaby said,

I was forced to be surgically mutilated and medically raped at the age of fourteen. And that's exactly what I consider it.

Participants also regularly reported that their genital exams routinely involved doctors' stimulation of their genitalia to assess genital responsiveness and size. Given the sensitivity of genital tissue and doctors' perceived need for direct manual stimulation to be conducted in these exams, patients sometimes become aroused. Certainly these early feelings are confusing, especially given the context of the clinical setting and relationship. Speaking of such an experience, Gaby said,

> I don't know about you, but your body betrays you. My body definitely
> betrayed me. And here was this guy who was being a clinician,
> looking at my crotch and meanwhile I'm getting warm fuzzies, which
> means I'm getting aroused. Okay and just the probing alone was
> arousing—inadvertently arousing. Nobody ever taught me how to
> deal with that.

Teaching oneself skills for dealing with sexually arousing and physically or psychologically painful exams was just one area where participants demonstrated resourceful coping skills. Just as Carol's unexpected hospitalization demonstrated earlier, intersexed children's feelings of powerlessness are often intensified by a perceptible lack of disclosure on the part of clinicians and family members. In order to explore the implications of this further, I now turn to examine participants' experiences with the impact of such silence and secrecy.

FEARING THE UNKNOWN: "WHAT KIND OF MONSTER AM I?"
One of the most common themes in intersexuals' stories centers on the lack of full disclosure on the part of clinicians and family members regarding the true nature of their intersexed conditions. Withholding information from the intersex patient compounds her/his feelings of confusion and shame because individuals are told that there is something wrong with them, but they cannot and should not know the specific details of their condition. For example, Sarah, a fifty-six-year-old retired community college professor and library cataloger, spoke of the silence and secrecy she experienced in her late twenties when trying to ascertain the details of her own anatomy from her physicians. In her words,

> They wouldn't tell me anything. I knew that there was more to it than
> all this. I knew that I wasn't being told the truth but there was no way
> anybody was gonna tell me the truth. It was such a mess. There was so
> much lying and symboling going on that there's a wonder I ever
> figured it out. Most everybody's figured it out for themselves.

Two other interviewees, Fanny and Peggy, both spoke of the profound sense of confusion that can stem from lacking accurate information about one's own body. Fanny is a forty-eight-year-old homemaker and mother with CAIS who had just found her local AIS support group and met others with AIS three months before we spoke. In her experience, "I was not told I was not going to have any periods. I was told [by my mother] to pray and hope a lot. So I did do a lot of praying and hoping that I would get periods. I think throughout my *entire* teenage years I prayed that one morning I would wake up and I would have periods. I was not told I wouldn't. So that was a lot of wasted energy." Lacking information may also lead to unfortunate and misguided self-blame. According to Peggy, who had been initially assigned a female sex, then reassigned as a male at three months of age and was raised as a male,

> I was thinking that [developing breasts at age thirteen] was caused by [a] personal failing on my part. I somehow had the feeling that I wasn't acting boyish enough and I was causing myself to develop this way instead of developing like a boy. I thought that somehow it was caused by myself not making enough effort to be boyish. I just felt that these breasts were the whole symbol of my personal failure to live up to what a boy is supposed to be.

Others, including Fanny, Greta, and Max, also spoke about how medical secrecy and scrutiny created both identity confusion and pressure to be successful in the gender role appropriate to the sex they were assigned. According to Fanny, "the idea often comes to me [that] 'my syndrome made me maybe less than a woman,' not quite the total woman. There's a part of me that's missing there." And in Greta's experience, "Because there was no information and it was withheld, it was a huge issue and it greatly affected my sense of self because I was constantly questioning who I was." According to Max, a thirty-two-year-old medical professional who was subjected to a clitorectomy in childhood for a female sex assignment and who began living as a man shortly before our interview, "Intersexuals aren't encouraged to be autonomous, period. I mean, who we are is dictated to us. That's been my experience. And that's why I had no identity and I struggled so hard to find one."

According to the participants, lacking information about their bodies and medical histories was far more difficult than actually learning the truth. As a means of coping with their confusion, many participants developed their own explanations for their physical differences that revolved around a self-derived diagnosis. For example, in an attempt to make sense of their families' shame, several imagined they had terminal illnesses or disorders too freakish to comprehend, let alone discuss. In Max's words, "What I knew myself to be was too horrible; I wasn't a viable fetus." According to Fanny, "I had been told that I had a very rare condition; that it was so rare that it didn't have a name." In another case Flora had the following experience with a genetic counselor when she was twenty-four:

> [The geneticist] said, "I'm obliged to tell you that certain details of your condition have not been divulged to you, but I cannot tell you what they are because they would upset you too much." So she's telling us we don't know everything, but she can't tell us what it is because it's too horrible.

For Peggy, whose gender reassignment was never revealed to her and who was desperately attempting to uphold a male sex assignment despite her body's inability to do so, lacking information about her body gave rise to intense feelings of shame and inadequacy. She recalled her schooling as particularly traumatic:

> In the second grade I started to realize that boys are supposed to stand up to urinate and it was sort of a source of perplexity to me. I tried doing it and it didn't work. I did have the feeling that this was not something I could ask anyone about. Somehow I thought this was something, like a skill, that I had failed to master. It was sort of a personal failing. [I thought] that if I just could figure it out I'd be able to do it. But what I actually started doing was just not urinating at school, which meant I just wet my pants in school. This was happening all through the second and third grades. I was wetting my pants in school. Then I stopped doing that, but I actually never used the public bathroom until I was eighteen and I went to college.

Lacking peer contact with other intersexuals only served to further an individual's difficulty in formulating a coherent and stable self-concept because they had few if any accurate points of social comparison.[18] Of this alienation, Tiger, who was subjected to sixteen failed genital surgeries in the hope that he would eventually be able to urinate from the tip of his penis, said, "The isolation is the *most* punishing aspect of this. You *really* do grow up with the internal sense of absolute freakishness." Having dealt with her difference in complete isolation all her life before finding the AIS support group in the United Kingdom, Sherri, a thirty-nine-year-old lawyer with PAIS, said,

> The cruelest punishment we inflict on prisoners is solitary confinement. And intersex people have lived lives of solitary confinement. And I think that that is such a personal holocaust. Because to be completely separated from others, to not know that there are others, to only know it intellectually, but not know it viscerally is, without a doubt, solitary confinement.

Recall that it is standard practice to sex individuals born with complete androgen insensitivity syndrome (CAIS) as female because they lack the ability to masculinize due to an inability to respond to male hormones. For young women with CAIS, puberty can be a challenge because they typically know nothing is different about them until, in adolescence, they notice their bodies are different from their peers. About noticing this difference for the first time, Carol said,

> [At the age of twelve] I started to notice in change rooms that friends had pubic hair and I didn't and that a lot of women's breasts grow out and mine grew sideways. I really started to notice things. And I noticed that things looked different and I started to just become *really* self-conscious.

When she was a bit older, Flora became concerned that boys would notice her body was different from other girls once she became sexually active. In her words, "I avoided getting involved with boys when I was in high school because I knew that there was something weird [about me]. I didn't want anybody touching my pubic area and discovering that I didn't have hair."

Women with AIS typically are not told that they possess both X and Y chromosomes as well as undescended testicles. Typically the testes of people with CAIS are removed through surgery in adolescence or earlier, due to the possibility that they could become cancerous. As in the case of Carol's surgery I described earlier, it is standard for doctors and family members to refer generically to the organs removed during this surgery as "gonads" or "precancerous ovaries" to downplay the discordance between a female sex assignment and testicular anatomy. Concealing the fact that testes are actually the organs being removed during this operation is widely accepted as medically ethical and was the experience of women with AIS I interviewed. For example, in 1995 a medical student won second place in the Logie Medical Ethics Essay Contest of the *Canadian Medical Association Journal* for an essay that justified deception of AIS patients, including adults.[19] Speaking to the consequences of having been lied to about having precancerous ovaries—when in fact she never had ovaries and in reality had her abdominal testicles removed—twenty-five-year-old Ana said,

> And then the doctor started talking to me about my ovaries. She probably actually said, "There's a great likelihood that you'll develop cancer very soon and we have to have your ovaries out immediately." But all I heard was cancer. I spent all my teenage years terrified I was gonna die someday riddled with cancer.

Having had a similar experience with a lack of complete disclosure during the removal of her undescended testicles, Greta also spoke of fearing that she would someday develop cancer or some other life-threatening illness. When she learned the truth about her surgery and about what caused her body to be different, Greta stated that not knowing the truth had been far more damaging than learning that she had AIS. In her own words,

> I was devastated because I sort of had an inkling of, "Oh my god, there's something not right here." I finally had a label for [it] and I had to deal with the fact that it had been withheld from me. [And] *that* was the big secret? *That* was the big secret? You know, like, "hello," that's nothing. That's like nothing.

If and when intersexuals do learn about their physical difference, they are frequently told that they should not tell others. Withholding information from intersexuals and encouraging them to keep secret what little information they might have is isolating and may actually impede the development of meaningful social relationships. In Carol's case, "I was told by the physician that I should never, ever tell anybody. It was not something they could handle. He said, 'This is *not* something people will be able to handle and still treat you like a normal person.'"

Consistent with theories of medicalization, gate keeping, and patients' overall lack of autonomy in medical settings, intersexuals are told that if information about their condition is shared with others, it should be mediated by a medical professional.[20] Meta, who was diagnosed with Turner's Syndrome in her adolescence, said, "[When I was sixteen years old] this doctor said, 'This is [the condition] you have, but don't be talking about it and when you get a boyfriend, bring him in here and we'll discuss things with him.'" Jenny is a forty-five-year-old businesswoman with a proclivity for political involvement. She was born with partial AIS and an incomplete vagina, and was explicitly instructed by her doctor to lie about the cause of her short vagina. Her doctor suggested that Jenny tell people she had Mayer Rokitansky Kuster Hauser (MRKH) Syndrome—a condition where women have XX chromosomes and ovaries, but no vagina (vaginal agenesis) and very minimal uterine development. Apparently Jenny's doctor thought it would be less troublesome if the cause of her short vagina was not associated with male genetic features such as XY chromosome and abdominal testicles. About this exchange with her doctor, she said,

> I was told by my doctor to tell [my husband] that I had a disease called Rokitansky Kuster Hauser. I was told that that was my story because

no one could ever handle [the truth]. I was told by the same [doctor]
to be very careful about politics. [He warned me,] "If you take a
political path, there is the opportunity for blackmail." So, at that
point in my life, I decided to end my journalism career and end any of
my political involvement.

Clearly, Jenny's story shows that the culture of secrecy that surrounds intersexuality can have unintended, yet profound consequences.

ERASING DIFFERENCE

In addition to experiencing their bodies as frightening and worthy of shame,
many who had genital surgeries emphasized that the very operations that were
intended to assuage feelings of difference only served to deepen their sense of
alienation. In reflecting upon the clitoral recession she underwent at age seven,
Faye, a thirty-year-old scholar, spouse, and mother, said,

I looked back on it and thought, this must have been really necessary.
And that sort of went with me through childhood. If they would do
this to me, it must be that I'm unacceptable as I am. The point is the
emotional damage you do by telling someone that "You're so fuckin'
ugly that we couldn't send you home to your parents the way you
were." I mean, give the parents some credit. Teach them. Help them
to deal with their different child.

While it is common to perform surgery on the external genitalia of young
children, internal operations such as vaginoplasty are sometimes not performed
until the teen years. Although the surgery takes place later, messages about
its impending necessity are common throughout childhood. These messages
lead to further confusion in that intersexuals often receive the conflicting message that they are "normal" yet require a little surgical "fixing up" nonetheless. For example, in reference to a conversation about vaginoplasty with a
physician at age fifteen, Max said, "I had always been told that I was a girl, I
just wasn't finished and I was going to need to have this surgery eventually;
that this would be necessary because I was a girl but I wasn't finished and this
is how they would finish me." Gaby also spoke directly to the contradiction
inherent in such logic:

Oh it's ludicrous, [being told] "You're normal, but you need this
operation, but you're normal, but you need this operation, but you're
normal, and that'll make you normal." "Well, if I was normal before,
and that's gonna make me more normal, what am I supposed to be,
dead? You know. Well, what? What are you gonna do? Sew a neon
sign saying, 'Cunt down there' or something?"

Normalization procedures are not only confusing, but are potentially humiliating and physically debilitating as well. That is, although an intersexual's visible differences may have been erased, the emotional and physical consequences of the process may be long lasting. For example, vaginal dilation is commonly used in conjuncture with vaginoplasty. Some intersexuals who are sexed as female do not undergo vaginoplasty, but may be encouraged to lengthen and widen their existing vaginal openings via manual dilation with a dildo. Many in my study told embarrassing tales of pubescent conversations in doctors' offices (oftentimes with parents present) where physicians instructed them on the use of medically produced dildos to increase the penetrative capacity of their vaginas. In her own words, Ana said,

> At that time she told me I would need to [dilate] like two or three times a day for at least twenty minutes at a time—just like hold it there. And I'm living in a dorm, you know? It was pretty impossible. I found it so humiliating and just degrading that I think I didn't do it [even a total of] three times. I just couldn't, you know. I just couldn't do it. And I felt a little like a failure about that.

As a teen, Max also found his/her doctor's suggestion that s/he regularly dilate his/her vagina both awkward and confusing.

> Even at fifteen I knew there was something incredibly wrong about this doctor suggesting that this would be a perfectly okay and natural thing for me to do as he held up this rack of phallic test-tube-like objects and this box of KY Jelly. Even if I'd been incredibly outgoing and sexual, I don't think I would have [been] comfortable with keeping myself dilated, so I didn't. And then when I decided I was ready to be sexually active I had to have another procedure. I mean I had always been told that I was a girl, I just wasn't finished. I was going to need to have this [vaginoplasty] surgery eventually because I was a girl, but I wasn't finished.

As I indicated above, the consequences of normalizing procedures are not limited to the psychosocial realm because they can also impact sexual function due to nerve damage or scar tissue formation in the genitalia. Compare the consequences experienced by intersexuals to those who received medical intervention to "correct" other forms of physical variation. Consider a principal character from Flaubert's classic fictional work, *Madame Bovary*.[21] One of the characters in the novel experiences discrimination due to his clubfoot. People persist in telling Hippolyte that his foot is abnormal and in need of aesthetic repair because it does not conform to social expectations. Oddly, the condemnation of his foot is contrary to his own experience. His "deformed" foot is the far stronger and more reliable one. Despite knowing this, he gives in to social pressure and undergoes "corrective" surgery, which in the end renders him disabled. When his foot was made aesthetically appealing to others, it lost its strength and reliability. The demand for social conformity and his desire to be considered normal caused his disability, not the variation in his anatomy.

The parallels between Flaubert's fictional Hippolyte and intersexuals' experiences are clear. Intersexuals consistently undergo surgeries intended to make their bodies conform to the norm. As with Hippolyte's surgical outcome, many complain of problems generated by these operations. For example, many adults report an inability to achieve orgasm, as well as irreversible nerve damage to their genitals caused by surgical procedures that were intended to correct their variation from the norm. Such outcomes are of great concern, especially if these problems were not apparent before medical intervention and the procedures were performed for social or cosmetic reasons, and were not life-saving.

Additional physical complications may result from personal attempts to uphold one's sex of assignment for intersexuals as well as others. Here I draw on Lynx's experience, who reported developing incapacitating carpal tunnel syndrome from years of plucking out her facial hair beginning at ten years of age (at the insistence of her mother), in an attempt to look more feminine. In her own words,

> I was spending up to a minimum of three hours a day [plucking out my facial hair]. I finally figured out [that my carpal tunnel] wasn't because of all the typing I was doing, it was more the issue of you know, twenty years of torque-ing your neck and plucking your face and keeping your hands doing repetitive motion. I couldn't pluck the hairs anymore 'cause my hands would go completely numb.

As an adult, Lynx decided to stop fighting a losing battle and let her facial hair grow in. Before a visit to her mother, she informed her that she had stopped shaving her face. As Lynx relayed the experience,

> My mother said, "I don't want you to come here if you have a beard." And I said, "Why?" I mean, talk about those moments when the whole world stops. And I can to this day, I can feel my throat closing up as I'm telling this to you. "I don't want to see you with a beard." And I said, "Why?" And she finally said, "I would feel very uncomfortable and would feel afraid of seeing you with a beard." And I was just so thunderstruck. And then she said to me, "So, are you gonna shave?" And I could literally *feel* myself disassociate. I literally felt part

of me just split off and leave. And that moment of being so conscious
that to be accepted and loved, I was going to have to meet *her* needs.
It was like the whole world had stopped. And I said, "Yes."

In the end, Lynx did shave before her trip home to ease her mother's discomfort. The process of shaving was identity changing for her. Again, in Lynx's words:

> Now I decided to go into the bathroom, and I knew in my heart of
> hearts that I was doing this to ease my mother's anxiety. Not because
> there was anything wrong with me. I looked at myself in the mirror
> and said, "I'll be back." And when I shaved I didn't cut myself once. I
> really understood that I was doing this so my mother would feel more
> comfortable. And that was the real reason I was doing it. So she could
> feel less anxious.

Iatrogenic complications (that is, problems resulting from medical intervention) were common among other interviewees as well. Here Chimera tells of the ongoing physical complications she endured following genital surgery as a young child:

> When I was eighteen months old, they performed surgery; removed
> the hood of my clitoris, most of my labia, which left me wide open for
> urinary tract infections, which I had on a real regular basis. Of course
> there were weekly examinations at the hospital. My childhood was a
> nightmare as far as I was concerned. They did try to stretch my
> vagina, which was altogether unpleasant. [There are] some things in
> life that really were not intended to be stretched, and that's one of
> them.

Presentation of Self

Although contemporary intersex medical protocol is intended to assuage stigma stemming from sexual ambiguity, these procedures create feelings of alienation, shame, and confusion on the part of intersexuals and their families. Because medical intervention draws continued attention to intersexuals' developing bodies and identities, their importance is maximized. Thus, the salience of widely held social expectations, such as gender binarism and heterosexual orientation, is increased. Recall that the heterosexual matrix presumes causal and linear relationships between physiological sex (i.e., genitals), gender, and sexual desire.[22] To be sure, people adhering to this model, whose physiological sex is in question, may come to doubt the authenticity of their gender and sexual orientation as well. Such is the case when one's sex is continuously questioned and little explanation is given to make such scrutiny meaningful, let alone sensible. Questioning the authenticity of their sex and gender was a common thread among participants. In Carol's words,

> I felt like I was a woman, but I was missing the ability to experience it fully. Not that I didn't feel feminine or female, but I didn't have either experiences or parts or rites of passage to really experience full feminine feelings. I don't think I had experiences that really affirmed [that] for me.

The importance of external appraisals of the self is clear for participants whose sexual ambiguity was not apparent until puberty, as was the case for 49 percent of the people I interviewed. In such cases, participants often lived for a decade or more with the understanding that they were typical females or males. When their sexual ambiguity did become apparent, participants reported a disruption to their sexual and gender identities. According to Sherri,

> When I figured out that I had XY chromosomes and had testes, I did at some point look myself over from head to toe and say, "Okay, what about me is male? Where is that male part of me hiding, waiting to come out at night? Where is it? What's visible to other people? What's visible to the world? What is it?" And I went through my body, pretty much head-to-toe.

And in Jenny's words, "I start[ed] wondering, 'Well gee, is there something wrong? Is there something that I'm putting out?' Was I projecting [something] that said, 'Hi! I'm a hermaphrodite. I'm ambiguous. I have ambiguous genitalia. Can you tell from just looking at me?'"

When one's concept of self is transient or unstable, an individual might engage in high levels of self-monitoring or self-objectification in an attempt to gain control over the image they project.[23] Such is the case for intersexuals who are uncertain about the authenticity of their membership in a given sex or gender category. For such individuals, issues of presenting oneself, self-monitoring, and "doing gender" in a manner that is believable becomes exceedingly important.[24] As forty-seven-year-old Martha, a probation officer, said, "I think you [are] constantly monitoring yourself. Is this the way women act? Is this what women think? Is this how women are? It's maybe not something that you do consciously, but it's a constant kind of trying to fit in."

REINFORCING THE LOOKING-GLASS:
THE IMPORTANCE OF EXTERNAL VALIDATION

As is common with other marginal populations, intersexuals develop creative means of coping with their anxieties about passing and fitting in.[25] Many managed their distress by attempting to project a convincing gender-appropriate performance. Goffman's use of the stage as a metaphor for social interaction is easily applicable here.[26] According to Goffman, individuals engage in the use of props and character study to ensure the fluidity of social interaction and believable character performance. For example, Joseph is a forty-four-year-old pharmacist who was raised male, despite clinical concern over the small size of his penis. He, like many others I spoke with about trying to "pass" as one gender or another, demonstrated skills of character study: "I was trying really hard to act like I thought men acted, so I watched my voice very carefully and I watched my mannerisms and I would observe how men were." In a similar effort to pass as a man, forty-two-year-old Jamie invoked the use of costumes and props: "I had a job where I was coming into contact with lots and lots of people. I was being expected to [be] male so I got a custom-made suit. That was part of my armor. I could go out in the world in full drag. Nobody would give me any problems and it felt very much like a suit of armor."

Because they lived with a pervasive fear of not passing or being "discovered" as a fake, some participants employed far-fetched tales to explain their difference to others, in case it was ever noticed.[27] This was often a concern for participants sexed as female who did not menstruate as their peers did. Some were exceedingly adept in creating their tales of defense. Carol and many others were highly inventive in the cover stories they told others. Several women with AIS felt that they needed some explanation to account for the fact that they didn't menstruate. As Carol acknowledged,

> I actively practiced lying in my head so that I could avoid the uncomfortable situations. The story [I told] to my friends [was] that I was born without a uterus [because] my mom took thalidomide when I was a kid. I said, "I'm one of the lucky ones from thalidomide because I at least have my external [organs]. Just my uterus got wiped out and I have this wall that goes transversely across my abdomen and blocks my vagina, so I actually have a closed vagina, but I won't bear children."

Swan, a fifty-seven-year-old chemical dependency counselor with AIS, told lovers that she had had a hysterectomy. Here she recounts this aspect of her story:

> Other than doctors, the only people that I would say *anything* to at all would be lovers, because I had a big scar on my stomach, and I would have to explain that and why I didn't menstruate and stuff. Usually I would try to lie about it, make up some reason. Like say, maybe I had a hysterectomy.

In addition to telling stories to allay questions or doubts, several participants engaged in behavior meant to ensure their sex/gender viability. Robin, a thirty-seven-year-old graduate student with CAIS who was working in educational publishing, notes,

> In high school my girlfriends were always asking me, "I'm gonna walk in front of you and check me if [my period is] spotting." I felt like, god, I wanna do that. I wanna be like that. You know? So I would walk in front of my friends and say, "Am I spotted?" Because I wanted them to know, I wanted to feel like normal back then. I wanted to feel like a woman, and I want[ed] them to think I'm normal.

Others turned to more drastic means of passing and engaging in behavior specific to one's gender role, such as getting pregnant. Thirty-two-year-old Julian, mother of a thirteen-year-old daughter, was living in a male role when we met. In his words,

> I [got] pregnant. I was desperately trying to be female and I was desperately trying to be heterosexual. My mother basically put me through female boot camp. It was like, "You will walk this way, you will act this way, you will dress this way, you will never forget that you are female and you will never try to be anything else and you will take your medication and you will pluck your facial hair out and you will shave." It took me years to get past this feeling of I have to try very hard to be female to compensate for the fact that my body doesn't seem to want to [be].

Still others turned to engaging in sexual promiscuity or exhibitionism in an effort to seek external validation of their gender performance. For example, Martha sought reflections of herself as sexually desirable. In her own words,

> I became very promiscuous. I think I was trying to find out who I was as a sexual being. I think I was trying to prove that I was female through sex. If I could get someone into bed, then I must be a female. It was my own reality testing. I felt awful about it. If your whole idea is just to get someone into bed, that's not hard to do. I guess that's what I felt I had to do to try to prove that I was female.

The salience of external validation to alleviate one's self-doubt is perhaps most evident in Ardea's efforts to be read as an "authentic" woman. Ardea, a thirty-three-year-old medical researcher, was born with a life-threatening heart condition in addition to PAIS and ambiguous genitalia. Her parents' and doctors' primary concern at her birth and throughout her childhood was to stabilize her heart. She was subjected to many heart surgeries in her youth. Given the real health concerns associated with her heart condition, the appearance of her genitalia took a back seat and she didn't undergo genital normalizing surgery until she was eighteen years old. According to her, social acceptance as an unquestioned female was essential to her acceptance of self. In her experience,

> I did nude modeling in college. I was having an identity crisis. I wanted to be sure that people perceived me as a female. [And] everybody's paying attention to me. I'm bare ass naked and they still like me. They don't know I'm an "it," you know? Nobody ever knew. I realized these people are accepting me as a full-fledged female and that's all I ever wanted. That's what I really wanted and that's what I got. I was validated. It really, really helped me. It was one of the best things I ever did.

Having received repeated messages about one's inadequacy as a female or a male, receiving external validation becomes increasingly important. Here Robin demonstrates the significance of not only external validation, but also the ability to participate in gendered rituals and rites of passage:

> When I got married was when I really felt so feminine with my bride's dress, my wedding dress, and a veil. I felt so pretty. I was so proud. That was a turning point and that was about the most significant time in my life that was special to me, where I felt like totally female, *totally* womanly.

Following the wedding, Robin's marriage and relationship with her husband continue to reinforce her womanliness. In her words,

> [My husband] makes me feel like a woman every day of my life. He touches me, he makes me feel sexy. I mean we have sex all the time 'cause he loves me. I mean he wants to always touch me. And he's very attracted to me. He's very muscular, very big. And so he makes me feel small, even though I'm not. I mean, he makes me feel all woman.

DOING GENDER: INTENTIONALLY ENGAGING IN DRAG PERFORMANCE
While the majority of this chapter has been dedicated to outlining the procedures that lead to an internalization of stigma, I will close with a brief section highlighting the critical self-awareness of participants who attempt to uphold their sex of assignment. Once individuals have begun to move out of the stage of shame and isolation so common to intersex medicalization, self-efficacy becomes evident on many fronts. Such is the case for intersexuals who

take part in gender performance voluntarily, rather than as a means to downplay their difference. As individuals move to greater self-acceptance, this freedom is commonly expressed. Several participants spoke of consciously playing a gendered part, oftentimes for their own amusement. Their empowerment is especially notable in participants' discussions of "drag." For example, when referring to the dress she was wearing during our interview meeting, Gaby said, "I kid myself. I sometimes say all I do is drag. And in this society, all I really do is drag. I do the execu-dyke drag, I do girl drag, I do boy drag. This is girl drag, what I'm wearing today." Portraying similar self-awareness and self-efficacy within his performance, sixty-two-year-old Jana said,

> I've been living as a male in a male role, and let's face it, the [ongoing injection of] testosterone has certainly enhanced the male appearance. The mastectomy has enhanced the male appearance. But I would say that what you see is really a chemically, surgically altered being. The physical appearance is a construct. I've at times said it's a lie; what you see is not what I am.

One does not wake up one day and magically possess the ability to be free from the stigma of medicalization and the constraining expectations of gender binarism and the heterosexual matrix. Rather, the resources of humor, critical social deconstruction, and self-reliance are cultivated carefully over time. When individuals are given so little affirmation about their basic constitution, developing a sense of self that moves beyond the looking glass is far from simple. Such a feat is part of a process.

I turn next to exploring that process further by examining intersex empowerment and mobilization, as another stage in the process of coming out and coming to terms with marginality. During this process, individuals shift from viewing and experiencing themselves as stigmatized, to rejecting a self-concept that is primarily shame-based.

Chapter 4   Seeds of Change

*It's almost like I've come full circle, like I know myself
now. It's almost like a part of me has been found. And
now it's like, [sigh] I can go on with my life. I feel like I
have a sense of satisfaction now—a sense of acceptance
of myself. I don't call myself a freak anymore. I don't
think there's something wrong with me. I mean I see
good things in me. I think it has a lot to do with finding
out everything about [androgen insensitivity syndrome];
what is really me. I've come a long way. I'm proud of
myself because I'm special.*

       —Excerpt from interview with Robin

THE PROCESS OF DESTIGMATIZING intersex is a long and arduous one. It begins,
as coming-out models articulate, with an ability to acknowledge one's own
difference to self and others. That is, destigmatization begins with an ability
to move beyond secrecy, isolation, and shame. Recasting the understanding
of one's difference in a more positive light requires a change of consciousness.
What's more, intersexuals and members of other stigmatized populations, such
as people with disabilities, often find this recasting of identity a difficult hurdle
to overcome.[1] This change of consciousness requires an ability to reframe one's
own "personal troubles" as "political issues."[2] That is, the process of
destigmatization requires that one regards the personal as political. Doing so
is essential to developing a positive self-image because the ability to do so relo-
cates the genesis of the problem as external rather than internal. In Gaby's words,

> I don't have a problem coping to begin with. I've always been
> comfortable with who and what I am. And be damned what anybody
> thinks, as long as I'm not harming anybody. And I'm not, so be

damned. I don't have a problem coping. The problems tend to arise with other people's reactions or society's reactions as a whole.

Individual and collective agency play crucial roles in appraising external reflections of the self as appropriate or inappropriate summations of one's own self-concept. In the previous chapter, I explored some of the processes by which individuals become stigmatized and internalize and perpetuate that stigma or mark upon themselves. I now turn to exploring the process by which individuals develop the capacity to reject stigma and come to see it as an inappropriate representation of the self. First I explore the recent mobilization success of other marginal groups.

I would be remiss in not connecting intersex mobilization to the particular sociocultural context within which it emerged. First, the intersex social movement of the very late twentieth and early twenty-first centuries is based on the accomplishments of earlier activists, such as those in gay, lesbian, bisexual, and transgender (GLBT) movements. The great strides these activists made in recent years have furthered achievements for GLBT human rights, identity politics movements, and the development of queer theory. The increasing visibility of GLBT-identified people has clearly provided an expanded level of social tolerance for those with nonbinary genders and sexualities, ultimately paving the way for the intersex movement to take shape. Both queer theory and GLBT activism parallel the politics of earlier difference movements, such as the disability rights movement, which caused understandings of disability to shift from moral to medical to minority concepts of difference.[3]

According to Leslie Feinberg, "Trans*gender* people traverse, bridge, or blur the boundary of the *gender expression* they were assigned at birth."[4] People who identify as transgendered (that is, people who cross or live beyond the standard binary categories of gender), garnered significant attention in the 1990s when they mobilized and created an identity-based social movement. Transgender activists participate in "social movements which seek to alter the self-conceptions and societal conceptions of their participants."[5] Rather than attempting to adapt and conform to normative expectations of gender and sexual expression, transactivists seek to normalize transgenderism.

While traditional transsexual hormonal and surgical interventions conformed to and reinforced gender binarism, the recent transgender movement challenges the necessity of matching one's genitals to one's gender, thus effecting a paradigm shift in the way transgender identities are conceptualized.[6] Today, a number of individuals born male and female are living differently gendered lives without the aid of hormonal or surgical treatments and with less emphasis on passing as standard women and men.[7] Many transsexuals are choosing to live with blended gender identities that blur the boundaries of female and male.

Identity politics movements such as the GLBT movements acknowledge the importance of the agency individuals have in constructing not only their own identities but also in responding to and negotiating social expectations of who they ought to be. In this way, identity movements expand Goffman's theory of stigma beyond its potentially deterministic stance on the "spoiled identities" of those who deviate from social norms.[8] Rather than passively accepting a socially stigmatized identity, individuals have both the capacity to transform their self-conceptions and the means to redefine how others see them.[9] The same trend of identity reconstruction is evident among intersex individuals as well.[10]

Identity Politics and the Intersex Social Movement

Recently, many people began questioning the ethics and effectiveness of medical sex assignment procedures.[11] Most agree that surgical sex assignment is not the best form of treatment for intersexuals and that performing surgery without the patients' (not the parents') consent is unethical. That's about where the similarity stops. Some, such as Milton Diamond and Keith Sigmundson, argue from a biological perspective that neonatal hormone levels to which a fetus is exposed will override gender socialization and in the end be the primary factor in determining gender identity. Thus, they argue, sex assignment must concur with the hormonal exposure a neonate received during gestation.[12] From a social constructionist perspective, Suzanne Kessler, Alice Dreger, Anne Fausto-Sterling, and I argue that intersex ought to be demedicalized because it is not in itself pathological.[13] Rather, the pathology lies in the social system and its strict adherence to gender binarism. We contend that in a culture where childbirth is treated medically, intersex variation is seen within a medical framework—that is, as a disease requiring medical intervention.

In addition, many intersexed individuals are openly expressing their dissatisfaction with this medical intervention.[14] Their dissatisfaction centers on the following: (1) certain medical interventions, from a strictly physical point of view, are not necessary for survival;[15] (2) as a result of medical intervention, both sexual and psychological satisfaction and functioning are often impaired; and (3) for intersex individuals the lack of open discussion of their intersex status results in feelings of shame and isolation. Evidence of their discontent is abundant in the writings and personal stories of intersexuals.[16] For example, in Morgan Holmes's words,

> Not that I would necessarily have kept my phalloclit. . . . But I would have liked to have been able to choose for myself. I would have liked to have grown up in the body I was born with. . . . But physically, someone else made the decision of what and who I would always "be" before I even knew who and what I "was" . . . [The doctors] used surgical force to make my appearance coincide with the medical and social standards of a "normal" female body, thereby attempting to permanently jettison any trace of intersexuality.[17]

And in Cheryl Chase's experience,

> Who am I? I now assert both my femininity and my intersexuality, my "not female"-ness. This is not a paradox; the fact that my gender has been problematized is the source of my intersexual identity. Most people have never struggled with their gender, are at a loss to answer the question, "how do you know if you are a woman (a man)?" I have been unable to experience myself as totally female. Although my body passes for female, women's clothing does not fit me. The shoulders are too narrow, the sleeves too short. Most women's gloves won't go on my hands, nor women's shoes on my feet. For most women, that wouldn't be more than an inconvenience. But when the clothing doesn't fit, I am reminded of my history. Of course, men's clothing doesn't fit either. The straight lines leave no room for my large breasts or broad hips.[18]

Chase continues:

> As a woman, I am less than whole—I have a secret past, I lack important parts of my genitals and sexual response. When a lover puts her hand to my genitals for the first time, the lack is immediately obvious to her. Finally, I simply do not feel myself a woman (even less a man). But the hermaphrodite identity was too monstrous, too Other, too freakish, for me to easily embrace. A medical anomaly, patched up as best the surgeons could manage.[19]

Despite the medical aim to erase or hide sexual ambiguity, some intersexuals are finding each other through their own activism and are attempting to reclaim their difference as a source of pride. In fact, in recent years intersexuals have been implementing their own networks of support and avenues for social change at a rapid pace. Here I provide a brief overview of a few of the significant developments on this front.[20]

Intersex Support and Advocacy Resources in North America

A.I.S. (Androgen Insensitivity Syndrome) Support Group U.S.
P.O. Box 75027
Duncan, OK 73575-0273
e-mail: aissgusa@hotmail.com
Web site: http://www.medhelp.org/ais

A.I.S. Support Group Canada
206 115 The Esplanade
Toronto, Ontario
M5E 1Y7
e-mail: sallie@ican.net
Web site: http://www.medhelp.org/ais

Ambiguous Genitalia Support Network
P.O. Box 313
Clements, CA 95227-0313
(209) 727-0313
e-mail: esagsn@hotmail.com

Bodies Like Ours
e-mail: info@bodieslikeours.org
Web site: http://www.bodieslikeours.org/

CARES Foundation (Congenital Adrenal Hyperplasia)
11 Hardwell Road
Short Hills, NJ 07078
e-mail: CARESfoundation@home.com
Web site: http://www.caresfoundation.org

Congenital Adrenal Hyperplasia Education and Support Network
e-mail: mail@CongenitalAdrenal Hyperplasia.org
Web site: http://congenitaladrenal hyperplasia.org/

H.E.L.P (Hermaphrodite Education and Listening Post)
P.O. Box 26292
Jacksonville, FL 32226
e-mail: help@southeast.net
Web site: http://www.jax-inter.net/~help/

Intersex Support Group International
Web site: http://www.isgi.org
e-mail: care@isgi.org

ISNA (Intersex Society of North America)
e-mail: info@isna.org
Web site: http://www.isna.org

K.S. & Associates (Klinefelter's Syndrome)
P.O. Box 119
Roseville, CA 95678-0119
(916) 773-2999
e-mail: ksinfo@genetic.org
Web site: http://www.genetic.org/ks/

The Klinefelter Syndrome Support Group
Web site: http://klinefeltersyndrome.org/index.htm

The MAGIC Foundation (Congenital Adrenal Hyperplasia)
1327 North Harlem Avenue
Oak Park, IL 60302
(708) 383-0808
fax: (708) 383-0899
e-mail: mary@magicfoundation.org
Web site: http://www.magicfoundation.org/

National Adrenal Diseases Foundation
505 Northern Boulevard
Great Neck, NY 11021
(516) 487-4992
e-mail: nadfmail@aol.com
Web site: http://medhlp.netusa.net/www/nadf.htm

Turner Syndrome Society United States
14450 T. C. Jester, Suite 260
Houston, TX 77014
(800) 365-9944
fax: (832) 249-9987
e-mail: tssus@turner-syndrome-us.org
Web site: http://www.turner-syndrome-us.org/

EMERGENCE OF INTERSEX SUPPORT AND
ADVOCACY ORGANIZATIONS

The Turner's Syndrome Society, founded in Minneapolis in 1987, was the first known support group for people with atypical sex differentiation. This organization was founded by women who have Turner's Syndrome and currently serves thousands of members nationally as a medical information clearinghouse.[21] A year later, in 1988, the mother of a girl with androgen insensitivity syndrome (AIS) founded the U.K.-based AIS Support Group.[22] The U.K. group has convened fall and spring weekend conferences since 1995, and many people from continental Europe and the United States travel to attend the U.K. group's meetings. Since 1995, other AIS groups have also been formed and hold their own annual meetings. The U.S. AIS group was formed in 1995 by a thirty-six-year-old woman who has CAIS, after she attended the April 1995 support group meeting of the U.K. group. The U.S. chapter currently has about three hundred members. The East Coast Canadian AIS support group began in 1996 and was formed by a forty-three-year-old woman with CAIS after she attended the first annual meeting of the U.S. group in September 1996. A west coast Canadian group was formed more recently, in 2001. At the time of this writing, the AIS group has chapters in seventeen countries, nine of which were formed since 2000. In addition to the groups in the United Kingdom, the United States, and Canada, there are active AIS support groups in India, Poland, New Zealand, Sweden, Greece, Italy, the Netherlands, Norway, France, Spain, Switzerland, South Africa, Germany, and Australia, and a widely distributed newsletter called *ALIAS*.[23]

In 1989 the mother of a child with Klinefelter's Syndrome founded the U.S.-based K.S. & Associates.[24] This organization now serves over one thousand families.

In 1993 the intersex activist and scholar Cheryl Chase founded the Intersex Society of North America (ISNA). Chase initially announced ISNA's existence by publishing a letter to the editor in response to Fausto-Sterling's article "The Five Sexes" in *The Sciences*.[25] In Chase's letter, she indicated that hermaphrodites weren't mythological or fictional characters and that she, herself, was intersexed and had founded and was president of an advocacy organization for intersexuals called the Intersex Society of North America. The society Chase referred to didn't exist yet. The organization was actually formed out of her letter to the editor. Chase was hopeful that by acting as though the organization was already in place, she would find others who had bodies and medical histories like her own. In the signature line of this momentous letter, Chase listed a post office box for ISNA, and it soon began filling with mail from other intersexuals around the world. The Intersex Society published the first issue of its newsletter, *Hermaphrodites with Attitude,* in the winter of 1994, started bimonthly support groups in January 1995, and went on-line with an Internet web site in January 1996.[26] In addition to the support it offers to intersexuals and their families, ISNA's mission is to destigmatize intersexuality and to legitimate genital variability.[27] By picketing at medical conferences, the Intersex Society's critique gained the attention of the larger public. In another political move, ISNA linked its objective of preventing genital surgery to the emotional and political movement against female genital mutilation. Since the October 1996 U.S. federal legislation banning female genital mutilation, the Intersex Society has been lobbying against "intersex genital mutilation."[28] The ISNA has grown tremendously since its formation in 1993. It currently has a mailing list of 2,600 and has 650 donors.[29] Under Chase's astute leadership, the Intersex Society helped give form to the intersex support and advocacy movement. In July 2002, however, Chase announced that she will step down as executive director of the organization at the end of the year. Even so, she will continue to serve as a member of its board of directors. Given its strength at the time of Chase's announcement, ISNA will likely continue to be a forerunner of intersex patients' rights under its new leadership, medical sociologist Dr. Monica Casper.

In 1995 the mother of an intersexed child formed the Ambiguous Genitalia Support Network (AGSN), an organization that fosters pen pal relationships among parents of intersexed children. In 1996, another mother founded the Hermaphrodite Education and Listening Post (HELP). This group offers peer support and medical information to its members. Both AGSN and HELP were started by mothers who were dissatisfied with intersex medical protocol. Both had children who at birth had male chromosomes, gonads, and genitals that were deemed inadequate. Each mother countered medical advice for feminizing surgery and is raising her young son as a boy.

More recently, in 1998, an American intersexed woman formed the U.S. and Christian-based Intersex Support Group International (ISGI). In support of its opposition to intersex medicalization, this group cites biblical passages referring to the sanctity of all God's creations. The following quotes come from the group's web site manifesto and director's page:

> ISGI provides information and support for genetic intersex persons and their families from a Christian viewpoint. Jesus said, "Some are eunuchs (genetic intersex) because they were born that way . . . Matthew 19:12." We know that God made no mistake when He made us. We are His unique creation. We believe that God's original creation design for humanity was that of male and female bodies, identities, roles, and relationships, which the Bible declares to

■ Intersex Society of North America ■

Hermaphrodites with Attitudes

Volume 1, Number 1, Winter 1994

$3

© 1994 ISNA
Free to copy and distribute

Welcome, readers!

Long promised, long delayed, but here it is. ISNA now has its own newsletter. I hope that many of you will contribute short articles, stories, poetry, and illustrations so that the next issue can be even more of a collaborative effort.

Who are we? In the 16 months since ISNA was founded, we have responded to hundreds of inquiries from intersexuals, therapists, educators, parents, physicians, academics, and journalists. The Intersex Society mailing list now reaches intersexuals in five countries and in 14 of the United States.

(continued page 6)

Case report
Will B. Dunn, M.D., FACS

The patient was a 2 year old reindeer (*Rangifer tarandus*) who was brought to the clinic by guardians for diagnosis of a disfiguringly prominent nose. Some even said it glowed. (fig. 1, left) Although no objective standards have been published for proboscal length in reindeer, it is a simple matter for the surgeon to judge.

Under general anesthetic, the offending tissue was excised and sent for frozen section microscopy. While awaiting the
(continued page 6)

The Awakening
Kira Triea

I really awakened about a year ago, though I realize that my awakening has had many stages. Some time before the onset of memory, I awakened to the knowledge that I was different; when I was thirteen I learned that I was not "a boy"... I was actually "a girl." Now I know that I am an intersexed person.

Before this last year I rarely thought about sex, gender or relationships. My "hermaphroditism" was completely off limits as a topic for introspection, except in vague despondent moments when I would reflect to myself that "people like me" were just not able to become involved in relationships or have sex. I absolutely never entertained the notion that I would talk about my biological status with anyone... it was too dark a secret even for me to contemplate for very long. When I was thirteen I chose my sex in a game of binary roulette at Johns Hopkins and with that choice I accepted the implied vow of silence: "Don't ask, don't tell."

On February 28, 1993 something happened and I awoke, I don't know why. I experienced what I can only describe as a *constructive breakdown*. The intense awareness of my life and the implications of being intersexed ripped through my existence and the implosion hurt. I couldn't continue in school with my math and computer science degree; I was too busy crying and wondering and hurt-
(continued page 6)

Figure 1 (*A, left*) Note disfiguring hypertrophy of nose. (*B, above*) Post-surgical aspect. An excellent cosmetic result was achieved.

Figure 6. The Intersex Society of North America's first newsletter cover. *Hermaphrodites with Attitudes*. Winter 1994. 1(1). (Note that subesquent issues of this newsletter are called *Hermaphrodites with Attitude*.) *Reprinted with permission.*

be a living picture of Christ and the Church. We believe that decisions in treatment of intersexuals both medically and socially have further complicated that distinction, creating unique challenges for intersexuals. Errant treatment of intersexuals is not exclusive to medical protocols. The response by the Church at large to these

---

Ideas & Trends

Intersexual Healing: An Anomaly Finds a Group

By NATALIE ANGIER

HERMAPHRODITUS, the son of Hermes and Aphrodite, was a beautiful young man, so fetching that the nymph of the fountain of Salmacis fell desperately in love and begged the gods to merge her body with his forever. They granted the nymph her wish, forming a being half-man, half-woman.

For most of us, the idea of human hermaphrodites

Society of North America, even has the requisite home-page on the World Wide Web.

Like the deaf who resist being forced to learn to speak or to accept cochlear implants, or the dwarfs who do not want to be prenatally diagnosed out of existence, intersexuals do not want to be seen as sick or defective or in need of pity. And while none of them who were interviewed are ready to declare themselves happy and proud and none would agree to be photographed for this article, they feel they have something to say about the androgyny inherent in everyone.

Figure 7. New York Times, Sunday, February 4, 1996:14E. Reprinted with permission.

specific individuals has alienated intersexuals and has also served to drive real people away from a personal relationship with God. That consequence is not God's will.[30]

In addition to the groups chronicled above, there are many others around the world developing at a rapid pace with the use of Internet technology. Accordingly, the intersex movement is technologically quite reliant upon electronic media and communications, including the Internet and electronic mail.[31] The use of the Internet as a primary means of contact, education, and support has afforded the development of a geographically diverse advocacy movement. This technology, with its relative accessibility, has given former patients and family members an opportunity to discuss intersex beyond the clinic, in their own homes and virtual communities. For successful mobilization of disparate individuals, such communication networks are essential. Many individuals and families have developed their own web sites that are linked to a larger support group's site, in order to tell their stories and connect with other people and families who are also affected by intersex.

POPULAR ATTENTION TO GENITAL SURGERY:
THE IMPACT OF THE DAVID REIMER CASE

Oddly, the most well known and widely cited case in the intersex medical literature involves *nonintersexed* identical twin boys, Bruce and Brian Reimer, born in Canada in 1965. The twins were not circumcised at birth, but at the age of eight months they both developed phimosis; that is, a painful tightening of the foreskin. The twins were scheduled for circumcision to relieve their pain. Bruce Reimer (known formerly as "John" in the medical literature) was scheduled for circumcision first. Tragically, he lost his penis due to accidental burning during the routine electrocautery procedure. After learning of Bruce's horrible outcome, the boys' parents canceled Brian's operation. As is quite common with this condition, Brian's phimosis resolved itself shortly thereafter without any medical intervention.[32]

Although Bruce was not sexually ambiguous and had been raised as a male for nearly a year, John Money and his colleagues recommended that he be reassigned as female because he lacked a penis and therefore could not develop a normal male gender identity.[33] Bruce was twenty-two months old before his parents consented to his surgical and social reassignment as "Brenda" (previously know as "Joan" in the medical literature), turning an unfortunate surgical accident into an "experiment of nature" for researchers and others interested in gender identity acquisition.[34] Money and colleagues used this surgical mishap and sex reassignment to test the impact of gender socialization by rearing a male child as female and using his genetic twin as an empirical control.

For more than thirty years, Money reported Brenda's gender reassignment as an undeniable success and used the case as unquestionable evidence of the value and success of surgical sex assignment for intersexed children.[35] Money's findings were widely cited by sociologists, feminists, psychologists, and others as proof that biology is not destiny, and that gender is socially malleable, at least in early childhood. Money's findings were promoted widely in classrooms and textbooks as incontrovertible evidence that environmental factors outweigh biological ones in gender identity development.

In 1997, biologist Milton Diamond and psychiatrist Keith Sigmundson revealed that Brenda was never satisfied with a female gender identity and that s/he began the process of male sex reassignment at age fourteen when s/he learned the history of the surgical accident and gender reassignment from his/her father.[36] When Brenda Reimer started living as a boy again at age fourteen, he took the name David. David spoke with Diamond and Sigmundson after learning that Money was still reporting "Brenda's success." David and his family chose to keep their identities under wraps despite a flurry of media attention in 1997.

In February 2000, Canadian journalist John Colapinto published his book *As Nature Made Him: The Boy Who Was Raised as a Girl.* Upon publication of the book, the Reimer family, at David's lead, made several talk show and news program appearances revealing their stories and identities to the world. Currently David is in his mid-thirties and married. He adopted his wife's children from a previous relationship. He underwent a double mastectomy to remove the breasts that were created when, as Brenda, he took prescribed estrogen pills in childhood. He also underwent a phalloplasty, among other procedures, to assist his gender transition back to male.[37] Diamond and Sigmundson seized the opportunity garnered by their publication to make recommendations for intersex clinical management.[38]

The major media were abuzz with reports of biological determinism within days of Diamond and Sigmundson's 1997 publication. The media also became interested in other cases of infant sex reassignment and turned to newly emergent intersex activists and parents for their stories. Print media reports in the spring of 1997 included front-page coverage in the *New York Times* and cover stories in *Newsweek, Rolling Stone, Time, On the Issues, Out,* and *Mademoiselle* magazines. In addition, television media featured the David Reimer story on *NBC Dateline, Inside Edition,* and *Prime Time Live,* and interviewed David Reimer himself, leaders of intersex support groups, as well as biologists Fausto-Sterling and Diamond.[39] Similar coverage followed Colapinto's 2000 publication of *As Nature Made Him: The Boy Who Was Raised as a Girl.*

The critical public attention to infant genital surgery garnered by the Reimer case and the growing intersex patients' rights movement spurred many study participants to begin an investigation of their own history of medical sex assignment.

Coming Out, Stage Two: Acknowledging One's Difference to Self and Others

Participants in my study reported that they engaged in medical detective work to make sense of their physical difference and the medical scrutiny they experienced as children. Their desire to do so represents an ability to move beyond a stigmatic label and identity to engage in a more complex process of self-concept development.[40] Participants reported their ability to reject the formerly shame-based notion of the self and to employ innovative skills to assemble the missing pieces of their identity puzzles. In an attempt to make sense of their anatomy and life experiences, participants served as their own advocates in gaining accurate information about themselves and their histories—a process that Paulo Freire calls liberation education.[41] In an attempt to make sense of their histories and bodies, participants interviewed their family members and physicians, ordered copies of their medical records, and spent time researching their piecemeal diagnoses or medical procedures in medical libraries and on the Internet. In doing so, they were able to locate and meet other intersexuals by stumbling upon the web sites or contact information of

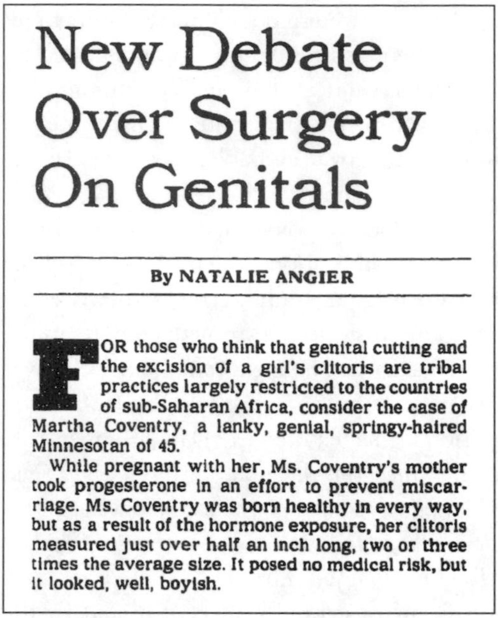

New Debate Over Surgery On Genitals

By NATALIE ANGIER

FOR those who think that genital cutting and the excision of a girl's clitoris are tribal practices largely restricted to the countries of sub-Saharan Africa, consider the case of Martha Coventry, a lanky, genial, springy-haired Minnesotan of 45.

While pregnant with her, Ms. Coventry's mother took progesterone in an effort to prevent miscarriage. Ms. Coventry was born healthy in every way, but as a result of the hormone exposure, her clitoris measured just over half an inch long, two or three times the average size. It posed no medical risk, but it looked, well, boyish.

Figure 8. New York Times, Tuesday, May 13, 1997:B7. Reprinted with permission.

newly developing intersex support groups. Having lacked a valid point of social comparison for most of their lives, locating complete and accurate information about their bodies and meeting others like themselves were essential turning points that facilitated the redefinition of self in a positive and empowering light.[42]

COMING TO TERMS WITH DIFFERENCE:
PUTTING AN END TO SECRECY

Most participants internalized feelings of stigma and shame about their intersexuality in childhood or early adolescence. Once they reached adulthood, however, they were able to skillfully garner resources to engage in critical self-reflection. In doing so, participants acted as their own advocates and educators in a quest to gain a comprehensive understanding of their histories and a concept of self that accurately reflected their experiences. This major reassessment of self most often led to a conversion of participants' personal beliefs about themselves from "Other" to "Okay," from feelings of shame to eventual pride in the self.

Relying heavily on interactionist notions of identity negotiation, Edward Jones and colleagues address the micro aspects of self-concept formation, noting the important role individual agency plays in the development of the self.[43] With specific regard to stigma, Jones et al. label individuals who possess a notable difference as potentially stigmatized or "markable." Conversely, they refer to individuals who are accepted as socially normal as the "markers" who have the power to mark or stigmatize the markable. Jones and his associates assert that those who are potentially markable have a choice as to whether or not to accept and internalize the social stigma of the mark or refuse the mark by seeing their difference as nonstigmatic.[44] They postulate that there are three primary ways individuals respond to social stigma. Someone identifies an individual as "markable," and (1) the individual accepts the stigmatic designation and comes to see her/himself as deviant; (2) the individual sees her/himself as stigmatized because of a pervasive concept of self as being deviant; and (3) the individual rejects the negative assessment and thus refuses to be stigmatized.[45]

In his instrumental work on stigma, Goffman focuses on the pervasive impact of stigmatization on one's self-concept.[46] As in point two above, he claims that once a person internalizes stigma, s/he perpetuates it internally without the necessity for stigmatization by others. Individuals who understand themselves in such a pejorative manner have a concept of self that is irreparably damaged—what Goffman refers to as a "spoiled identity." Goffman claims that once individuals reach this state of internal despair, they are never able to fully recover from their general sense of self-loathing or from a spoiled identity, despite appearances to the contrary. Goffman sees claims of liberation from stigma as reflecting only a lessened degree of stigma, rather than a comprehensive normalization of the self. In his words,

> Where such repair is possible, what often results is not the acquisition
> of fully normal status, but a transformation of self from someone with
> a particular blemish into someone with a record of having corrected a
> particular blemish.[47]

My data suggest that Goffman's belief in the permanence of stigma may not apply to all cases of stigmatization. In fact, the work of identity negotiation may be ongoing and never quite permanently fixed. I now turn to a detailed exploration of participants' attempts to reject stigma and reclaim formerly spoiled notions of the self.

Like others, I see labeling theory and, more specifically, Cooley's metaphor of the looking-glass self as an overly passive view of self-concept formation which ignores critical links between self-understanding and social structure.[48] In fact, as Viktor Gecas and Michael Schwalbe claim, Cooley himself regarded the formation of self-concept as a complex process, with the reflective appraisal of others constituting only one part.[49] According to Cooley, the self-concept will be necessarily weak and incomplete if it is entirely dependent on the reflections of self from others. The significance of individual perception in evaluating these looking-glass reflections is made clear by my research.

Participants repeatedly told of having a strong and positive enough sense of self to eventually reject the mark of stigma that was prevalent in external appraisals of their bodies. The ability to redefine oneself in this manner and deflect external devaluation of the self is a skill that participants honed and cultivated over time. Participants often spoke insightfully about the necessity of engaging in self-definition and self-validation in order to liberate the self from social stigma. Their efforts to do so appeared to be motivated by their desire to find an unmarked, "authentic" or "true" self.[50] As is common for survivors of emotional trauma, the ability to validate the self plays a pivotal role in moving from a state of victimization to one of empowerment. Speaking to the significance of cultivating these internal resources, Julian said, "You will live or die by your ability to be the only one in your life who can say anything that makes a difference about who you are. To get to a point where no one else validates you. That is what will save or kill you."

Study participants' ability to serve as a source of appraisal for themselves is not universal across the sample. Some participants were far better than others at detaching from negative social evaluations of themselves and coming to view these reflections as entirely or partially inaccurate. Certainly one's social resources, both material and nonmaterial, have a major impact on her/his ability to renegotiate a stigmatized concept of self.

Participants shared with me their beliefs about their personal relationships and sense of empowerment frequently throughout the interviews. Several made emphatic statements about the role of certain beliefs in furthering their ability to validate themselves. I turn to their articulate expressions to facilitate the illustration of meaning here. According to Julian, intersexuals who have been most able to avoid a permanently spoiled self-concept are those that have an active sense of spirituality. In his words,

> [A member of the support group] took a poll on [an intersex chat line] once [that asked], "Who here has been utterly and completely smashed by their [intersex] condition and wishes it never happened and who here is okay with it?" And [the results] kind of fell into fifty-fifty. All the people on the more or less [had] "come to terms with it" side had one thing in common and that was our spirituality. That was *it!* The *only* thing that we all had in common was that we had some kind of spiritual [understanding] and the people on the other side had no spiritual anything. [Spirituality] seems to be what saved us; what saved our lives.

Notably, 76 percent of the sample identified some spiritual or religious affiliation. Because all interviewees were affiliated with support groups when I interviewed them, these are people who also turned to the social support of community ties in order to come to terms with medical secrecy and trauma. Others spoke of the importance of having a spiritual connection, albeit an internal sense of spiritual power. In Carol's experience,

> I learned early to rely on myself and not my parents. I didn't think God was around me, I thought God was inside of me. I felt like He was somebody I had put inside me, so I had things inside of me that would help [me] get to a future place or future time.

The ability to develop and strengthen one's sense of empowerment may be, in part, dependent on one's material resources and station in life. Gecas and Schwalbe detail the role of economic and other structural factors in one's ability to impact her/his own self-concept. Their work in this area provides an essential balance to the micro-level work of Jones et al.[51] For example, Gecas and Schwalbe assert that one's chances to engage in "efficacious action" largely impacts one's sense of self. Those who are not able to exert their independence suffer a decreased sense of autonomy and self-esteem. Gecas and Schwalbe outline three specific criteria which they deem most significant in assessing material and nonmaterial resources in the development of strong self-esteem: (1) the degree of constraint on individual autonomy, (2) the degree of individual control, and (3) the resources which are available to the individual for producing intended outcomes.[52] As I outlined previously, intersexuals severely lack such resources as children and are especially susceptible to others' assessments of themselves. Adults, however, have far more ability to be discerning in choosing relationships and self-sentiments.

As was the case for many participants, children who feel socially stigmatized and isolated may come to reject social support and community ties, learning to rely primarily on themselves. Such action may lead them to become high achievers in an effort to form an internal sense of control to compensate for their feelings of difference and shame—a potentially fortunate outcome of unfortunate circumstances. Such achievement is notable among the people I interviewed. As I noted in chapter 1, participants, on the whole, were exceptionally well educated. All were high school graduates, 97 percent had at least some college education, 78 percent were college graduates, 43 percent had at least some graduate education, and 27 percent had graduate degrees. These rates of educational attainment are far higher than the U.S. average, considering that on average, 33 percent of U.S. citizens graduate from high school, 15 percent attain a college degree, and only 5 percent attain a

master's degree.[53] At the time of interview, 86 percent of the sample were employed, and several participants were working in high-profile and high-income
careers. Most were computer users and had Internet access, providing them
with wide-ranging opportunities for self-education, self-diagnoses, and participation in electronic communication networks.

Perhaps these resources, combined with a sense of empowerment and
hope, led participants to seek information about themselves, for in order to
change one's situation, one must first have the belief that change is possible
and that they have the power to effect it. Learning to reject stigma is a way
to liberate oneself from various forms or sources of oppression. The ability to
do so is dependent on the awareness that a hardship does exist and that one
has been treated unfairly. Educating oneself is a crucial step in overcoming
injustice, during which an individual normalizes the aspect of self that has
formerly been stigmatized.[54] During this process, one confronts the source of
their devaluation, and thereby dissipates the power it once held over them.[55]
By taking an active role in their own self-definition, participants rejected
stigma by putting an end to secrecy, shame, and isolation. In Suegee's experience,

> Now I don't really care [about my sex chromosomes]. I mean, that has
> nothing to do with who I am. I am this way; this is my body. Who
> cares what my chromosomes are? I know a lot of people who look a
> hell of a lot more female than me that have XY chromosomes. It's like
> I don't really care. I mean, it just really doesn't matter.

PERSONAL ARCHAEOLOGY

Participants engaged in innovative and varied means of searching for information in their attempts to solve an identity puzzle to which they were missing several key pieces. Many told of frustrating attempts to retrieve their
medical records and information from their parents, to no avail. In their per-
sistence and desperation to make sense of their bodies and medicalized histories, several began searching for information about themselves in medical texts
at public or university libraries. Speaking of the tremendous impact of this
process of self-discovery, Peggy stated, "When I read all those medical books
in college, I was reading basically about a way of saving my own life and about
how I could have a better life than the [one] I thought I was going to have."
Participants' initial searches were often motivated by their desire for autonomy
over their bodies and the ability to exert control over their lives. Speaking of
this process, forty-two-year-old Cheryl, who was initially sexed male and then
reassigned female at eighteen months of age, said, "I needed the [medical]
records to find out who [the doctors] were. I wanted to get every single scrap
of the records and judge for myself what they had done."

Participants engaged in various means of gaining information about themselves. As is common in other forms of research, their initial searches often resulted in disappointment or confusion. Those whose difference was apparent to them at a young age began the search for information in early adolescence. For example, in J8's case, "By the time I was in ninth grade, I was reading anything I could find about intersexuality. I didn't know the word yet. I knew the word 'hermaphrodite.' I was reading [John] Money." Others didn't begin their investigations until much later, but also turned to publications as a primary source of information. Cheryl and Fanny described their use of public resources during their missions of self-discovery. In Cheryl's case,

> I read *everything*. I would pick up all kinds of books that looked like there was even the slimmest possibility that they might mention intersexuality and I flipped to the index and looked for intersex and hermaphrodite and pseudo-hermaphrodite and clitorectomy. Usually there was nothing, or if there was something, it was utterly irrelevant.

And in Fanny's experience,

> I would go to the arboretum and try to get any kind of book that I could find on the subject. I just had to do it on my own and so I looked at some books, I learned a little bit more about the syndrome. I tried to understand this androgen insensitivity. It all sounded very complicated. I was not in nursing yet and that was part of the reason I wanted to get into nursing, just to get a little bit more control of the medical aspect; that helped a lot.

Like Fanny, others were motivated to gain mastery over the medical aspects of their intersexuality and sought careers in health care professions. Forty percent of participants were employed in medical or social service-related fields.

Some participants were skilled at using information in medical publications to perform accurate self-diagnoses. I quote one participant's experience at length here because her story illustrates this process quite well. According to Sherri, a thirty-nine-year-old lawyer with complete AIS whose abdominal testicles were removed when she was two or three weeks old because of inguinal hernias:

> I knew that something didn't make sense about removing the ovaries of a month-old child. [So,] when I was twenty and in my first year of law school and I had surmised that probably I had not been told the truth, at the first opportunity I got to be let loose in a medical school library, I went in search of the information. I started out researching under "oophorectomy" because I'd been told I'd had my ovaries

removed and I wanted to see what the indications would be for doing [that]. From there it was a pretty quick hop, skip, and a jump to figure out that it was [androgen insensitivity syndrome]. It was an easy diagnosis. Things finally made sense; the pieces finally fit together. The logical part of my mind found [it] somewhat comforting to find a resolution of why all of the pieces [fit].

For Sherri and many others, finally having the pieces come together in this way allowed them a feeling of relief and empowerment they had longed for throughout their lives. But unlike Cheryl, Fanny, and Sherri, others were not initially as intentional about their search for information. For some, the investigation began as a matter of coincidence. In Tiger's case,

When I got to college, I was in an abnormal psychology class and [the professor] was talking about hermaphroditism. I didn't really know what any of that was. He threw up this slide that said hypospadias on it. I recognized the label [from my medical chart] and I, kind of shaking, walked up to him after the lecture and said, "I'm one of the people you were talking about. No one's ever talked to me about this. I've never understood what all this was about." [The professor] immediately took me under his wing and I did three years of independent study courses with him. I learned *everything* there was to learn. Between [the ages of] nineteen and twenty-six, I became a world-class expert in my own syndrome.

Regardless of how the quest for information was initiated, once individuals made a commitment to learning more about themselves, they invariably turned to medical professionals and resources for answers. Such efforts often proved to be irritating or fruitless when many medical professionals denied them access to accurate information about their diagnoses or medical histories. For this reason, participants often found it necessary to be both cunning and assertive in their quest for information. Carol recalls one such attempt to acquire additional information from the surgeon who removed her abdominal testicles when she was nineteen years old. Here she relays a conversation with this doctor when she was twenty-one years old, during which she chose to lie in order to elicit her true chromosomal makeup. Her method was successful in the end. Here I relay a portion of our interactive conversation where she conveyed this story:

C: I said [to my doctor], "I have one more question for you. I would like to know what I have that necessitated that you removed my gonads." And he said, "Well, you're just fine, there's nothing wrong." I said, "Listen, for *years* I thought I had a debilitating condition. I thought I perhaps had a progressive disease. I really believed that I possibly could still have cancer, even though you removed the unusual cells. I need to know what I have." And he said, "You don't need to worry about it, *really*. It's not something that you need to know." I said, "I need to know." And I thought, "He's not going to tell me. He's not gonna tell me. I *know* he's not going to tell me." And so I thought, "I've gotta either walk out and find somebody else [to tell me the truth] or I gotta nail this guy to the wall." And all of a sudden it hit me, I said, "Listen, I need to know because I am going into the Olympics this summer and I need to know if I'm going to test XY or XX."

S: Was that a lie?

C: Oh yeah. [Clapping hands, shared laughter] Yes.

S: That's terrible! What was your sport? [Laughter]

C: Knock-kneed high jumping. [S's laughter] And he just froze. And he just looked totally panicked. And then he just dropped all pretense and he leaned over, he shook my hand with those great big long penetrating fingers, and he said, "Congratulations. You are such an intelligent woman. Congratulations for figuring it out." I said, "What did I figure out? Do I have AIS? And am I XY?" and he said, "Yes." And I said, "Well, thanks for finally telling me the truth. Do I have cancer?" And he said, "No." And I said, "So, why did you remove them? Did my, did my . . . " I couldn't say testes at the time, because I sort of didn't feel like it. But I just said, "Did my gonads have cancer? Were they cancerous?" He said, "There was some abnormal cell growth but, no, they weren't cancerous per se." "Where are my gonads?" I said. And he said, "Well, I sent them to the Clark Institute for inclusion in a research project." And I said, "And *what* did they learn about my gonads?!" And he said, "Um, ah, well, ah, I, I . . . " I said, "I would like to have copies of the research, please. Would you be able to get me copies of my research? I would like to find out *what* my gonads were all about, please." And he said, "Well, I suppose I could," and I said, "I would also like to know if you have any more information on AIS because I would like to read about it, and learn more about it." He said, "If you insist."

Like Carol, Tiger found it necessary to be persistent in his attempts to retrieve medical information relevant to his history. Here he tells of having to threaten legal recourse before he was able to acquire his medical records:

I fought, but I got 'em. My birth records took me about a year and a half of doctors' letters and requests and finding out where things actually existed and doing all that. It didn't really happen until I actually presented myself at their records warehouse and said, "You've refused. You haven't responded to any of [my previous requests], and I'm not moving until you get a supervisor. I'm gonna look through your stacks myself if I have to, but I want those records. And if I don't get them, I'll sue this place." That's the level of threat you *must* do with these people 'cause the last thing they wanna do is release those records.

Like Tiger, many dealt with obstacles when recalling medical records. In fact, some participants eventually did resort to employing legal counsel in acquiring their medical records. Even though they were adamant about retrieving their complete set of records, many did not. For many, this included an inability to retrieve photographs doctors took of their bodies. According to Tiger, "They destroy all medical photography. It's very, very hard to get that stuff. And if they do see your record request, dollars to donuts, 90 percent of the time they sanitize 'em before they release 'em." Many participants speculated about the reason doctors and hospitals were so reluctant to release their medical records. Several interpreted clinicians' unwillingness as evidence that doctors were both trying to "protect" former patients from what doctors perceived as the horrifying nature of their conditions, as well as trying to protect themselves from potential lawsuits and accusations of medical malpractice. Due to the obstacles they encountered, some participants felt they were unable to fulfill their objective of comprehensive record recovery.

Others chose to forgo or supplement physician- and family-supplied information by using advanced technological resources in their quest for self-knowledge. This included the use of laboratory equipment and the Internet as diagnostic tools. Of the former, Jana spoke about his efforts to assess his fertility: "In college I was pre-med. I had suspected that I was sterile [and] I confirmed that with a microscope. I compared my sperm samples with that of my roommate's. His was teeming with life; mine was as barren as the Sahara." Not surprisingly, many participants turned to the rapidly expanding computer technology in their search for information. Many participants told of conducting Internet searches for information about themselves the very first time they had access to the technology. Because most were unaware of their diagnoses, they relied on the scant medical terminology used in reference to them that they had acquired over many years of determined listening. Speaking to the cryptic information she garnered over the years, Swan said, "It was never anything direct [or] out in the open. I'd hear rumors or snatches of conversations or something like that and get impressions, but that would be all." Applying these tidbits of information about the self in Internet searches was often fruitful, as in Robin's case. She recalls,

> I remembered [the] name [my doctor had given me for my condition].
> When I was thirty-five [years old] I got my computer and set up my
> modem. I got onto AOL, I [thought], "Now, I'm gonna get on the
> Internet. What do I wanna search for?" I just remember seeing [the
> word] "search." I could type anything in there, and I could find out
> anything I want[ed]. So what did I type in there [but] feminizing
> testicular syndrome. And lo and behold, I got gobs of information. I
> think I stayed up 'til like two or three in the morning reading all this
> stuff and printing it out. That's when I found out everything.

Although they often met their goals of gaining knowledge about themselves, participants usually did so in isolation because they had few useful resources to acquire information. Their choice to engage in self-initiated and directed research endeavors highlights the isolation they experienced as children, as well as the resulting impact on their ability to trust others. Lacking information about oneself leads to a failure to know oneself and prevents the validation of identity that is typically offered through social interaction. Having tremendous insight into the level of internal despair and social detachment that is common among intersexuals who have been medicalized, thirty-seven-year-old Kiira, a computer analyst, said,

> You can't become a real person until the reality of your life is acknowledged. And if you're an intersexed person, you can't be real
> until you can say, "I'm an intersexed person; I was born different."
> And no matter what path you take from that reality, it can't be
> surgicalized away. If you try and destroy that reality, you destroy big
> pieces of human beings. And people who've had big pieces of
> themselves [changed], surgically and psychologically, do not develop
> enough "self" to be able to enter into real live relationships.

The power of receiving such validation speaks to the major social consequences wrought by secrecy and isolation. In order to develop connections with others, one must be freed from obsessive secrecy and shame. While it is clear that many intersexuals find medical attempts to normalize their bodies stigmatizing, their efforts to break free from that oppression are not always easy. Generally speaking, emancipating oneself from a stigmatized role requires that one develop new feelings of self-value and efficacy.[56] Seeing the self as valuable and deserving is an essential part of liberating the self, as those who have been outcast often internalize a concept of self as an object of persecution and as less than human.

THE ONLY WAY OUT IS THROUGH:
THE PAINFUL JOURNEY OF RECLAIMING THE SELF

The social desire to fit in and to belong is well known across geographic borders and historical time periods. Negotiating identity, one's basic sense of place and self, is a challenge for many of us, and is no doubt more challenging when something as rudimentary as one's sex is called into question. In a culture whose emphasis on dichotomous sexual categorization touches nearly every aspect of social life, contesting a person's sex is tantamount to shattering their core sense of self. This disruption of identity occurs whether a person learns of their sexual ambiguity at puberty or later in adult life. The reason that learning the "truth" about one's sex is so jarring is because it differs from how they viewed themselves before that moment. Seeing themselves as sexually ambiguous is incongruent with their past identity and with their plans for the future. What's more, one's sense of identity is developed over time, and is dependent on time.[57] A current concept of self is reliant on one's past, whereas one's plans for the future are based on who they are in the present. Perhaps if intersexed children were raised with complete and age-appropriate information about their bodies on an ongoing basis, they would not experience the jarring disruption of self experienced by intersexuals who learn of their difference for the first time in young or later adulthood. It only makes sense that identity negotiation might be easier if current and future conceptions of self blend well with those of the past.

Because most intersexuals grow up without accurate and complete knowledge of their physical sexual differences, they experience intense identity confusion when they finally piece together the mystery of their "gender trouble."[58] The revelation of sexual ambiguity may be likened to dealing with major physical changes. For example, coming to terms with one's chronic illness or disability may similarly destabilize one's concept of self. In such cases, one may see her or his body as having failed or betrayed them.[59] Feeling that one's body is unpredictable, unruly, or out of control is a common theme in intersexuals' stories. For instance, shortly after learning that she had XY, male-typical chromosomes, Martha's hair started falling out in clumps after she put a chemical straightener in it. In her mid-forties at the time, she worried that her loss of hair was evidence of an internal male-self emerging against her will. In her own words,

> [My hair] started falling out at the temples and systematically fell out
> from the edge in. Well, I just freaked out because I thought, "I'm
> really a guy and this is what's happening. I'm middle-aged and I'm
> losing my hair." My way of interpreting it was, "I'm really a man. I'm

really a guy. I've been raised as a woman, taught to act like a woman [and am] still trying to portray myself as female."

Concern that one's genetic sex was somehow trying to exhibit itself against their will was a common theme among interviewees when they were initially coming to terms with what had been hidden from them for so long.

According to Paulo Freire, the process of breaking free from oppression is painful because it makes "real oppression more oppressive still by adding to it the realization of oppression."[60] He equates this transformation to the process of rebirth, where individuals engage in the laborious task of confronting their difficulties, transforming themselves, and emerging anew. Having internalized a stigmatized notion of the self, some may be afraid to try to change their self-concept for fear of failing or feeling overwhelmed in the process. Realizing that they are able to attempt to reshape their identities may actually be experienced as overwhelming, rather than as a relief. This is the point at which the prospect of moving beyond the familiar, despite its many acknowledged consequences, seems daunting rather than liberating. In Sherri's case,

> I felt such an utter sense maybe of decay of my own life—[of] what I had not been dealing with—and I knew that I was desperately in need of going to a therapist to start talking about things. I was either going to go into therapy or I was gonna kill myself—that was the level at which it was at. I started in therapy two days later. In the beginning, I couldn't even tell the therapist what this was all about, but over time I started talking with her about things.

Sharing one's most personal insecurities and doubts with others is a basic building block in being able to acknowledge and accept oneself, and to build trustworthy, meaningful relationships with others. Such transformations are often filled with grief and discomfort, but result in tremendous freedom from living a life of secrecy. Participants spoke frequently about this metamorphosis of self, often using metaphors to refer to their "shamanic rebirths," "conversions," "awakenings," and "constructive breakdowns." In Julian's case,

> There was this six-month period of time where I went crazy and was reborn—in a very real sense. I think that this is the closest we [can] come to a shamanic rebirth in this society [where] you tear everything down that you were and you start over. I threw out everything that I was, basically, and started over. The conversion experience is indistinguishable from a psychotic break, so this madness is all wrapped up in there. Once I got sane again, got over it, and said, "OK, now what happened there?" I couldn't go back [because] the world opened up;

the heavens opened up. You can die physically, or you can die and be reborn in the same body. My life was shredded and put back together again.

As Julian notes, reformulating the self requires the ability to start fresh with new information about the self. Despite its many potential rewards, this initial period of self-seeking and self-acknowledgment often left participants unable to integrate their newfound information into a coherent concept of self. This resulted in bouts of denial, depression, and overall difficulty comprehending the implications of this newly acquired information about themselves. For example, Swan, who recovered her medical records when she was fifty-five years old, less than two years before we met, said,

> [The] first time I read [my medical records] it was pretty painful. I just kind of sat there and cried with it. I don't do that anymore. [The records are] just kind of like the way I was treated. It's just cold, you know. Now I'm clearer about what happened. It's good to have [the records] to put stuff in chronological order.

Even though they elected to seek information about themselves, some relayed that they felt emotionally unprepared to handle what they unearthed. In Sherri's experience,

> [Finding out I had androgen insensitivity syndrome] wasn't seamless. It was very disturbing and emotionally very distressing to find out that I was intended to be my parents' son and not my parents' daughter. I think I was smart enough to know that it was too overwhelming for me to deal with and that I didn't have either the time or the resources emotionally to deal with it. And so with a sort of intuitive kind of wisdom, [I] just put [that information] in a box and shut it and put it in my mind, and was aware that it was there but knew that it was a Pandora's box I wasn't prepared to open. [I didn't open it] for fifteen years.

Participants engaged in creative means of coping with this initial despair, including sealing off the information until a later date, as in Sherri's case. Others were less able to go on without giving immediate attention to the newly discovered facts. Once they chose to proceed with their attempts to complete the identity puzzle, however, most proceeded with vigor.

COMPREHENDING ONE'S DIFFERENCE THROUGH THE LOGIC OF BIOLOGY

Initially coming to terms with the news that they had conflicting sex chromosomes and gender assignment left many participants startled and confused.

Most found such inconsistencies significant enough to be disruptive to their concepts of self. Several noted that their formerly stable gender identities were initially shaken by these revelations. For example, Sarah and Flora said that discovering they had XY chromosomes after a lifetime of believing otherwise caused them to question their female identities. In Sarah's words,

> My whole world had shifted because suddenly I found out that I was XY. It left me feeling very uncertain about what I was, although I didn't feel any different. I mean I still function as a woman. I didn't know how to be anything else. I mean this is what I was. I would sit and pray, like "What am I? Am I some kind of freak?"

In Flora's case, her doctors' lack of skill in communicating with her about this discordance caused her identity as a woman to be undermined. In her words,

> There have been ways in which people have sort of threatened my sexual identity. I've had at least two doctors say, "You shouldn't feel bad that you're male." I bought into this for a long time. I'd been led to believe that chromosomes were the be all and end all when it came [to] gender.

Such disruptions illustrate the power of others' perceptions of self, conveyed through daily social interaction, even into adulthood.

One's sense of self, one's very identity, is formed through ongoing interaction with others. For Sarah, Flora, and other women with AIS, learning that they had male-typical chromosomes and gonads led to feelings of self-doubt. Most often these women perceived themselves as unambiguously female until puberty; others perceived them as unambiguous females up until that point as well. When they failed to experience characteristic female rites of passage, such as menarche and the development of secondary sex characteristics, such as pubic and underarm hair, they went in search of medical assistance. Generally, these women did not question their femaleness until after they sought outside information about why they didn't experience female-typical puberty and after they learned of their genetically male makeup. Thus, even though their physical state of being remained the same, their self-understanding changed dramatically when medical professionals reflected a male-typical, rather than a female-typical appraisal. Up until that point, they expressed feeling different only because they were different from their female peers in that they did not share their coming-of-age rituals, not because they saw themselves as anything other than female.[61]

After learning that they had male-typical genetic makeup, several expressed fear that they would somehow turn into men, as though their genetics operated as a live entity yet to be fully realized. Living with this fear that one's "true" genetic self would somehow emerge against their will often induced feelings of insecurity, powerlessness, and stress. According to Martha,

> I was programmed to be male, but by some fluke of nature, I turned out to be female. This lie is what the world sees. Somehow or another, this part of me is going to come out, this male part of me. I used to be afraid that I would turn into a man. I was fearful that if I was ever elderly and in a nursing home they might say, "You've been on [female] hormones all your life. What do you need them for anymore?" They take me off, and I turn into a man. It was like nobody knows that every day I have to take a little yellow pill just to be able to [be a woman].

As in Martha's case, some found the revelation of their genetic sex to be so disruptive that they initially felt as though their lives as women had been somehow false or fraudulent. The knowledge of their genetic "maleness" led them to question not only their presentation of self, but also their internal sense of identity as well. For example, Greta learned that she had XY chromosomes when she was twenty-eight years old. In her experience, "There was that [sense of], 'Oh my god, I'm XY. Oh my god, I'm really a guy.' I was a mess because I [felt like] a fraud. On the outside I'm a girl, [but] on the inside I'm a man."

The notion that one's "true sex" ultimately resides in the body, and manifests itself physically in chromosomes, gonads, or genitals, is suggestive of biological explanations for gender that Butler and Kessler and McKenna critique in their theories of the heterosexual matrix and gender binarism.[62] Privileging the biological in this way led many participants to devalue their own experiences with gender and sexual identity. This was especially true for those who adhered to the heterosexual matrix and found arguments for genetic causes of homosexuality convincing. For example, some women with androgen insensitivity syndrome saw their attraction to men in a new light upon learning of their XY chromosomes. Having considered themselves to be heterosexual prior to learning of their chromosomal makeup, some concluded that since they were genetically male, their sexual attraction to men must actually be reflective of a homosexual rather than a heterosexual orientation. As Melody illustrates,

> I like men. I've never felt gay until the seed was planted. Then I searched. I searched. I wondered if perhaps I'd been deluding myself. I was told I was a male. So that meant to me, if I'm a male, I would be attracted to women. And I thought, "No, that's bizarre. I'm not." So what is going on?

Others understood the implications of chromosomal sex to be even more defining of sexual attraction, even thinking that they should change their sexual attraction to maintain a claim on heterosexuality. In Mel's case, "I guess when I learned [I was XY], I was like, 'Well, should I like girls instead?'" Despite their initial difficulty comprehending this newly discovered yet contradictory information about themselves, as participants came to terms with it, they were able to see the inconsistencies and limitations within this dualistic thinking itself. For example, take Ardea's experience, which literally exposes both the simplicity and the limits of binary understandings of gender and sexuality. In her words,

> I used to think, "Well, if I like boys then that must mean I'm gay because I was supposed to be a boy. Then if I like girls, that means I'm a gay because I was raised as a girl." Now I've gotten to the point where, I feel like a girl, I'm raised like a girl [and] I wouldn't have any problems getting married to a man at all. But if they win that Defense of Marriage Act, I would be breaking that because I would be a genetic male marrying a genetic male.

Given the recent rulings in Texas and Kansas and the fact that most intersexuals are given a female sex assignment, regardless of their chromosomes, many intersexual women may find themselves being unable to legally marry, should state and federal government continue to pursue chromosomal definitions of sex.

According to Edward Jones and colleagues, the origin of the stigma plays a significant role in determining the dimension or level of disgrace assessed.[63] That is, when an individual is held responsible for the origin of their difference, in addition to being seen as somehow stigmatic, the level of moral judgment associated with their difference increases notably. Conversely, individuals who are deemed victims of unfortunate circumstances often receive sympathy rather than condemnation. This distinction became increasingly clear when participants spoke of deviant aspects of their lives deemed to be of their own choosing, versus those attributed to biological certainty. Their narratives focused on two key examples of difference that often lead to blaming the individual and assigning moral judgment: homosexuality and transsexuality.

Several participants expressed relief upon realizing they would not be blamed for their physiological differences. As Carol stated, "I think there's an element of, 'Well, if it's not your fault or your choice, then it's somehow acceptable.'" Despite the fact that they benefited from a biological excuse, several conveyed the idea that moral judgments based on a stigma's origin were not sensible. This was the case for Chimera, who unexpectedly developed male secondary sex characteristics, such as facial hair and male pattern balding, when she stopped taking her medication for congenital adrenal hyperplasia at age eighteen. In her experience,

> My twenty-year high school reunion was a complete disaster because everybody in my graduating class thought I'd had transgender surgery, thinking that I had changed into a man. I had to tell them over and over, "No, I haven't. The hormones kind of lost their minds after high school. This is caused by a hormone imbalance. I can't fix it; I can't change it. It is what it is and I've gotta live with it."

Unlike Chimera, those who did initiate a gender transition became aware that, to many, the outward appearances of an intersexual gender change and a transsexual sex reassignment had the potential to be interpreted as one in the same. Realizing that they could be assessed more blame for changing genders if they were mistakenly thought to be typical men or women undergoing sex reassignment, several maintained the import of distinguishing intersexuality from transsexuality. For example, when Peggy transitioned from her male gender assignment back to her original, infantile sex assignment of female in her early twenties, she was concerned that she would be incorrectly assumed to be a male-to-female transsexual. This concern motivated her to conceal her history of gender change. In her own words,

> I wouldn't want the people I work with and the people I see every day to know about all this, mainly because they wouldn't . . . even my relatives don't perceive all the facts correctly. They don't have a clear picture of things. They have a lot of misinformation. It's the misinformation and the misperception that I don't want. I think they don't know what my original physical condition was. I don't know what they imagine. There isn't really a convenient or easy way for me to explain it to everyone and I think even if I did, they wouldn't really come away with an accurate picture of the facts even if I gave them that.

Despite her desire to live as a woman throughout her adolescence and young adulthood, Peggy was unable to fully accept her decision to transition into a female gender role until she learned that she had androgen insensitivity syndrome. Once her biology became clear to her, she felt vindicated in her decision to do so. The moral blemish associated with a stigma is relieved if one is able to cast off blame through the rationalization that "it's not my fault; it's my body's fault." Speaking to the impact of this relief, Peggy said, "Basically at that point I had the idea in my mind that I was doing a reasonable thing. I had every right to do this. And I was no longer ashamed of what I was doing. I could explain everything to everybody." Others also noted that their intersexuality made their gender transition easier to accept, for themselves as well as their friends, colleagues, and families. In Max's words,

> I have a medical excuse [to do a gender transition]. I have a letter from my doctor. It's okay for me to look like a boy. If you get right down to it, the fact that I'm intersexed and my body has been butchered and I've been in and out of hospitals forgives my going on testosterone and growing a beard at work. [It] condones it and allows it. It clears up so much anxiety and confusion for people about who and what I am.[64]

Participants also communicated that they were often not stigmatized for their intersexuality, simply because it was invisible, but were condemned for their apparent homosexuality. Constance was the youngest person I interviewed. She was twenty years old when we met, and a college theater major, living in a sorority on campus. Constance had been raised as a woman, but had many physical features, such as height and body build, that are associated with men. In her experience, "Being gay is a bigger challenge because people see me holding hands with a girl or kissing a girl at a party; they don't see my chromosomes at a party." Even though this was the case, some participants found their intersexuality easier to comprehend than their homosexuality. As Barbara noted,

> Coming out [as] AIS is so much clearer, so much more factual than being lesbian. It's sort of a yes or no thing. I feel I can justify AIS just like that [snaps fingers], that nobody in the world can stand against me, or will dare to. I think that [the] issue is simpler. The facts are simpler. I mean, I know why I have AIS. I don't know why I'm a lesbian.

FROM SHAME TO ANGER AND EMPOWERMENT

Participants' process of self-discovery not only resembles the stages noted in most "coming-out" models, but those identified in grief research as well. As I detailed above, when they initially gained accurate information about their bodies and began to understand why they were the focus of medical attention, participants often experienced feelings of shock, denial, and depression. As Carol demonstrates, "When I first started learning about [intersex], it was like, 'Oh, I'm not an intersexual. Why am I grouped as an intersexual?'" In later stages of self-discovery, many came to feel angry with their families and physicians over the way they were treated as children. Eventually, as I describe below and in the next chapter, participants resolved these feelings of angst when they developed greater understanding and acceptance of their difference.

As Elizabeth Kubler-Ross and others have noted, the movement from depression to anger is essential for recovery from loss.[65] Before they were able to do so, several participants found it necessary to grieve the pain and isolation they endured as children. In Sherri's case, acknowledging the isolation was especially significant in her attempt to fully understand her history. Doing so gave her the opportunity and ability to nurture an internal aspect of herself that remained vulnerable, tentative, and afraid. Here she describes the value of grieving her history:

> I mourn and grieve for an eleven-year-old who just had no support. I cry a lot. Not for the me now, but for the me then—the eleven-year-old girl who had no one, who had to deal with it entirely on her own without any support. But mostly I mourn and grieve really for the ordeal of living through this myself. It's like looking at a five-hundred-pound boulder and knowing that you've carried [it] your [entire] life. And it scares you to know that you've carried it. It's like you look at it and you go, "My god. How did I ever carry that?" And it's almost frightening to know that you have. I guess I have had to reach back to that eleven-year-old girl and take her by the hand, literally, and tell her that it's okay now. And to move forward with her life. I'm not there yet, but I'm a hell of a lot further along the journey than I was a few years ago.

Oftentimes the point at which one moves from depression into anger is quite remarkable. This transformation from a rather passive state into one that is active often results in individuals' feelings of empowerment and motivation. For some, the shift from depression to anger signals the beginning of their restoration, in lieu of the fact that their process of reformation actually began long before, when they felt their initial reactions of shock and despair. Because of its import, some recall this change with clarity, as Cheryl does in the following account of suicidal despair.

> I started to get more angry again and I thought, "This is just unacceptable that they could treat me so horribly and I'm gonna kill myself in back of the temple behind my house and [the] people who did this to me will never be confronted with what they did. So if I'm gonna kill myself in such a messy way, at least I should go to the [United States] and do it in the office of the doctor who did the surgery." And that was really making that shift from "I am going to kill myself" to even as small a shift as "I'm gonna kill myself in front of the people that did it" was the beginning of getting better. I just decided that I was too angry to let my life be lost like that. And I was going to really throw myself into feeling better and healing myself.

In this story, Cheryl tells of her decision to end her life after countless futile attempts to attain information and support for herself. In this particular portion of that account, in a move from depression to anger, Cheryl realized that killing herself would do very little to resolve her feelings of anger at the doctors who performed her clitorectomy at age five. She relayed her sudden insight that her dissatisfaction lay not with herself, but with the doctors who had objectified her.

Once they moved to a place of externalizing the dissatisfaction with their bodies and themselves and refocusing it on the source of that shame, as Cheryl conveyed above, participants were able to progress toward a greater acceptance and understanding of themselves. This development was easily notable in participants' rejection of pathological references to the self. As Jana explains,

> Intersexuality is not a disease. Nobody dies from Klinefelter's Syndrome, for example. It's not a disease. I'm not even gonna say it's an abnormality. I simply say it's a variation. Now I like my body and I think I would have liked my body when I didn't like my body if I had known *why* it was like it is. This is the way I am and I can accept that now. And I think I could have accepted it then, had I known, but I didn't know.

Learning to demedicalize their identities and accept themselves as healthy human beings oftentimes left participants with feelings of pride in their difference. As Robin said,

> I feel special. My AIS has made me feel special and it finally makes me understand why I am the way I am. It has made a big difference because I feel complete. I have found a part of myself that was lost. I always knew there was something wrong with me, there's something about me that I don't know.

As I outlined earlier, acknowledging one's difference to oneself and to others is the second part of the coming-out process. As Robin illustrates, when one is able to fully acknowledge their difference, the experience may indeed be positive. Here I turn to Flora, Faye, and Mel's stories, which also illustrate the positive aspects of self-acknowledgment. In Flora's words, "[The doctor] told me what it was and I was relieved. Not only was I relieved, but what I first felt about it was . . . I felt kinda special. I thought it was kinda neat." According to Faye, "I don't think I would turn it in. I mean I've thought about this a lot. I really don't think that I would choose to be other than I am." And for Mel, a twenty-one-year-old medical student, "Every now and then I'd start to think about being XY, and I think it's kinda neat; it's kinda unique. You know? [It] sets me apart from everybody else." Moving into one's secrets rather than away from them in this way allows individuals to "come into" themselves. Many participants spoke of this movement as discovering and living in an identity they called their "authentic" self.

TELLING OTHERS ABOUT THE SELF:

BREAKING FREE FROM OPPRESSIVE SECRECY AND ISOLATION

By speaking out and externalizing their reality, individuals take an active role in reframing and transforming their identities. This is especially significant for those who take personal action to transform an oppressive reality, such as ending a lifetime of silence, secrecy, and isolation. As Lee points out, the consequences of being closeted or "passing" are quite high and may lead to pervasive feelings of anxiety and guilt.[66] Remaining secretive about a central aspect of one's identity may in fact impair the development of a stable and congruent identity. As Lee notes, "the achievement of a healthy personality *requires* significant and substantial self-disclosure to others."[67] Engaging in acts of self-disclosure often proves to be cathartic, especially when the response is positive. As a participant wisely noted, telling one's story to others is a narrative form of restoration. In his own words, Michael, a forty-two-year-old family therapist with hypospadias,

> Breaking secrecy—I would say that was the biggest challenge. I think
> that in itself was healing. I've been studying a lot about narrative
> therapy, which is a form of family therapy. They talk about the
> therapeutic value of restoring your life. It's based on the idea [that] by
> telling your story you externalize the problem, the so-called problem.
> You put it out there for you and others to look at so that it's separated
> out from you. So that it can be looked at and changed and worked with.

In short, Michael and others conveyed that they were unable to make meaningful connections with others without first revealing themselves. Before seeking out other intersexuals, most participants disclosed their intersexuality to their nonintersexed friends, family members, and therapists. Voicing the truth about their differences served to dissipate the feelings of shame and self-loathing they had acquired over years of self-concealment. In Michael's experience,

> [Telling others] really was a powerful experience because it disarmed
> the secret and the hidden quality of my experience. It brought me
> into a relationship with people. I think a lot of what I was suffering
> was the secret life I created around my so-called physical problem.

An ability to be open, to confess and share one's secrets, is key to establishing connections and strong community ties.

As John Lee demonstrates in his interactionist work on gay liberation, externalizing one's identity by verbalizing it results in feelings of internal legitimacy and validation. As a means of illustrating the relief they felt when they first came out as intersexed, I turn to Martha and Max. Each one spoke of the overwhelmingly positive experiences they had when they told others about their intersexuality. In Martha's words, "I would recommend [talking about it] to anybody. It's a good thing to do. It's the best thing I ever did. I think the more I think about it, the more I read about it, the more I talk about it, the more confirmation it gives me." Max spoke to the importance of having one's experiences and identity validated by externalizing them through coming out: "Nothing has been better for me than telling as many people as possible—telling it to people who mirror it back to me."

Telling others about one's secrets becomes easier over time, especially if the people one tells are also somehow marginal or deviant. Because the recipient of the disclosure is also "markable," the exchange may be especially empowering. For example, Robin and a gay male co-worker "traded" secrets. He told her that he was gay, and she told him that she had XY chromosomes. The interaction proved to be lighthearted, affectionate, and supportive for both because they bonded with each other through their marginality in a realization that everyone's got a secret and that disclosure undoubtedly leads to intimacy and trust building. In Robin's own words,

> I've only told one friend, he's a friend of mine at work, and he's gay. I feel like we both have a secret. He told me his, then I told him mine. He was so sweet. He [said], "Robin! I never would have guessed! Oh my god, Robin, you're a guy!" And we were laughing *so hard*, you know? And so we were just laughing about it.

The decision to come out as intersexed was not always motivated by a desire for support. Others told of their political motivations for self-disclosure. Some "went public" in the hope that doing so would destigmatize intersex and thus prevent harm to intersexed infants and children. In this case the decision to disclose was often morally based. For example, in Suegee's case,

> [I] realiz[ed] that my silence was not gonna help anybody. It wasn't gonna keep me safe, it wasn't gonna keep all the babies that are being born safe. That's when I really started coming out as being intersexed. That was really, really it. I realized how important it was for me, specifically, to be speaking about it because I *hadn't* had the surgeries, I *had* grown up this way [and] I was perfectly fine with it. I knew that I had to start talking because things have just gotta change.

Others were also motivated to disclose their intersexuality to model pride rather than shame, hoping that doing so would encourage others to venture out of the closet. This was especially true for those serving as leaders of intersex support and activist organizations. In Cheryl's case, "Ultimately I realized that if I'm saying that intersexuality is not shameful, then I have to stand up and own it. Everybody doesn't need to do that, but somebody needs to do that. And I can't ask anybody to do it if I won't do it."

According to Mason-Schrock, we come to know ourselves by relaying our histories verbally to others.[68] Our identities become more clear and meaningful when reflected through the response of others. As both Suegee and Cheryl found, verbalizing one's difference is just one of several crucial steps toward reclaiming and destigmatizing the self. One who has been without power is often paralyzed and incapable of action. Once one is able to acknowledge her/his secret, the next logical step is to find others who have the same secret and are engaged in similar efforts of self-affirmation. Often, their ability to act is restored by identifying with a similar person or group of people who possess a great deal of power.[69] Affiliating with those who are strong provides a model of hope and potential achievement for those who have been long-suffering and disempowered.

Coming Out, Stage Three: Validation of Self at Long Last

Recall that in stage three of the coming-out process individuals seek similar traits and affirmation in others.[70] Overcoming the mark of stigma requires that one finds others who are similar to serve as adequate peers for social comparison. This kind of social comparison is necessary for adequate self-concept development. Finding peers enables one, perhaps for the first time, to construct a positive, coherent, and stable concept of self. Meeting others who have lived successfully with the same difference provides an alternative to feeling confusion and shame about the self.[71] According to Jones et al.,

> Comparison with others who are similarly marked or stigmatized
> should allow individuals to focus on attributes and qualities other
> than the stigmatized ones, and thereby provide the opportunity for
> them to view themselves as complex and differentiated individuals
> with valued attributes and abilities.[72]

As I noted above, several participants became aware of other intersexuals' existence via electronic and print media, such as the Internet, television, and newspapers. While this initial association was certainly powerful, the connection remained incomplete for some until actual face-to-face meetings took place. Speaking to the importance of physically meeting with one's peers, Dana, a twenty-one-year-old college student with PAIS, said,

Until then I was really alone. I could read all about [intersex]. I could read all the letters and all the papers and all that stuff. But until I met an intersexual, they'd still be fictitious, they'd still be this fantasy, this wondrous fantasy. These people that were just like me and who could relate to me and would have compassion for me. For exactly what is causing my pain. [It] was really just a watershed event.

Schwalbe and Mason-Schrock claim that affirmation of one's identity, especially when it is contested, is essential to maintaining its reality and function, for "Without affirming, the identity in question remains an ephemeral notion, connected to no real persons."[73]

Even though meeting other intersexuals offered participants the validation they had been seeking for so long, some found the prospect of meeting others face to face daunting at first.[74] This was especially true for those who were consciously seeking validation of themselves. In this case, participants often felt fear associated with meeting other intersexuals because doing so had the potential to powerfully impact their notion of self. What if these "similar others" they had sought out over the course of a lifetime were somehow bizarre or apparently different and would reflect a similar strangeness about oneself? For example, in Cheryl's experience,

I decided I'm gonna have a peer support group meeting where I'm gonna invite the ones who are close enough to come and sit and talk to each other. And it took me a long time to do that. I was really afraid to [meet others]. Partly I was afraid of how much pain there was gonna be there. And partly I was afraid that they were gonna be freaks. Intersex people, hermaphrodites, they're all freaks, right? They were afraid of that too. The people who came to the first support group meeting, they all told me that, "We were afraid we were gonna come here [and] everybody was gonna be a freak." If they were freaks, then maybe I was [too].

For most, however, the opportunity to meet other intersexuals signaled the end to a lifetime of seclusion. Recounting the isolation she experienced prior to finding other intersexuals, Faye said, "Up until that point I was sure . . . I thought I was the only one."

Here, Melody, Claire, and Martha articulate the power of finding out they weren't the only intersexuals after a lifetime of being sure that they would never encounter another human being with a body like theirs. In Melody's words, "You can't imagine what it was like! What a relief to find people and not to be alone! It was just incredible. It's like being green in a world of blue and suddenly you find another green person. It was unbelievable. It was just really unbelievable." In Claire's account, "It's been incredibly freeing because there is that sense of not only finding someone like you, but finding a whole community where you belong. There's that wonderful sense of, 'Oh my god, I'm not alone.'" In a very similar conversation, Martha added:

> After having lived all my life in isolation with this, suddenly to hear another person speak the words that I have spoken in the past; share the thoughts that I've had. Well, what it felt like was that I've been living on this alien planet, portraying myself, passing myself off as an earthling and I've met someone from, one of my people, from this other planet. You know?

Still, meeting others evoked an emotional hardship similar to that encountered when they first gained access to information about their differences. Such encounters elicited emotions of grief and sorrow for some by serving to validate the reality of the trauma endured by many during medical procedures of normalization. Here, Suegee relays her shock and emotional pain when seeing other intersexuals' genitals for the first time.

> The really intense part about the retreat was the part where we all did the [genital] show and tell. I remember at the beginning of it, I started feeling very light-headed. Actually seeing [the surgeries] it made it just so much more real—seeing what could have happened to me. After we'd done all that, everybody just broke down and started crying.

Despite initial emotional difficulties, coming into contact with other intersexuals served to validate participants' experiences to a great extent. According to Vivienne Cass, seeking peers helps those who have suffered from stigma move toward identity tolerance and eventual identity acceptance.[75] A positive self-image is directly related to one's opportunity to interact with others who have been similarly stigmatized.[76] In fact, as Schwalbe and Mason-Schrock argue, many participants found that they were best able to "locate" themselves by associating with others who had similar life stories.[77] In Sherri's experience,

> It was so validating to be able to talk with other people who had had similar experiences, because part of what happened in my case was that I blamed myself for how I was reacting [and] thinking; that if I was only more capable, more emotionally together, I would be dealing with this better. Then you start meeting other people who coped exactly as you coped, and you suddenly forgive yourself and you start to understand that how you dealt with it was the most normal reaction under the most abnormal of circumstances.

Having one's worth reflected through others' appraisals not only gave participants self-confidence, but also valuable insight into the social context for their experiences. Furthermore, meeting others and finding out they had been similarly stigmatized gave many participants political understanding of their histories. As Michael said,

> The key thing for me was that I expanded my personal experience
> from an isolated one to a more communicative one, where I could see
> that hypospadias existed socially. That was a big shift for me and an
> important transition 'cause [that] helped me to see that larger picture.

Finding others serves to contextualize intersexuals' medical experiences as social, rather than individual problems. Learning that others had undergone similarly alienating medical procedures led to an ability to recast the personal as political, rather than as an individual failing. Realizing that others had been similarly traumatized by medical intervention led some to become active in organizing social support. As Cheryl commented, "I realized, 'Wait a minute! This isn't rare; this has gotta be utterly common. This is more common than all kinds of things. All these people are traumatized and silenced.' That's when I determined to create a support group."

Social support has been shown to be extremely effective in developing a strong sense of empowerment for those who are marginalized.[78] As I demonstrated previously, intersex stigmatization leads to feelings of alienation, powerlessness, meaninglessness, social isolation, and self-estrangement.[79] People who are singled out as different often come to devalue and distrust themselves. Such self-doubt leads to high levels of self-monitoring and an inability to relax in social situations.[80] In direct contrast, when people who are marginalized encounter social support, especially through interaction with similarly stigmatized peers, their sense of self-efficacy increases dramatically. As Jenny illustrates,

> [Social support has] increased my sense of self-worth one hundred
> percent. I no longer walk around with that little voice in my mind
> saying, "Am I okay? Do they know what's going on?" It's gone. I mean
> it was just really a major thing. It started changing immediately when
> I saw, face to face, other women. It changed things big time.

Being labeled as deviant and without peers fosters feelings of social detachment and hopelessness and may even prevent the development of significant social relationships. When individuals are treated as though they are outside the social norm, they may elect to remain socially detached. In Sherri's case,

> I fully assumed that I'd live my whole life without ever meeting
> someone else. I guess it's all I wanted. I didn't want to be alive without

knowing someone else. I felt completely untethered to the planet. I was just floating out in space. And I wanted some kind of connection to the rest of the world and I didn't have it. There was no point of reference. There was this Plexiglas barrier between myself and [others] because I had this terrible secret, and I couldn't talk to anyone. And even if I could have talked to them, they would have not [had] a clue as to what I was talking about.

As Sherri and others so clearly illustrate, secrets serve as barriers to self-knowledge and social intimacy. Countering the social barriers of isolation that Sherri describes is perhaps achieved most readily by interaction with members of one's own peer group. The identification felt with those having similar experiences often assists those living in isolation in forming meaningful social relationships for the first time. As Kiira stated,

When it *finally* happens, when you finally meet another intersexed person who will stand face to face with you and say, "Yeah, that happened to me too," honest to God, it's like being in the desert and finding an oasis—a beautiful, emerald blue, cold oasis in the middle of the desert. That's exactly what it felt like to me. When we meet, there's this gush; it's just like, "Yes!" There's a great deal of love between intersexed people for that reason. A great deal.

Although participants demonstrated that they had clearly internalized feelings of humiliation, estrangement, and shame, they also exhibited an inspiring desire and ability to overcome their self-loathing. In doing so, they empowered themselves through self-education about their physical differences. The rather personal nature of their quest led to archival research within familial and medical establishments. As they became more competent in understanding their own bodies, participants demystified their feelings of secrecy and alienation about their bodies. Once they had unearthed accurate information about themselves, they elected to share it with others. In addition, they began to associate with other intersexuals, putting an end to many years of isolation. Thus, the search for the "authentic self" led participants to an initial and more positive concept of self. I turn now to an exploration of participants' further renegotiation of self via intersex social support and political activism.

Chapter 5   Intersex Pride

We have the power to shake people's foundations. You can't touch one of us and come away unchanged. At least you'll come away questioning things. We infect people, just by being. We are walking carriers of the gender questioning disease.
                     —Excerpt from interview with Julian

THROUGH THEIR ASSOCIATION with intersex support groups and activism, participants' experiences help them to realize the next two stages in the coming-out process. Through these activities, intersex individuals gain pride in their stigmatized identities through associating with others like themselves and by engaging in political activism that gives a new sense of autonomy and visibility.[1] Through the processes of self-education and self-awareness, participants met other intersexuals, often for the first time in their lives. In doing so, some of them became actively involved with other intersexuals by participating in support groups, while others became engaged in political efforts to reform contemporary medical management practices. Identifying with others who have been similarly outcast increases one's sense of personal power and autonomy and enhances their ability to recast their own identity in a more positive light.[2] While active participation in intersex support and activism is strongest during one's initial association, being a part of the intersex community both normalizes and politicizes one's previously stigmatizing intersex experience and identity. During the early stages of coming to terms with their identities, intersexuals, like others who are similarly outcast, often want close affiliation with support groups. During this stage, however, people are often engrossed in their marginal identity so that it dominates their self-concept, but it can become less important as they come to see stigmatizing character-istics as less defining.[3]

Recall from previous chapters that individuals initially internalize stigma and shame, then engage in medical research to gain accurate information about themselves in an effort to reshape their marked identity. Here, I turn to an exploration of how individuals recast their identities further by engaging in intersex support and activism. By doing so, they realize stages four and five of the coming-out process: developing pride in their marginality and integrat-ing their marginal identity within a larger sociocultural context.[4]

Identifying with others who have been similarly outcast increases one's sense of power to create their own identity in a culture where identity forma-tion has largely been a process *external* to an intersexed person's sense of self.[5] What's more, moving successfully through the first three stages of the coming-out process establishes a solid sense of self and autonomy. This process, how-ever, is difficult to complete because intersexuals' early identity so often relies on external medicalized notions of the self.

In order to understand the difficulties many intersexuals face in creating a workable identity, it is important to understand the influence of medicalization on an intersexed person's sense of self. For example, some medi-cal models treat intersexuals as passive objects whose bodies are acted upon to correct their physical "pathologies," which are seen as deviating from so-cial norms. This approach devalues intersexuals' own life experiences with the very phenomenon or condition under consideration. Rather than listening to intersexuals' critical perspectives on the negative impact of surgical sex as-signment, many clinicians focus single-mindedly on the development of new technologies and techniques for performing genital surgeries and administer-ing exogenous hormones. Thus, physicians maintain the necessity for surgery and for developing ways to improve surgery and increase accuracy in sex as-signment decision making. This medical approach is founded on the belief that intersex itself is pathological. Similar to the medicalization of other natu-rally occurring phenomena, such as menopause, intersex is perceived as need-ing treatment, despite inconclusive evidence demonstrating the effectiveness of the current treatment protocol and recent studies that in fact depict medi-cal treatments as harmful. As is the case with menopause, intersex is also seen as potentially disease causing, as is evidenced by emergency gonadectomies performed on some intersex children and young adults to prevent cancer.[6]

Negative connotations of difference reinforce normalcy, in that they tend to assume that the person who is different is damaged and that the person who labels them is normal. In addition, the persistent focus on the abnormality of intersexed bodies further reifies the "normalcy" of bodies that are not intersexed.[7] In other words, affirming intersexuals' difference as deviance confirms a normal/abnormal opposition.[8] As Lennard Davis says of the deaf/hearing dichotomy, "the 'problem' is not the person with disability; the problem is the way that normalcy is constructed to create the 'problem' of the disabled person."[9] While Davis writes of disability, his sentiment is easily applicable to other types of difference that have been stigmatized, including intersexuality. Or, in the words of one study participant named Meta:

> If a person of my condition defines themself as neuter, you're basically defining yourself by what you are not, and then you're less than. I don't feel that I'm less than. I don't feel that I'm a genetic mistake. I don't feel that I'm genetic junk. I don't feel that I'm a genetic failure; [I'm a] genetic variation.

Paradigm shifts, such as demedicalization, are very hard won.[10] And once a situation has begun to be treated clinically, it may seem illogical for those who adhere to the dominant framework to attend to it in any other manner.[11] For example, clinicians are often not the initiators of treatment reform because they are frequently served by, and benefit from, work which may be deemed disempowering by their patients. In order to enact change, however, clinicians must interact directly with those they serve and be affected by their patients' personal experiences and efforts.[12] In the case of intersex medicalization, physicians who are far less eager advocates of surgical intervention on intersexed infants and children are those who have had personal contact with adult intersexuals who are critical of medicalization.[13] This shift is due, in part, to the persistent vocal and visible efforts of some intersexuals.

Contemporary intersex activism emerged as a reaction to intersexuals' broad societal marginalization and aimed to critique medical interventions and disempower the secrecy and shame associated with intersexuality. Recall that prior to actively seeking information about themselves, all participants reported having a lack of accurate information about their medical histories, conditions, and diagnoses. Before the presence of intersex support and advocacy organizations, intersexuals were dependent on their physicians for information. What's more, before finding a support group, an intersexed person might have only discussed intersex, albeit scantily, in a doctor's office. Before associating with support groups, all participants reported feeling a lack of control over their own bodies because they did not have accurate and comprehensive information. Ironically, though, Cleo Berkun reports that even though they may be disappointed with the information they receive from their physicians, individuals turn to medical authorities for assistance with their medicalized condition, rather than personal means of social support. They do so because the social dynamics of secrecy, oddity, and shame mix potently with those of the medical power structure. Berkun uses the example of menopause to illustrate this phenomenon:

> Because of the perceptions of the private, medical, and moral nature of their [menopausal] thoughts, they did not turn to their usual sources of support and information but, rather, sought "factual" information from physicians with which they were not satisfied.[14]

But for too long, those "facts" were not found by intersexuals in a physician's office and as a result, intersexuals were forced to rely on themselves and other intersexuals to learn the reality of their own anatomy. Developing an ability to be one's own source of information is possible over time, and this newfound autonomy is critical to one's self-concept. In fact, it is so critical that Jones and colleagues claim that "The self-esteem of stigmatized individuals will increase to the extent that the individuals come to view themselves as other than helpless, dependent, and worthless."[15]

The possibility of developing new clinical guidelines or alternatives to the current medical treatment of intersex is expanding rapidly as a result of intersex activism and new research in this area. It is possible that through their continued efforts, meaningful exchanges can transpire between intersexuals and the clinicians who desire to serve them. Perhaps, through the development of alternative understandings of intersex, the negative meanings associated with it may begin to be cast off. In order to further discuss the viability of transforming social discourse in this way, and to see how social support networks can serve as a vital agent of change, more consideration must be given to research on small-scale social movements.

Collective Action: Theories and Evidence

In theorizing the internal workings of social movements and collective action, William Gamson and Jo Freeman postulate that there are several processes essential to small-group social change.[16] Each of these elements parallels the efforts of support groups working to counter a stigmatized identity, such as intersex. Both Gamson and Freeman argue that collective identity and established communications networks are essential for successful social change. For example, through involvement in a social movement, one begins to shift the social location of her/his identity from an individual notion of self to a group identification. That is, the problem that was formerly individualized is now recognized as a social problem that others experience as well. My study participants described this process most clearly during stages two and three of coming out, where the development of a group identity served to enforce the social solidarity and the "we-ness" of a group of individuals drawn together for a common purpose and through common experiences. But to be successful, groups must be defined as a common entity and its members must have shared views of the social environment, shared goals, and shared opinions about the possibilities and limits of collective action.[17]

Groups must also have a sense of solidarity. Solidarity here serves to connect group members to that which initially drew them together. According to Gamson, criteria for recruitment into social movements rest upon prior social relationships, common personal experiences, and the gratification of personal/individual needs through group membership. Many participants described their dedication to intersexuals, intersex rights, and a willingness to go to great lengths to help others. As one study participant named Kiira said,

> I'm really happy to be able to be one of the people who's working
> hardest to provide communication and contact between people.
> That's my big thing, finding contacts for people and also giving people
> a chance to speak; [giving] them their voice, that's my theme.

An important aspect of helping or healing oneself is to assist others who have experienced similar hardships.[18] Seeing that one's experience, courage, and tenacity can assist others gives individuals a sense of importance, purpose, and reason to remain actively involved with support groups and other outreach efforts. As Kent Sandstrom notes, some people with stigma develop an "ideological embracement" related to their difference.[19] Doing so gives them a purpose, a mission to fulfill their calling to educate and help others who may be affected by the same stigma. As J8 recalled, "I decided this is important work to be doing. I could see that what I had to offer and what people were drawn to was self-acceptance and being proud of who you are."

Many participants spoke of the ease with which they interacted with their newfound peers, oftentimes using humor and insider knowledge to support one another through stressful, intimate, and sometimes delicate situations. For example, many participants spoke of fearing that they were sexually inadequate or unable to perform. This was an issue for many who wanted to engage in vaginal intercourse or to accommodate penetration, but did not know if their vaginal cavities were deep enough. For example, for Barbara, a sixty-five-year-old retired social worker and self-identified lesbian with CAIS,

> I didn't get physically involved sexually until I was thirty-five. I was so
> scared to test out how short or long my vagina was. This was a really
> important fact. It held me back in some ways from becoming involved
> with men. I was scared to become involved with men. I thought,

"What if I can't do it?" It caused me a lot of distress in my twenties and early thirties.

Because women with AIS typically have short and "blind-ending" vaginas (meaning they have no cervix), the ability to talk to others and negotiate sexual intimacy was especially important. Speaking of the reassuring ease and humor with which her support group discusses sexual intercourse, Sherri said,

> In the support group, we call them "docking maneuvers." I'm probably the only person in the world who, moments after [sex], would be on the phone with about thirty different women talking about it, from all over the world. We do tend to talk about this a lot.

Negotiation of these delicate issues with others who share similar experiences, fears, questions, and desires, was an empowering experience for study participants.

As social movements continue their development, groups develop a consciousness that bridges the gap between individual and cultural beliefs. The widespread medical framework that dominates the understanding of intersex persuades individuals to adhere to "proper" (read: medical) intersex treatment protocol. Thus, becoming aware of the cultural constructions of deviance offers one an increased ability to transform both self-identity and cultural discourse. For example, in trying to ensure that her niece had a more empowering experience during her gonadectomy than she did, Carol spoke directly to her, in front of the girl's parents. She said,

> So many of my friends that I've made have had experiences and me included, where people did exams, or took pictures of us, without our consent. And we didn't know that we were allowed to say, "Stop it." And so please, if they ask, know that you can say yes or no. It's up to you. Not your mummy or dad, or *any* of them. It's up to you.

A final phase of collective action is micromobilization, which challenges both individual and institutional belief systems. In Bert Klandermans's words, "Collective action proceeds from a significant transformation in the collective consciousness of the actors involved."[20] Writing of the importance of social support garnered for menopausal women, Geri Dickson writes that:

> Free, open discussion with other women could lead to questioning the assumption behind the scientific and medical discourses and the resulting expectations of menopause. Other knowledge of menopause might then be free to emerge from women's experiences.[21]

Note that much of the information exchanged in intersex support and advocacy organizations contradicts pathological and pejorative conceptions of intersex. In telling their stories, participants spoke of a sense of frustration with the information and resources readily available to intersexuals prior to their association with support groups. This desire for more information corresponds with Irving Zola's notion of the political foundation of self-help groups.[22] According to Zola, gaining knowledge is a primary source of empowerment for those engaged in self-help groups. As I noted above, leaders of intersex support groups oftentimes initially formed their groups in order to provide an accessible and centralized source of information for others.

Building communities based on social support is a common response to coping with a stigmatized identity, role transitions, and physical difficulties.[23] Similar to the consciousness-raising groups that emerged out of 1970s American feminism, support groups serve the purpose of altering social norms and rejecting stigma. John Suler refers to these groups as "redefiner groups."[24] Some groups are more focused on supporting the feelings of its members while others are more pragmatic in their objectives, such as providing education and affecting legislation.

Further outlining possible similarities between social movements and self-help or support groups, Kurt Back and Rebecca Taylor outline Herbert Blumer's five stages of social movements.[25] In summary, these stages are (1) the mobilization of members due to frustration and social needs, often witnessed as a dissatisfaction with professional services pertaining to the issue of concern; (2) peer exploration of this agitation; (3) the development of group morale and inspiration; (4) the formation of an ideology and justification for the existence of the group/movement; and (5) goal achievement. This model is useful in demonstrating the orientation toward change that may be present in self-help and support groups. According to Back and Taylor, once a self-help group has moved through Blumer's five stages, it "may now go beyond its expressive origins; [and] it may be looking for social change on a larger scale."[26]

Focusing on the political aspects of self-help groups, Zola also speaks to the mistrust of professional help as grounds for group formation. In his model, a primary function of self-help groups is to demystify the common "problem" that initially brought members together. According to Zola, clarity is found through increased lay knowledge surrounding the issue of concern. This lay education creates an empowered and informed lay group membership. Group members actually experience membership benefits beyond what they could receive from professionals, in that they not only receive direct help with their concern, but also experience the emotional benefits of community.[27]

Others demonstrate the importance of support group membership, group cohesion, and social reinforcement in decreasing alienation and cultivating a sense of control over one's own situation.[28] As one participant named Drew insightfully stated about the importance of social support,

> The peer support was just an added bonus. I guess you can compare it to a gay experience where you can feel okay about being gay [and] know that there's support out there, but if you live in a town where you're the only one, it's like you just can't share it as much or you can't live it as actively and share it with your friends. So here I feel like I can actually share it with people and have that, and that's wonderful.

Clearly the importance of group social support systems cannot be underestimated, even though little empirical research has been conducted to determine their impact. For example, Davis claims that there has been little empirical work on the area of social support networks as they impact women's experiences of menopause.[29] The same is true of research on intersex. But as Davis argues, lay referral and support systems may serve as a valid route to the "renaturalization" of menopause, and I argue that the same holds true in the case of intersex. According to Davis and the anthropologist Emily Martin, "learning about female bodily processes from a combination of personal experience and the experiences of one's peers is an important counterforce to the hegemony of the scientific, medical view."[30] Surely, one can also use this lens to view the experiences of intersexuals who use lay systems of social support as a primary means of demedicalizing sexual ambiguity.

Coming Out, Stage Four: Pride in the Marginal Identity

According to Michael Schwalbe and Douglas Mason-Schrock, individuals engage in "oppositional identity work" when reclaiming a formerly stigmatized self. Schwalbe and Mason-Schrock define oppositional identity work as "A matter of trying to transform discrediting identities into crediting ones, that is, to redefine those identities so they come to be seen as indexes of noble rather than flawed character."[31] By rejecting normative values, individuals gain pride in their marginal identity and come to see it as valuable, worthy, and sufficient in its own right.[32]

As I outlined in previous chapters, several scholars have explored individuals' means of living with various stigmatized characteristics, such as physical disability and transsexuality. Many successfully cope with stigma by organizing themselves to transform a stigmatized identity into one of dignity and pride. We are witnessing the same trend among intersexuals with the recent emergence of well over a dozen intersex support and advocacy groups in North America alone.

Support groups provide meaning and structure for individuals who have lived with feelings of anxiety, uncertainty, and ambiguity. They encourage people to overcome feelings of powerlessness and provide role models and assistance for group members who also want to learn how to rely on their own internal resources for problem solving. Sharing one's difficulties with those who have suffered similarly is often an emotional catharsis. In addition, when one's secret or shameful identity is validated, the need to engage in consistent self-monitoring may slip away. In Melody's words, "We finally had our rite of passage. Finding everyone. You have no idea what it was like. I can't even begin to tell you. It was like suddenly it was all okay. I went through [a] flourish of freedom. I no longer had to analyze what I did."

Support groups also provide role models for their members to emulate in the process of reworking their self-concepts. For instance, while conducting research on people with AIDS, Sandstrom found that support groups provided members with a "buddy system" that offered individuals a chance to be themselves—to test and legitimate their identities.[33] In the case of intersex, where individuals are often taught that sexual ambiguity is pathological, meeting others who embrace that aspect of their identity is liberating. Here, individuals can rethink their own self-concept while others model intersex as a viable and worthwhile aspect of self. For example, in Max's experience, "I don't think that I could really identify as intersexed if I hadn't come to find out that that was actually a viable alternative." Meeting others not only validates one's difference, it contextualizes it as well. Learning that their experiences of medical trauma were not isolated incidents gave participants a political lens through which to view their own histories. Speaking to the social psychological value of situating her marginal identity in a broader social context, Barbara said,

> I really have a place in the world. I really am a human being, a very
> valid human being. It's just wonderful. I am very proud to come out as
> an [intersex] person. The world has tried to make us feel like freaks.
> We have felt like freaks. I felt like a freak most of my life, but look at
> me. I'm just a human being just like everybody else.

In their stories of collective action, it is evident that participants are working together to redefine intersex in more positive and empowering ways. Contrary to Western medical views and lay understandings of intersex as an aberration in need of correction, many participants spoke of intersex as a prideful aspect of themselves. Joseph and Robin exemplify the fourth stage of many coming-out models: the ability to develop pride in one's marginal identity, by making statements of self-worth directly related to their difference. In Joseph's words, "I mean, think of it...what if this was a culture that really honored intersexuals [so that they were] really special, really desirable and that then they would be looking. They'd say, 'Don't you think this kid is a hermaphrodite? Oh no, he's a regular one.'" Speaking more personally about herself, Robin said, "I feel like a super female. I'm both; I'm the yin and yang. I'm the epitome of yin and yang. Genetically I'm a male, but physically I'm all woman. So, I'm not one or the other; I'm both. And I just feel so powerful about that."

As participants developed pride in their intersexuality, some notably developed gratitude for their difference as well. In their writings about overcoming stigma, Jones et al. address this phenomenon of appreciation for personal challenges. In their own words, "[some]…may feel that a stigma provides them with an opportunity to change their life course, to alter the flow of events, something that would not be possible without the special circumstances created by a stigma."[34] Transforming one's difference from bane to virtue in this way is similar to victims who, having worked through a trauma, refer to themselves as "survivors." Some argue that survival of hardship builds character. As Deborah stated,

> *Nobody* is strong from having just sat in a chair. They're strong
> because they've gone through endurance testing—physical things or
> emotional things. Nobody has any mettle to their life if they haven't
> gone through something hard.

Formerly stigmatized individuals may feel not only prideful about their difference, but also superior or heroic about it as well. According to Julian,

> I wouldn't call it a messiah complex, but I do firmly believe that I'm
> different from most people in a way that is better, that gives a greater
> perspective. [Being intersexed] has given me the ability to look at so
> many different people's perspectives, through *so* many different
> people's eyes. I almost feel sorry for people who haven't had this
> experience.

Clearly, by this stage in coping with their difference, these participants have moved beyond intersex as a primarily stigmatic identity, and they are able to reflect back on their life with critical insight. In addition to having feelings of heroism, after coming to terms with their differences, others see divinity and purpose in their intersexuality. As Carol said, "Having AIS brought me my [adoptive] children, it brought me my husband, it brought me my friends. It's what I love about myself."

Having countered one's own internalized sense of shame for being different, some individuals choose to become politically involved in an effort to destigmatize their marginal identity at a larger, sociocultural level. That is, some segments of self-help movements enter the political arenas in an attempt to effect social and legislative change.[35] Once again, individuals demonstrate here their ability to reject the former pivotal status of the stigmatized self, and thus avoid continued "identity engulfment" or a permanently spoiled sense of self.[36]

HERMAPHRODITES WITH ATTITUDE: EVIDENCE OF INTERSEX PRIDE
One strategy for self-presentation is for stigmatized individuals to embrace their difference and find ways to exploit it. Sometimes people do this by associating with groups that emphasize positive aspects of difference, as is shown in stage four of coming out—pride in one's marginal identity. According to Jones et al., "drawing attention to the mark may occasionally take the form of idealization ('Black is beautiful,' 'Gay is the way'), but more often than not, it serves as a rallying cry for self-protection and political action."[37] Examples of groups that highlight their differences include Queer Nation, an activist group for members of GLBT populations; CRIPS, an activist group for people with disabilities; Little People of America, an activist group for people of short stature; and the Intersex Society of North America's activist branch, Hermaphrodites with Attitude.[38] Other, less politically active groups still highlight their difference in the group's name, but serve a primary purpose of social support. Examples of these well-known groups include Alcoholics Anonymous, Weight Watchers, Gamblers Anonymous, and the less-known Androgen Insensitivity Syndrome Support Groups.

Politicizing identity was important to a number of the participants in this study, regardless of the type of support group with which they were associated. Some of the groups were committed to working on improving current medical treatment, as seen in the efforts undertaken by the Androgen Insensitivity Syndrome Support Groups. Others who were equally committed to effecting medical change worked from outside the medical establishment; for example, Hermaphrodites with Attitude picketed the 1996 Annual Meeting of the American Academy of Pediatrics in Boston.[39] Study participants demonstrated various means of stating both their pride and their politics. For example, recall that 27 percent of those interviewed chose to use their real names for the study. Furthermore, another 24 percent changed their first and sometimes last names as a form of reclaiming themselves.[40]

Many participants spoke of the importance of experiencing a sexual awakening at the same time that they came to terms with their intersexuality. For some, this was perhaps viewed as a political act, in that 14 percent of the sample was sexually active with other intersexuals. Regarding the development of a broader concept of self, participants spoke of being unable to freely explore their sexuality until they had overcome the barriers inherent to secrecy and shame. These barriers were heightened for participants who were repeatedly subjected to genital scrutiny. Breaking free from shame and inhibitions was often associated with learning about and acknowledging one's intersexuality. As Kiira illustrates,

> I was asexual and anorgasmic until I was thirty-two years old. Then I discovered my sexuality, my identity as an intersexed person, and I learned how to become orgasmic. I'd never had any sexual feelings, but it was almost like my sexuality just kind of awakened at that time in my life. Before, I would think about sex and go, "Oh, people like me don't have sex."

Similarly for Greta and Claire, learning to accept and respect their bodies for, and not in spite of their differences, led to enhanced self-confidence and freedom of sexual expression. In Greta's experience, coming to terms with her intersexuality dissipated her earlier fears of inadequacy and inauthenticity. In her own words, "I love having sex. I'm not afraid to let myself go. My response is very normal, so I know that I'm not a freak, as I at one point thought." Claire also articulates the deeper level of trust and appreciation she developed for her body after accepting her intersexuality. In her words,

> And then I came to really love my sexual self. The way I felt, and the way I smelled, and the way I responded, and the way I tasted. I came to love my body that way without any judgment about how it looked in a societal way or how it performed or what it could and couldn't do. I just loved its "itsness" for what it was.

While recognizing one's sexual awakening as a form of political activism was important to some study participants, others were engaged in forms of activism that were more explicitly political. Several spoke to their commitment of being "out" and visibly intersexed in an effort to counter and overcome their experiences with shame and isolation. In Julian's words,

> Closets are bad. Closets are awful. Closets are the enemy. Sometimes they can be necessary for short periods of time, but one should always be working towards getting out of the closet, no matter what you have to do. It's so much easier to be out than to be consumed with shame. When you're in the closet it looks horrible to be out. But when you're out, you look back at digging the closet and you say, "Why did I do that? Why was I such an idiot for so long?"

But being "out" as an intersexual can sometimes take effort because similar to other types of "invisible" difference, such as some forms of learning disability or chronic illness, intersexuals are often assumed to be typical women and men because clothing quite easily conceals intersex ambiguity. Some participants spoke of wanting to be accurately categorized as intersexed, and as a result, they occasionally engaged in political acts of destabilizing and subverting their social identity by intentionally living in opposition to normative gender roles and expectations.[41] For example, in young Constance's experience,

> Who I am is a person that doesn't have to conform because in my very DNA I don't agree with the societal norm. There's just no way I could fit either [gender] role. Then why the hell should I bother to try? Why don't I have a little fun? It's been a really freeing experience. I'm a lot happier. I don't blend in ever, so I may as well have fun if I'm gonna get noticed anyway. I might as well get noticed for what I really want to be.

And in Julian's case,

> Part of the reason I'm out is I *want* people to know what I am. I want people to know that I'm gender ambiguous. I don't feel female, but I don't necessarily feel male either. I feel like I am in the middle and feel that very solidly. And that seems very natural. When people say, "Do you identify as male or female?" [I hear,] "What do you pretend to be?" I don't pretend. I just am what I am, which is something in between.

Many participants spoke directly to the importance of using social visibility as a strategy for destigmatization and empowerment. Here Tiger speaks of his appearances on television talk shows in an effort to educate lay audiences about intersex and to externalize his feelings of shame.

> Becoming a person who is comfortable standing up in public, literally on television and saying, "No matter what you think of how I look or how I speak, no matter what I've done to fit into this world, I am not male or I am not female. And probably neither are you." To be in the position [of] making those kinds of statements and having all the signs and facts to back up my position, it's very exciting. This is a dramatic level of self-acceptance that I have fought with and been tortured by all my life. And to have come to a place where I realize that mine is a position of strength, not of disadvantageous exclusion, which is all it had ever been before…it's a good place to come to.[42]

Some participants also spoke openly about their strategies to reappropriate particular words and activities that were formerly associated with medical trauma and social stigma. For example, some members of intersex support groups find it important to not only meet others like themselves, but also to see each other's bodies as they search for validation of their own social and biological experiences. For example, upon meeting another woman with AIS for the first time, Jenny asked:

> "Do I look intersexed?" [The other woman said,] "What do you mean?" [Again, Jenny asked,] "Do I look intersexed?" "No, what do you mean? Do I?" "No." She goes, "Oh yeah, that's right. This is the first time you're meeting anybody. How does that feel to know that no one can walk down the street and 'make' you?" [Jenny] said, "It's like really a relief."

As I have noted throughout this book, most forms of intersex are visible only when an individual is undressed. Participants consistently demonstrated that fully acknowledging one's difference with others who have been similarly outcast is validating and transforming. Some participants involved in intersex retreats wanted not only to meet and compare themselves to others, but also to see and show others what it was about their bodies that had caused them to be cast as different. Those who described how they participated in these encounters of "genital show and tell" said the experience was empowering for them simply because they had choice regarding when and to whom they exposed their bodies. For many, being able to exert choice increased their sense of autonomy. In addition, seeing other bodies that had been similarly medicalized or had not been medicalized at all provided even further validation for some. For example, speaking of his intersexed partner's body, Tiger said,

> My partner is somebody who escaped surgery. So when I look at the genitals on my partner, it's like, "Oh, I see." It really wasn't until just a year ago now that I had my experience with my current partner and it's like, this is what I've been missing. *This* is what I have hoped for. This is what being with someone who is like me is like.

In addition to these experiences, many study participants found the medical terminology associated with their difference to be shameful and distressing. Moreover, many participants felt that they lacked appropriate language to express their difference in ways that were free of negative connotations. Oftentimes, the ability to express themselves without shame resulted from their association with intersex support and advocacy organizations. For example, in Gaby's experience, "It is only in the last three to four years that I've been able to have the vocabulary to express myself as an intersexual." For many, the term *hermaphrodite* itself was particularly painful. In a rather gutsy and subversive move, the founding director of the Intersex Society of North America chose to embrace the word in the group's newsletter title. Speaking of her decision to do so, Cheryl said,

I was so tickled with the fact that we had made this incredibly traumatic thing into something with humor in it. And we came up with the name *Hermaphrodites with Attitude*. I thought of myself as incredibly subversive here. Here are all these little subversive messages winding their way out into the world. And [the newsletter] got *all* over the place. So many people told me, "I just saw the words *Hermaphrodites with Attitude* and it changed my life in that moment. I was petrified and traumatized; that word had been so painful and yet, there it was out there. Just out there and then I picked up the newsletter and it was my story on every page."

THE USE OF HUMOR TO TRANSFORM STIGMA

While most group leaders chose medical phrases to label their organizations (e.g., the Androgen Insensitivity Syndrome Support Groups and the Congenital Adrenal Hyperplasia Network), some chose to be more subversive and humorous, such as the Middlesex Group, conveniently located in Middlesex County, Massachusetts. For many, the use of humor also proved to be a successful strategy in overcoming stigma. In addition to using creative names for their groups, some participants used their organizations for political commentary through the production of provocative goods for sale. Most notably, the Intersex Society of North America produced "phall-o-meters" intended to expose the arbitrary measures used for genital adequacy. In their initial printing in 1997, these colorful plastic rulers poked fun at the standard medical

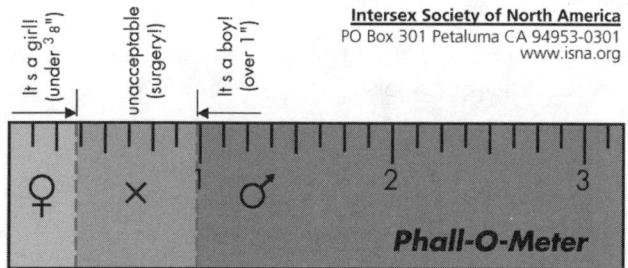

Actual scale. The above are actual current medical standards. Challenging these arbitrary standards, ISNA works to create a world free of shame, secrecy, and unwanted genital plastic surgery for children born with mixed sex anatomy.

Figure 9. Phall-O-Meter. The Intersex Society of North America created this colorful plastic ruler to challenge the arbitrary medical classification of babies as female and male by the size of their phallus. Note the shading gradations. These various shades represent three distinct gender sections of the ruler: the area of the ruler that is 3/8 of an inch or less is colored pink for girls; the area of the ruler between 3/8 of an inch and 0.9 inches is colored purple for "unacceptables"; and the area of the ruler that indicates one inch or more in size is colored blue for boys. *Reprinted with permission of the ISNA.*

measures for female and male genitalia by noting that someone whose phallus at birth measured 0.9 cm. or less was "just a girl"; someone who measured between 1 cm. and 2.4 cm. required "Surgery! Fix it quick!"; and the remainder who measured 2.5 cm. or greater were deemed increasingly male. (The current version of the phallometer is shown in figure 9.) Other political goods for sale by the Intersex Society include ISNA T-shirts printed with the "Hermaphrodites with Attitude" logo.[43]

Other groups embraced their ambiguity through the use of clever logos as well. For example, the Androgen Insensitivity Syndrome Support Groups recently adopted the orchid as their symbol.[44] The group chose to use this particular flower to intentionally emphasize their intersexuality; the word *orchid* stems from the Latin root "orche" or testis. They now use the flower in their publications, including their quarterly newsletter, *ALIAS*. As a means of further embracing the genetically male aspects of AIS, participants use humor to diffuse the tension many individuals and families feel about their sexual ambiguity. Sherri spoke of a group portrait taken at the 1997 AIS Support Group meeting in San Diego that helped to ease many attendees' feelings of anxiety about their difference. Of the experience, she said,

> In our last support group meeting, we took pictures of the parents [with] the fathers of AIS daughters and the AIS women forming Y's with their arms and the mothers forming X's. And I think that that illustrates that parents who have such anxiety about this chromosome thing are able to relax about it and see that it's not so horrible, and [that they can] become comfortable and kid around about it.

In addition to using humor to make light of their differences in group activities, several participants spoke of doing so in their personal relationships as well. Being able to cultivate tools, such as humor, that one acquires in a group setting within their own interpersonal relationships proved to be especially enriching. For example, Carol told of using humor in her relationship with her husband to make light of her genetic male components. In her words, "With my husband, it was such a great relief. If he said something like, 'You're really weird.' I'd say, 'I'm not the weird one, I'm not the one who married a guy!' It was *such* a relief to say things like that." Robin, who also has complete AIS, spoke of similarly beneficial encounters with her husband. "Occasionally [my husband and I] make fun of it. He'll say, 'Come here my pretty boy,' or something like that. And we laugh; we think it's funny. We work out and stuff like that."

Having achieved the ability to acknowledge their difference to themselves and others, having sought out a peer group with which to relate, and having developed pride in their formerly stigmatized identities, many participants spoke of a time when their intersexuality became less of a concern and was more fully integrated into a broader concept of self.

Coming Out, Stage Five: Identity Synthesis and Integration

The final stage proposed by many coming-out models is that of integrating one's marginal identity as merely one aspect of the self rather than one's most important, master characteristic or trait.[45] According to Marc Vargo, once individuals come to terms with their differences, they no longer find it necessary to spend considerable time and energy focusing on those differences.[46] Speaking to how gay men achieve this level of self-acceptance, Vargo writes:

> During the years when [a gay man] was struggling to accept his orientation, it may have been necessary for the man to invest the matter of his sexuality with much time and energy, such that this one component of his personality became amplified to the point of eclipsing other essential features. Once he reconciles himself to his homoerotic nature, however, his sexuality may become less of a concern. He may now find himself incorporating it, naturally and spontaneously, into his overall self-image until he achieves a more complete identity, that of a fully functioning person, his sexuality woven into the larger tapestry of characteristics, traits, and predilections that comprise his being.[47]

Furthermore, learning to be prideful about one's marginality with those who appear "normal" makes the integration process complete.[48]

Vargo notes that along with the identity integration common to stage five of coming out, individuals will maintain a level of commitment to the marginal identity as well. But rather than remaining a compartmentalized aspect of self, the formerly stigmatized characteristic is synthesized into one's daily life in a positive manner. As Dana said, "I am getting [to] where I can wake up intersexed, go to sleep intersexual, have sex intersexual. You know how awesome it is?"

As I discussed earlier, Goffman claims that once an identity becomes "spoiled," as in the case of stigma, it is not possible to fully recover from that mark.[49] It is interesting to note, however, that my study participants demonstrate an ability to overcome the trauma of stigmatization, at least partially.[50] Perhaps the stigma or mark remains for participants who engage in intersex support and activism, but the importance of that mark becomes transformed. Perhaps the stigma no longer serves as a source of core identity or master status, but becomes integrated within a more complex and varied understanding of the self. As Cheryl noted,

I'm certainly not all healed, but I'm not desperate for specific interaction with intersex people now. I am healed enough that it's more apparent to me that the pain that intersex people feel is not utterly unique in the world. And there are lots of ways that people are hurt.

Because the length of time that participants were associated with support groups varied from just two weeks to more than ten years, there was a significant range of involvement with the groups themselves. For those who were involved in early stages of coming out, close association with support groups was particularly significant. For others who had moved through the stages of coming out and had reached the final phase of integration, however, an affiliation with some aspects of the groups became not only less important, but also tedious as well. For example, despite a commitment to providing support for other intersexuals, some participants spoke of outgrowing the need for or attraction to intersex Internet chat lists. In Gaby's experience,

> I don't actually subscribe to the [e-]mail anymore, the chat[list]. I find it really dysfunctional. Very much full of people who still have a lot of heavy, heavy issues to work out. Been there, done that, [and] washed the car with my T-shirt.

In addition, several participants expressed feeling that they were near to completing their coming-out process and desired a life less concentrated on intersex. For example, of his experience with hypospadias, Michael said,

> It's really been a big part of my life and sometimes I feel I can't really separate myself out from that experience. I certainly didn't feel I could when I was younger and I think what's happening now is that I am able to be more individuated from that experience and [be] more freely related to it. So I still think [it] continues to influence my sense of self. My hope is that I don't have to spend too much more time putting my attention in that area of my life.

Others expressed similar feelings, even those who were very active as leaders in intersex support and advocacy efforts. Despite the central importance of intersex resources and community at one point in their lives, coming to terms with that aspect of self meant developing an ability to finally move on. As Cheryl said, "I need not to spend the rest of my life on this."

Like those in other research on marginality and identity, participants in my research demonstrate both the determination and capability of coming to not only accept, but also celebrate their difference from others. The ability to do so seems to correlate strongly with an association with peers who are able to model pride in their identities. Elements of small-scale social movement formation are clearly visible among intersex support and advocacy groups and their members.[51] For instance, the excerpts above demonstrate a sense of collective identity and solidarity experienced through support group formation. The role of support groups for these individuals seems to best approximate Gamson's notion of an "affinity group," which serves to provide emotional support and friendship for its members.

In addition, participants demonstrate an ability to engage in self-concept formation that contradicts the predominant pejorative view of intersex. More specifically, participants conveyed their commitment to challenging the medically institutionalized view of intersex as a form of pathology, in order to supplant it with a view of intersex that is not only positive, but liberating as well. As Gaby put it,

> [I breathed a] big sigh of relief, [a] big psychic sigh of relief. It was a big sigh of relief because even though I knew there were other people out there, it had been so long since I was able to be frank, open and honest, that it was a sigh, big sigh of relief. "Oh, I'm not nuts! I was right all along. *They* are the ones who are crazy! The medical society is crazy; the medical establishment is nuts. Which I always knew but I felt like one voice in the wilderness. And of course, if you're one voice in the wilderness, you're a nut. If there's a group of you, you're not so crazy anymore.

Jamie had recounted a similar experience when she realized there were others like her/him as well:

> [When] I read Fausto-Sterling's piece and I saw those numbers [that 1 in 2,000 are intersexed], *that* really changed my life. Understanding that it was far more common than I realized. And I now had a name to call myself. I was no longer a defective male or a disfigured female. I was a reasonably good-looking, moderately well functioning hermaphrodite. Oh, OK! That's OK. It was much less of a defective feeling. If I let myself think about it, I realize that pretty much anybody who is intersexed; it is a kind of defectiveness. But, at least I got a lot of company.

While individuals may still suffer depression and self-doubt due to years of alienation and shame about their bodies, associating with support groups that largely focus on the positive aspects of intersex led to the ability to integrate one's intersexuality within a broader concept of self. These findings indicate that both the power of the individual and the power of the group are necessary to rework meanings of intersex and personal conceptions of the self.

Chapter 6 — Implications of Intersex Mobilization

I didn't even go to the graduation ceremony in school;
didn't have my picture in the yearbook; didn't have an
entry. I tried the best I could to have my name left off the
yearbook. I wanted to disappear. If I could have just
sucked up all the references, all of the memories [that]
people had of me, as if I had never existed, that's what I
would have wanted to do.
                    —Excerpt from interview with Jamie

IN THE PRECEDING CHAPTERS, I have explored the historical creation of the intersex category, the intersex "emergency," and its impact on identity as experienced by thirty-seven North American adult intersexuals. The implications of this study extend far beyond those I interviewed, or even those who struggle with sexual ambiguity, for all of us live in a gendered world.

In exploring intersex narratives, I analyzed the process by which people who are perceived as intersexed cope with the stigma of being labeled as deviant. This process mirrors the efforts of others who have struggled to overcome socially stigmatized characteristics as reflected in models of coming out and community empowerment. Research participants were persistent in their attempts to educate themselves about their difference by engaging in personal research in medical libraries, with clinicians, and with family members. They consistently demonstrated an ability to overcome stigma and to feel pride in their marginality through their association with intersex support and advocacy resources. Their specific process of coping with intersex "deviance" involves their attempts to overcome medical trauma and to gain access to accurate and complete diagnostic information, as well as their eventual sense of self-empowerment through participation in intersex support and advocacy organizations. Here I aim to identify and summarize the theoretical and clinical implications of my research and address this study's implications for policy reform and future research in this field.

The narratives I have discussed throughout the book illustrate that in addition to accentuating rather than de-emphasizing sexual variation, medical sex assignment serves to isolate intersex children and adults from their peers and from a means of social support unless they seek it out or create it on their own. Indeed, ongoing shameful medical experiences in childhood may lead to disastrous consequences for intersexed adults, including a disinclination to pursue medical care. As a direct result of distancing themselves from medical care and hormone therapy, many adult intersexuals develop early onset osteoporosis or osteopenia—the precursor to osteoporosis. But for some, the consequences of this separation from medicine may extend beyond weakened bone density. For example, in Sherri's experience,

> I was really traumatized by my pediatric endocrinologist as a teenager. There were many points in my life where I genuinely felt like I would rather die than seek medical attention. And I used to think that if I was in a horrible car accident, I would just much prefer that they leave me to die than to take me to a hospital where they would undress me [and] see me naked. I mean I was *terrified* of that.

Without doubt, medical efforts to preclude alienation, stigmatization, and shame, have, at least in part, failed.

Theoretical Implications: Gender Identity and Performance

Participants demonstrated an adherence to binary understandings of gender as well as to the biological construction of gender and sexuality, perhaps as a result of being exposed to a repetitive emphasis on the importance of standard female- and male-looking bodies. Because 95 percent of participants underwent medical procedures to "normalize" their differences, the vast majority experienced repeated medical attempts to "correct" intersexual anatomy. These efforts do not meet the medical objectives of destigmatization, and in fact contribute to rather than counter intersexuals' feelings of shame and isolation. With so much emphasis placed on the significance of appearing like typical females and males, many participants became overly concerned with their ability to "pass" as normal females and males, especially during early adolescence and young adulthood. Despite the variation of their anatomy, most participants were socialized to believe in the importance of gender binarism and thus went to great lengths to uphold the sex of assignment they were given, even if this binary understanding of sex and gender did not validate their own anatomy or sense of self.

Similarly, study participants' impetus to privilege biological features of their anatomy further reinforces a binary sex and gender system and Butler's concept of the heterosexual matrix. This phenomenon was especially notable as participants spoke of discovering their "true" sexes, revealed by their gonadal or chromosomal makeup. In the same manner, research participants spoke of what it meant to be biologically intersexed as well as their insistence in patrolling the boundaries of the newly emerging category of "True" (read: biological) intersexuals.

Theoretical Implications: Efficacy and the Looking-glass Self

The findings from this study also warrant a reevaluation of Goffman's work on stigma, especially concerning his concept of a "spoiled" identity. Goffman claims that stigmatized individuals are classified and defined by belonging to a group of similarly stigmatized others.[1] Goffman also argues that once a person becomes stigmatized, they are incapable of ever entirely overthrowing the shadow of that mark. But despite the overwhelming feelings of shame and humiliation they experienced during medical procedures, study participants engaged in purposeful actions to refute negative reflected appraisals of self. Having "renegotiated the self" in this way, it is possible that the stigma or mark remains intact to some degree, but the weight or importance of the mark becomes transformed and thus eventually holds less meaning and power over time, as long as one is able to talk openly with others to disable the power inherent to secrecy. Furthermore, it is likely that after one accepts her/his difference, the stigma no longer serves as a source of core identity or master status, but that the formerly stigmatized characteristic will become integrated within an overall understanding of the self. In fact, the formerly stigmatized aspect of self may eventually be transformed into an aspect of self that is prideful.

Theoretical Implications: Social Movements and Identity Formation

The future success of intersex activism may be linked not only to growing social tolerance of sex and gender variability and the continued development of electronic communications, but also to the ability to connect the fight against genital surgery on intersex children to the human rights-based movement against female genital excision. Intersex activists have participated in this effort for several years already, attempting to expand the language banning female genital mutilation (FGM) in the 1996 U.S. federal bill to include a ban on intersex genital mutilation (IGM).[2] At the time of this writing, their efforts to pass this legislation have not yet been successful.

The social context within which contemporary intersex identity is emerging is not the only consideration of significance. It is also important to examine the concept of a group identity and its potential for essentialism on a far broader scale. Identity-based political movements, such as the intersex movement, are problematic in that they simplify social categories as unified and generalized phenomena. Critics of these generalizations claim that there is no such thing as *the* gay or straight or intersexed identity. Speaking to the constraints of this essentialism, Steven Seidman writes, "Positing a gay identity, no matter how it strains to be inclusive of difference, produces exclusions [and] represses difference."[3] In a similar vein, Ki Namaste asks several questions that are pertinent to the discussion of identity-based social movements. As Namaste has noted,

> How do categories such as "gay," "lesbian," and "queer" emerge? From what do they differentiate themselves, and what kinds of identities do they exclude? How are these borders demarcated, and how can they be contested? What are the relations between the naming of sexuality and political organization it adopts, between identity and community? Why is a focus on the discursive production of social identities useful? How do we make sense of the dialectical movement between inside and outside, heterosexuality and homosexuality?[4]

Moving away from traditional definitions of identity, Seidman offers a poststructural approach to identity, saying that poststructuralism

> dissolves any notion of a substantial unity in identity constructions leaving only rhetorics of identities, performances, and the free play of difference and possibility. Whereas identity politics offers a strong politics on a weak, exclusionary basis, poststructuralism offers a thin politics as it problematizes the very notion of a collective in whose name a movement acts.[5]

According to Seidman, Davis, and others, identity politics movements create a new kind of nationalism, in that identity-based social movements serve to erect artificial boundaries and borders, and thus increase the potential for in-group/out-group assimilation and separatism. According to Davis, "the deaf have created their own 'nationalism' as a resistance to audist culture."[6] Have intersexuals participated in similar exclusion of nonintersexuals from their activities?

Participants' tales of what it means to be intersexed and how one goes about proving their authentic intersexed identity made this issue of exclusivity especially apparent. This was most notable regarding the issue of medicalization as a defining characteristic of intersex identity. Despite their visible physical variation, those participants who did not undergo medicalization questioned the validity of their membership in intersex groups that were so heavily focused on recovery from medical trauma. Their doing so supports the notion that claims to an intersex identity are strongly tied to a history of medical trauma and social pressures to conform to a dichotomous understanding of sex and gender. Consider the case of a newborn whose clitoris was deemed too large and in need of surgical recession. Her parents waited a couple of months before consenting to surgery. During that waiting period, the baby's clitoris receded on its own, and she was thus not considered intersexed after all. But, she may have been classified as intersexed for the rest of her life had she undergone surgery.[7]

By continuing to focus and foster the category "intersex," we may be creating a whole new set of problems and issues. While demedicalization is indeed a noble and ethical goal, reformers should be wary of creating an essential intersexed identity and narrative in their process of making that critique and telling stories of medical trauma. Classification lends itself all too easily to thinking in simplistic ways about the characteristics of the people represented by each category. Classification also breeds exclusion.[8] For instance, take Drew's experience with adopting an intersex identity.

> I didn't hear the word *intersex* until 1995. That's when I began to
> think that I could be intersexed and I found out for sure that I was
> intersexed in 1996. I didn't quite think that I was a hermaphrodite
> because I still equated that only with what they call true hermaphro-
> dites, having ovaries and testes. I knew I didn't have that, so I was
> kind of flattered by having that [word] used in reference to me
> because I had heard of hermaphrodites in the past and thought it was
> really [a] fascinating identity, particularly spiritually.

After intersexuals initially found one another and put to an end their life-long isolation and internal struggles within the movement over the very definition of intersexuality, participants faced encounters with further alienation. Indeed, some were turned away and denied membership in support groups if they were read as posers or "intersex wannabes" because they did not conform to newly accepted definitions of intersexuality.

Before intersex mobilization and political and media activism, most North Americans didn't know the meaning of the word *hermaphrodite,* let alone *intersex*. Within recent years, the topic of sexual ambiguity has been featured in national magazines, popular and educational television shows, and local news media. With the breadth of activists' important and effective efforts to demedicalize and destigmatize intersex, scholars have placed the topic of sexual ambiguity under the rubric of queer or gender studies. As a result, a new field of intersex studies, replete with its own cannon (of which this book may be a part), is currently in formation. In fact, some university and community groups have extended the customary GLBT classification (now GLBTI) to demonstrate their inclusion of intersex issues among queer rights and politics. Indeed, as they have with political movements of the past, universities embrace and promote their discourse on ethics, inequality, and human rights related to the intersex movement.

When I speak to various community groups about intersex, almost without exception someone in the audience approaches me afterward to inform me of their personal connection to the topic. Most often, they tell me that a relative or friend of a friend is intersexed. Occasionally, they convey that they are themselves. One such instance occurred when I met one young person during a guest lecture on intersexuality in a colleague's gender studies course. This person revealed that she had been diagnosed with mixed gonadal dysgenesis at the age of sixteen, but had never identified as intersexed until she heard me speak in her college class. She reported running home to call her mom after my guest lecture because she finally realized there were others like her and that she was not alone. She took the support group contact information I offered to the entire class and began the process of self-education and connection with others who identify as intersexed.

What was stunning for me about this experience, and others like it since, is that while this person was able to access invaluable information and support, she also got a heavy dose of the newly emergent intersex narrative in the process. Sadly, it appears that stories of medical trauma and attempts to erase sexual ambiguity have become standard in intersex narratives. These repeated survivor accounts may serve to exclude nonmedicalized people with sexual ambiguity like Suegee and Drew from this newly formed identity category. Thus it seems that children won't experience their difference in categorical or negative terms unless they are labeled and socialized to do so.

Implications for Clinical Reform

The implementation of radical, invasive, and life-changing medical sex assignment procedures for children born with bodies whose sexual anatomy is labeled as different from the norm was standard practice until very recently.

However, the intersex patient advocacy and medical reform movement that began in the 1990s has gained tremendous legitimacy and ground in a very short period of time. What's more, the patients' rights movement has upset this formerly unquestioned approach in medical education and practice and placed it into its current state of flux, crisis, and reform.[9]

As evidence, consider the January 2000 formation of the North American Task Force on Intersex (NATFI). The task force was convened by pediatric urologist Ian Aaronson of the Medical University of South Carolina in response to the increasing debate over medical sex assignment in order to re-evaluate medical care for children with ambiguous sexual anatomy. A first of its kind, the committee is comprised of specialists from various medical fields, as well as ethicists and members of intersex advocacy organizations, including former patients and critics of medical sex assignment themselves. The committee represents the first "decision-making body" to bring patients and doctors together on the topic of medical treatment of sexual variation.

The mission of the task force is to improve the standards and experience of medical treatment for people who are subjected to sex "normalizing" procedures. In addition to establishing new medical guidelines, the group has set out to address the previously ignored legal and ethical issues of informed consent and quality of life for intersex patients following medical sex assignment. In the words of founder Ian Aaronson,

> We are committed to learn from past mistakes in order to offer the
> best advice and treatment to our patients in the future. Long-term
> outcome data is very sparse and selective, and this puts surgeons on
> tenuous ethical grounds. I was very gratified at the positive response
> from members of the professional community and the patient
> advocate groups to the notion of forming a Task Force.[10]

Psychologist John Money, the now infamous harbinger of the current medical paradigm in question, is notably absent from the thirty-person executive committee; however, strong proponents of the current model, including the pediatric endocrinologist Claude Migeon and the pediatric urologists John Gearhart and Antoine Khoury, may make up for his absence. In an apparent balancing act, some of the committee's members are among the most vocal critics of intersex medical management, including the Intersex Society of North America's founder Cheryl Chase and the social psychologist Suzanne Kessler. Perhaps one of the biggest indicators of change is that the primary professional medical associations that have even recently touted the merits of conventional sex assignment have signed on as supporters of the group.[11]

The American Academy of Pediatrics (AAP) is among the list of task force endorsers. Their support of this path-breaking patient-doctor dialogue comes just four years after Chase and other members of Hermaphrodites with Attitude picketed the AAP's annual conference when they were refused the opportunity to present patients' perspectives to conference goers.[12] But despite their willingness to back the efforts of the task force, the American Academy of Pediatrics published an article in July of 2000 that reaffirmed the organization's commitment to prompt medical intervention. I take the following from this article, on which Ian Aaronson is listed as a consultant:

> The birth of a child with ambiguous genitalia constitutes a social emergency. Abnormal appearance can be corrected and the child raised as a boy or a girl as appropriate. Parents should be encouraged not to name the child or register the birth, if possible, until the sex of rearing is established. Infants raised as girls will usually require clitoral reduction which, with current techniques, will result not only in a normal-looking vulva but preservation of a functional clitoris. [These children's] diagnosis and prompt treatment require urgent medical attention.[13]

Even though the AAP and others may be strong adherents of the "intersex is a social and medical emergency" paradigm, their willingness to be informed by former patient critiques is undoubtedly a dramatic shift. Instead of being relegated to picketing medical conventions, intersex activists are now being featured as invited keynote speakers at prominent medical conventions. Chase, for example, spoke at the May 2000 meeting of the Lawson Wilkins Pediatric Endocrine Society, giving "the grand finale to a four-hour symposium on the treatment of [sexual] ambiguity in newborns."[14] More recently, in May 2002, Chase addressed the First World Congress on the "Hormonal and Genetic Basis for Sexual Differentiation Disorder," informing them of the agenda of the intersex patient advocacy movement.[15] Clearly, the intersex patients' rights and medical reform movement has garnered significant attention and has begun to effect change. As further evidence, consider the 1998 publication of the *Journal of Clinical Ethics* special issue on intersex, which brought together essays written by intersex activists, scholars, and physicians in one volume. This special issue was republished in book form as *Intersex in the Age of Ethics* in 1999, and featured photographs of the authors on the cover. Notably, this was the first time that photographs of intersex doctors and patients appeared alongside one another without featuring patients' genitalia or other physical characteristics. In fact, by looking at the photos alone, there is no way to discern between doctor and patient; intersexed and not. (See chapter 3, figure 4.)

The findings from my research and additional recent reports on intersex quality of life call into question the effectiveness of medical sex assignment. It is my conclusion that contemporary attempts to destigmatize intersexuality via surgical and hormonal "sexing" and lack of disclosure about a child's condition do not serve intersexuals or their family members in the manner in which these procedures are intended. While I believe that these sexing procedures are motivated by a sincere desire to assist intersexuals and their families in achieving social acceptance, the data from my research and others', however, indicates that the very procedures intended to normalize a child are actually experienced as degrading and shaming.

There are currently no policy-based clinical guidelines for working with children born intersexed. Current clinical procedures are largely based on the limited empirical findings published on outcomes of intersex surgery and hormonal treatment. Recently, Diamond and Sigmundson published their own guidelines for intersex medical management.[16] Still, nothing formal is in place. One result of the formation of the North American Task Force on Intersex may be more comprehensive research and recommendations for clinical reform. My research plainly demonstrates the value of social support in increasing intersexuals' autonomy and self-esteem. Recent research has illustrated the significance of a strong social network for parents of intersexuals as well.[17] Moreover, my study participants benefited significantly from gaining accurate and complete information about their bodies.

Physicians are faced with a difficult dilemma. They are taught to intervene when doing so could improve the lives of their patients. Surgery is unquestionably warranted in the rare intersex cases that require medical intervention to save a child's life (as in cases where elimination of feces or urine is not possible without such intervention). However, the vast majority of intersex conditions are indeed not life threatening.[18] Given that physicians should "do no harm" and that we lack systematic data that conclusively demonstrates the success of more cosmetically based medical interventions, it is my suggestion that clinicians opt for the least invasive treatment or no treatment at all. That is, doctors should conduct no irreversible surgical or hormonal intervention without their patient's (not the patient's parents') direct consent. In fact, doctors and parents should focus far more on performing cultural, rather than surgical, operations for the well-being of intersexed children.

Perpetuating treatments that seem to be both noneffective and nonempowering raises ethical questions. Gecas notes that autonomous control over one's own existence is exceedingly important in the development of a positive and empowered self-concept.[19] As he writes, "It is the quality of the individual-environment interaction, primarily with regard to the opportunities it provides for engaging in efficacious action—that continues to be the major condition for self-efficacy throughout a person's life."[20] Why would there be reluctance to discontinue a course of treatment when there is reason to believe it is noneffective and even potentially harmful? Resistance to clinical reform is evident in historical uses of non-esteem-building treatment, especially in the case of various aversion or "reparative" therapies for GLBT individuals whose families hope for their "heterosexual conversions" or "shifts." According to Freire, people in positions of power, such as medical authorities, may disregard critiques and mobilization efforts of those they serve because supporting such action would only undermine their efforts to perpetuate and uphold the status quo.[21] This trend is apparent among intersex clinicians in that many disregard intersex activists as "radical zealots" who represent perhaps only 3 percent of the entire surgically altered intersex population.[22]

As Kuhn and Freire demonstrate, paradigmatic shifts are hard won, especially when attempted by a disempowered or marginal population.[23] In order to effect change, open communication and collaboration must occur to ensure that those operating from within the prevailing model are directly affected by the personal experiences and efforts of those seeking change. It is through personal interaction, when both parties approach the discussion with the elements of compassion, humility, and hope, that change is possible. Both sides must be willing to listen, to care for the other person's perspective, and to be flexible enough to make change in order for compromise and eventual action to be effected. Effective dialogue relies on both sides' openness to hear the other and to be influenced in their thinking.[24]

As a direct result of intersexuals' vocal critiques, clinicians are beginning to reform their practices and are claiming to be far less eager advocates of surgical intervention on intersexed infants and children.[25] Those who have made these changes are physicians who have had personal interaction with adult intersexuals who are critical of medicalization. The critiques that are deemed most credible are adults' complaints of sexual dysfunction, due to medically induced nerve damage, and complaints of incorrect gender role assignment, as was apparent in 24 percent of my sample who were living in a gender different from their medically assigned sex.[26] This shift was notable in the NATFI council member and pediatric urologist Yuri Reinberg's 1999 grand rounds presentation at the University of Minnesota's Medical School. During his presentation and discussion thereafter, several noted proponents of intersex surgery spoke of their newfound reluctance to perform genital operations on infants and children due to adult intersexuals' critiques of sexual dysfunction and inappropriate sex assignment.

Unanswered Questions

Despite the recent mobilization and activism of thousands of intersexuals worldwide, the social focus on gender categorization and genital regularity continues to be strong, in both medical and nonmedical sectors. In order to improve the quality of life not just for those labeled intersexed, but for us all, we must remove or reduce the importance of gender categorization and the need for gender categories, including the category of intersex itself. A more realistic and tangible goal is to respond far less to sexual variance. That is, to focus on the health of children born with genital variation, not on their difference. An outcome of this philosophy would prevent physicians from cutting into the bodies of intersexed patients unless a clear physiological need presents its necessity. Moreover, this philosophy would ask us to hold off on rushing kids into a patient mentality and instead send them to speak with counselors or other kids with divergent sexual anatomy. We should refrain from identifying them as different in any way, unless a child demonstrates a need and a desire for such special attention. Pushing the label of sexual ambiguity, sexual difference, or "sexual problem" onto children through medicalization, or remedicalization via social services, leads to stigmatization of the self. What's more, there is no inherent need for children to have therapy unless a need presents itself. We shouldn't restigmatize intersexuals by assuming a need for therapy or "preventative treatment" on the basis of physical variation alone. While these support resources are invaluable for people who have already been adversely affected by negative socialization—and family members and clinicians should be prepared to call on support services if necessary—we shouldn't assume that genital variation itself creates a pathological need.

Will the category and identity "intersex" disappear altogether if doctors stop treating, studying, and classifying children in this way, or will this category continue to expand further into academic and social realms until its presence is solidified in a way similar to the presence of transgender, gay, or alcoholic identities? Focusing less on articulating the category "intersex" may indeed be a step in the right direction toward the ultimate goal of focusing less on gender and sexual categorization. After all, returning to the elementary school children and the "gender lines" to which they are socialized to adhere, the clear message from my research is to decrease sex and gender categorization rather than to create yet a third rigid sex or gender line for us all to ponder. Instead, we should focus on loving and accepting children as they are, not because of or in spite of their differences, but rather just because they are terrific kids in their own right with or without bodies that vary from some mythical standard.

While my research addresses many questions about the construction and negotiation of contested sex, several important issues related to assessing and revising the treatment of sexual ambiguity remain untouched. Future research in this area should include intensive research on two additional groups: parents of intersex children and clinicians who specialize in intersex management. This research should focus on parents' and clinicians' personal and professional experiences with intersexuality and their perspectives on genital variation and the management thereof. Additional research should include observation of family consultations with medical staff and follow-up visits regarding the "sexing" of intersexed infants, in order to offer further insight into the interactional aspect of the social construction of sex and gender. Timely research in this area may provide further empirical data to inform the current debate and potential shift in intersex clinical management.

Despite my systematic analysis of former patients' experiences with medical sex assignment, the void remains for a rigorous analysis of the experiences of those with variant sexual anatomy who are not associated with intersex support and advocacy organizations and those who did not undergo medical sex assignment. This research is critical because proponents of surgical sex assignment will most likely resist clinical reform until the experiences of these populations are better understood. Until then, critics of my research and that of others will continue to shrug off the overwhelming dissatisfaction and trauma reported by intersex activists as representative of a disgruntled but vocal minority.

Far more could also be learned about the impact of peer social support as a means of reframing sexual ambiguity in a more positive light. In order to develop effective recommendations for clinical practice as they relate to peer advocacy, further investigation is needed that focuses specifically on the role of social support in coping with difference. Clinical mandates should also be informed by further research on the impact of age-appropriate disclosure of information to intersexuals and their family members. Developing a longitudinal research program with this focus is possible now that some children deemed sexually ambiguous are being raised in a new era of social support and have access to complete and accurate diagnostic information.

Finally, the strategies and efforts of intersex activists warrant further attention, as does the overall concept of the intersex social movement. Due to their prolific appearances in print, film, and radio media, substantive content analysis of their activism efforts is possible. This analysis could inform a more

nuanced understanding of models of coming-out and community empowerment rather than assimilation to an existing social norm. This research is now
possible because there are already substantial archives related to this area, and
because intersex patient, parent, and doctor communication, education, and
support networks continue to emerge.

Conflict often leads to change because critique brings with it an opportunity for reevaluation and movement in a new direction. The overlap of intersex mobilization, the call for clinical reform, and the follow-up reports on
the cornerstone David Reimer case are not accidental. Reimer came forward
after learning that thousands of other children were being subjected to the
same alienating treatments he received, and that they were being treated in
this way largely based on the reported success of his sex reassignment in early
childhood. That Reimer went public with his account of traumatic clinical
neglect has, in turn, opened the door for intersex rights activists to tell their
stories and influence medical reform. Seemingly in response to the Reimer
follow-up, coupled with vocal intersex critiques, the United States National
Institutes of Health issued a program announcement in 2001 for monies dedicated to new and continued research in this area, and in May 2002 convened
a committee dedicated to overseeing research on intersex.

Concluding Remarks

I have confronted several ethical issues throughout this research and continue
to do so as I publish and present papers on its findings. While my approach
to the topic and methodology employed in my research are aimed to empower
study participants and intersexuals at large, I struggle with my role in expanding the field of gender and sexuality studies to be inclusive of intersexuals'
voices. I am disquieted by the notion that despite my aim to create a meaningful and nondisruptive experience for the intersexuals who participated in
my research, I have furthered the exploitation of intersexuals, albeit through
an academic rather than a medical lens. In short, I am wary of perpetuating
intersex objectification.

Rather than studying and portraying intersexuals as deviants, I aim to explore the social context within which the very categories of deviance and identity are created. Garfinkel illustrated that studying breaches of normative
expectations leads to an increasing awareness of the nature and scope of the
norms themselves.[27] Here Namaste writes about a poststructural approach to
identity:

> A poststructuralist queer theory, then, offers sociology an approach to
> studying the emergence and reproduction of heterosexuality. Rather

than designating gays, lesbians, and/or bisexuals as the only subjects or communities worthy of investigation, poststructuralist sociology would make sense of the manner in which heterosexuality is itself a social construct.[28]

Thus, when studying "deviance" one must simultaneously also study "normalcy" in an effort to comprehend the very production of normalcy itself. For,

> If we focus only on the "subculture" of homosexuality, and if we never interrogate the conditions which engender its marginalization, we shall remain trapped within a theoretical framework which refuses to acknowledge its own complicity in constructing its object (or subjects) of study.[29]

Paying attention to the aberration merely serves to enforce its difference from that which is considered normal, thus perpetuating the categories of normal and abnormal or "inside" and "outside."

Critics of my research will likely argue that the lessons provided by the narratives I explore throughout this book are limited because I spoke only with members of intersex support groups. Certainly not all people join support groups, and those who do are most likely drawn to doing so because of a need for support or to effect change. Even so, given that thousands of intersex individuals have mobilized to undo the damage of a medical paradigm whose intention is to heal is evidence that clinical reform is urgent.

One of the major lessons from these narratives is that sexual variation is nothing to be ashamed of and that it wouldn't be experienced as shameful if it were recast as normal. Because sexual anatomy occurs on a continuum, diversity and variety are to be expected. Doctors, parents, and teachers have the ability and authority to reframe sexual variation in this way by responding to it with indifference. In addition to suspending unnecessary surgery on people with sexual anatomy deemed ambiguous, these key socializing agents can truly destigmatize sexual variation by paying very little attention to it.

Doctors, parents, and others have the ability to normalize sexual variation. In the meantime, they can help tremendously those labeled as intersexed by clearing the skeletons out of the closet and focusing on how best to love and support people cast as different. As the people in my study demonstrate, one of the most effective means of coping with difference is through relationships with others who are similarly alienated. Doctors and parents can easily assist those they care for by connecting them with the tremendous resources offered by intersex support and advocacy organizations. Doctors and parents can also engage in their own networking with the rapidly developing groups aimed at family and medical support, advocacy, and information exchange.

To the Stories One Last Time

I opened this book with the words of one of the women I interviewed. I return to her words again, at the close, because she so eloquently conveyed the value of normalizing intersex through peer support, humor, and advocacy. Throughout her interview, Sherri spoke of feeling both grateful for and indebted to the AIS support group for quite literally "saving her life." In closing, I turn to her resolution to carry her activism to her grave:

> I'll never repay, *ever*, in this lifetime I will never repay what I've been given. After I die, it all goes to the support group. My will is set up so that it all goes to the support group. My instructions in my will are to make my funeral as cheap as possible so that more money will go to the support group. That's where I want it to go. That's all I want it to go for. With the instruction that my headstone have the [support group's] web site address on it so that at least after I'm dead, people can still, hopefully, pass by my gravestone and find information.

Chapter 7	Methodological Appendix

Becoming a sociologist is a process of intense socialization. Some would go so far as to call it a period of training.[1] The language of training is applied to humans in many respects, especially in times of transition such as acquiring a new job or other skills. Most often, I think of the word *training* in relation to animals—especially dogs. I raise this issue here because occasionally I see myself as a dog, sometimes obedient and often not, in my role as researcher. Even though I conducted inductive research, I went "into the field" much like a dog does, with one or two purposes in mind, very focused on my goal. As is classic in field research, I found that the data from the field led me in directions I did not expect and often resisted. In conducting analyses on intersexuals' life histories, I was once again drawn to the metaphor of feeling my leash pulled in a precise and persistent manner—oftentimes feeling that I had become the data's dog.

Inductive research is far different from the better-known deductive practice. Deductive data collection and analysis test specific hypotheses generated by literature review, prior empirical findings, or the investigators' expectations. In contrast, inductive data collection and analysis are guided by issues of importance, which emerge from the data themselves.[2] I began my data collection with a specific set of questions, but no hypotheses in the deductive sense. Instead, I attempted to allow for an ongoing interplay between my initial questions and those that arose during the interview and analysis process. Despite my initial interest in sexual identity, participants' views on broader issues of identity development and management were the focus of the interviews and subsequent analysis.

In conducting my research, I attempt to inform and reshape existing theory about and clinical practices related to sexual ambiguity. I began by studying the issues intersexuals themselves identified as important because of my interest in creating scholarship that serves the populations I study.

I engaged in a process of self-reflection throughout my research. Doing so may seem self-indulgent and inappropriate to traditional, positivistic social scientists. In contrast, feminist researchers have come to see a discussion of the self in relation to the subject of study as traditional in its own right.[3] In Krieger's words,

> I wish to suggest that the self is not a contaminant, but rather that it is key to what we know, and that methodological discussions might fruitfully be revised to acknowledge the involvement of the self in a positive manner. The self is not something that can be disengaged from knowledge or from the research process. Rather, we need to understand the nature of our own participation in what we know.[4]

Here I engage in such reflection.

I am not intersexed. I am a white married Jewish woman who was born and raised unambiguously female in a wealthy suburb of Minneapolis. I also identify and present my gender as somewhat feminine. Why do I raise these issues here? My own identity and overt characteristics came into play continuously in every phase of this project, but most notably during recruitment and interviewing.

In making initial telephone contact, prospective participants utilized their own screening mechanisms, examining my methods and motives to do this research. The underlying question was "Are YOU intersexed?" Typically, participants posed this question, whether directly or indirectly, in the first few moments of our telephone conversations. My answer was always, "No." The next question was sometimes blatant, but more often not: "Then why are you interested in studying us?" My response was systematic, explaining the convergence of my theoretical interests in gender, medicine, and social psychology and my personal struggles with being a blond, Minnesota Jew who does not conform to the socially accepted stereotypes of what Jews look like and is forever being asked, "When did you convert?" to which I have always responded, "In the womb."

In lieu of this rather well developed succinct answer on my part, I always felt as though I were stumbling over my words because I left out a key component of my draw to the subject: I, too, experienced medical intervention upon my body in early childhood. As a toddler, I had chronic urinary tract infections and spent part of my childhood visiting the urologist, being examined, and even having urethral surgery—a procedure described by many participants in relaying their own life stories. Despite these similarities, there were clear and immediate in-group/out-group distinctions as intersexed and not, and as participant and researcher.

Research Instruments

I found it crucial to employ methods that would minimize any potential disruption my research could generate. By sampling intersexuals who self-selected into intersex support groups, the likelihood of unsettling participants' lives was diminished. In addition, my attention to this issue was of central concern in the construction of sensitively articulated interview and survey questions. I attended to this awareness by developing methods that served to empower participants and by using a sampling base of intersexuals networked with support and advocacy resources.

I found that participants were surprised and pleased by my methodology in its personable and conversational style and tone. All participants gave thoughtful and engaging responses to each of the questions posed during the interview conversation. A few, however, expressed difficulty or dissatisfaction when completing the portions of the survey instrument that most closely resembled clinical assessment, stating that the closed-ended options didn't represent their attitudes or behaviors well.[5]

I developed the interview guide through relevant literature review, identifying unanswered questions and debates in the field of intersex sex assignment. In the interview guide, I address three central themes from the literature. The first, which was related to the analysis of Money's sexing theory and management of a potentially stigmatized identity,[6] posed questions about intersexuals' experiences with and responses to social expectations of gender identity and performance. I expected participants to have struggled for a sense of gender identity and for ways in which to present a gendered self. Because of this, I included questions regarding participants' self-definitions of gender identity, presentation(s) of gender, experiences of gender, and presentations and experiences of sexual orientation.[7]

The second theme in my interview guide was also related to Money's notion of gender acquisition following surgical and hormonal sex assignment and addressed the development of a gendered self. These questions were included to gain insight into how participants developed their gender identities, gender presentations, and sexual orientations.[8]

The third theme included questions meant to assess participants' perceptions of their physiological sex both before and after sex assignment to more

Interview Questions

What follows are the questions I used as a guide during the interviews. Although I posed all of these questions to each interviewee, the interviews themselves were conversational and sometimes the order or phrasing of the questions changed slightly. The sequence and scope of the questions seemed sensible and comprehensive, as participants often led me through the interview schedule, with very little prompting on my part.

A. Introductory Questions
I began the interview with a brief questionnaire that I administered to research participants. I recorded their responses on the questionnaire.

What name would you like to use to refer to yourself in this research? Do you have a pseudonym you would like to use for the study?
How old are you?
What is the highest level of education you completed?
What kind of work do you do?
What is your current romantic relationship status?
What is your religious or spiritual identification?
What is your racial or ethnic identification?

B. Intersex Diagnosis and Treatment
This next set of questions is where the interview really began. Even though I included only two questions in this initial interview section, interviewees' responses to them were often lengthier than for any other questions during the interview. The first question alone often elicited a half-hour response.

When and how did you first become aware of your intersexuality?
Did you receive any medical intervention related to intersex? If so, tell me about that.

C. Sexual and Gender Identity
How do you, personally, define your sex at birth (sex assignment)?
I'd like to talk with you now about your gender. How do you define your gender?
How do you express this gender identity to others?
I am also interested in issues of sexual orientation. How do you characterize your sexual orientation?
What have been the most significant events that helped you to develop your sense of gender and sexual identity?
Has your sexual identity changed over time? If so, tell me about this.

D. Social Support, Identity, and Activism
Has social support been significant for you in developing your sense of self?
In your mind, how is intersex perceived and responded to socially?
How has your history of intersex affected your overall sense of self?
Are there any challenges associated with being born intersexed? If so, what are they? Tell me about how you have responded to these challenges.
What would you like to see happen for children who are born intersexed in the future?

directly extend Butler's theory of the heterosexual matrix.[9] Here, I included questions that addressed my broader interests in issues of social support, sexual satisfaction, self-esteem, and overall self-concept of the participants.

I arranged the interview questions by grouping them into four topical categories: (1) How do intersexuals define their sexual identity with regard to sex assignment, gender identity, gender performance, and sexual orientation? (2) From their perspectives, what were significant factors in the development of their sexual identities? (3) Are there challenges associated with being intersexed? If so, what are they? and (4) How have the participants responded to these challenges? Participants were not given these general topics to consider; instead, they were asked the questions listed, within each category.

While I used the same interview guide each time, participants attended to many related issues that I did not explicitly address. The guide served as a form of structure for the interviews, much like a shell or container, articulating the bounds of discussion. The contents of each story relayed within that container varied extensively because participants relayed issues of personal importance that were either not addressed by my guide or were merely sparked by it. I posed the fourteen questions in the guide to each participant in the same order, and participants wove their personal threads of discussion within and throughout this framework.

For the purpose of gathering general descriptive data about the participants, I administered a six-point questionnaire at the beginning of each interview that covered the topics of age, education, occupation, romantic relationship status, religious/spiritual identification, and racial/ethnic identification. I then posed my first question, "When and how did you first become aware of your intersexuality?"

As I stated above, the interview guide was intended to elicit a temporal account of participants' life histories, beginning from birth to the time of interview, with particular attention to issues of identity. As a means of increasing the validity of the interview data and accentuating this focus, participants completed a gender identity timeline at the interview's completion. I developed this life course gender identity map, with the help of my colleague Walter Bockting, to assist me in assessing particularly important times in the negotiation, experience, formation, and presentation of a gendered self.

The last item I asked participants to complete was a five-item, self-administered questionnaire (SAQ), based on the work of Michael Shively, John De Cecco, and Eli Coleman, that contains sexual orientation and gender identity measures.[10] I included this questionnaire as another means of enriching the interviews and in an attempt to assess the validity and reliability of my interview guide. In this regard, some questions from the interview guide

---

Life Course Gender Identity Map

Using the gender referents of your choice, please complete the following life course gender identity map.

Indicate how you identify your gender at the time of birth and how that gender identity changed over the course of your life. Please write in significant moments in your personal history when your feelings of gender identity changed or remained constant. For example, I identify my sex/gender at birth as ambiguous; I was surgically assigned female; at puberty I questioned my gender identity; in adulthood, I felt more resolved about my gender identity; at time of interview, I identify as a woman.

Indicate important shifts in perspective by drawing in new vertical lines and labeling them, as indicated in the sample gender identity map.

SIGNIFICANT HISTORICAL MOMENTS

Birth   Gender Identity
                                                                         at Interview

|———————————————————————————————————————|

---

and SAQ overlap. For example, in the interview I asked, "How do you characterize your sexual orientation?" and in the SAQ, participants responded to the questions, "I am sexually attracted to . . . "; "I engage in sexual activity with . . . "; and "I have sexual fantasies about . . . " by selecting one of seven categories.

Finally, I took detailed field notes during all phases of the project to assist me in the process of data analysis, reflection, and theory construction. I began keeping these notes during the conceptualization and recruitment process and continued doing so through the end of the data collection and into the analysis. These notes were transcribed and analyzed along with the interviews.

Initially, I planned to request permission to access participants' medical records to verify intersex status, acquire additional demographic information, and to gain insight into socio-medical responses to intersexuals. But because the primary focus of my study is on intersexuals' subjective experiences and perceptions, I did not pursue access to these records. Although I expected the records to be helpful in developing a more complete understanding of participants' experiences, I also expected difficulty gaining access to all participants' files in that I would not be granted permission and many do not have all or any of their records. In the end, several participants referred to or read

Self-Administered Sexual Identity Questionnaire

The following questions refer to your CURRENT identity. Please CIRCLE ONE for each question.

1) I am sexually attracted to:

women only	more women than men	women and men equally
intersexuals	transgenders	more men than women
men only	no one	

2) I engage in sexual activity with:

women only	more women than men	women and men equally
intersexuals	transgenders	more men than women
men only	no one	

3) I have sexual fantasies about:

women only	more women than men	women and men equally
intersexuals	transgenders	more men than women
men only	no one	

4) My primary emotional attachments are with:

women only	more women than men	women and men equally
intersexuals	transgenders	more men than women
men only	no one	

5) I identify my gender as:

woman	more woman than man	woman and man equally
intersex	transgender	more man than woman
man	not applicable	

from their medical records during our meetings, setting them out before my arrival and offering to show them to me.[11]

The Sample

Aiming to maximize the sample's diversity, I used Barney Glaser and Anselm Strauss's concept of theoretical sampling; that is, I sampled the population with the intention of including a diversity of perspectives.[12] Attention to diversity within the intersex population was one of my central concerns because I was working with a sampling base that cannot be considered representative of the entire intersex population. For example, it is certain that some intersexuals associate with support groups and others do not. In addition, some of those who are networked with other intersexuals are more inclined than others to participate in research, let alone in a project that required the disclosure of such personal information.

I utilized theoretical sampling in two ways. First, unlike other studies in this area, I interviewed people with all types of intersex conditions, expecting to find similarities among a given type of intersex as well as significant differences across physiological variation. I was especially interested in studying potential similarities in those with disparate intersex etiology. Second, I recruited not only for diversity of intersex conditions and experiences, but also for diversity in geography, age, race and ethnicity, sex of assignment, social class, and outlook about what it means to be intersexed.

Initially, sampling was a challenge because intersexuals are not generally identifiable by visible or socio-demographic characteristics and are a largely unmobilized population. During the course of my research, however, several intersex support and advocacy groups either emerged or came to my attention. Members of these organizations cannot be expected to represent the diversity of experience within the intersex population. In fact, because there has been so little follow up on intersexuals, I don't presume to know what the constitution of that population actually is. Rather, these organizations serve as a strategic and theoretically promising sampling base, given the social context of an emerging intersex social movement and my interest in the experience and process of social marginalization.

It is important to note that there is significant diversity within and among the existing sixteen North American intersex support, advocacy, and education organizations. Unlike some who view the members of these organizations as a cohesive community represented best by the Intersex Society of North America—which has been perhaps the most vocal of these advocacy groups[13]—I encountered a rich diversity of sexual identities and opinions about medical intervention on intersexed infants and children among the people I interviewed. In fact, several disassociated themselves from the category of "intersex," even though diagnostically their physiology would be so classified. Many individuals also seemed to participate in upholding a two-sex system by engaging in classically "feminine" or "masculine" behaviors and roles and participating in what would be outwardly perceived as heterosexual activity—that is, sexual activity with partners who were sexed "opposite" to the individuals whom I interviewed. Among some of the more gender traditional participants, I encountered individuals who distanced themselves from the well-publicized lobbying efforts of certain intersex activists to stop cosmetic genital surgery on intersexuals, saying such things as, "You know I'm not part of that radical lobbying group, right?"

I began recruitment efforts in February of 1997 by sending an initial letter of introduction to leaders of the North American intersex support and advocacy organizations of which I was aware. Of the initial eleven groups I contacted, I received responses from 82 percent and participation from 45 percent. The four groups that did respond but did not aid in recruitment were groups that specialized in parents' support or information and education, and did not have adult intersexuals as members. To my knowledge, the two groups that did not respond were also parents' support organizations and did not have adult intersex members. Throughout the course of my research, I became aware of four additional intersex support groups and received participation from each one.

Calculating the precise response rate is impossible because I relied on others to send recruitment packets to people they knew who may qualify and be interested in participating. I sent out approximately seventy-five recruitment packets to unknown recipients through leaders of intersex support groups, people I interviewed, and professionals who work in the field of sexuality. I received inquiries from forty-five individuals and conducted a total of forty-one interviews,[14] thirty-seven of which were with adult intersexuals.[15] After completing the interviews, some individuals returned unsent recruitment packets to me. I am not sure how many of the recruitment packets I sent actually reached potential participants. I am aware that several were never sent out by support group leaders. It is likely, given the small network of the groups, that some individuals received multiple packets from various intersex friends/ acquaintances. In addition to the recruitment mailers sent by members of the intersex support community on my behalf, study announcements were posted twice on two private intersex Internet chat lists.

The majority of participants became aware of my project via mail recruitment or personal endorsements from intersexed friends and acquaintances, which is typical in snowball sampling. Fourteen percent contacted me after seeing my Internet postings. Personal endorsements from participants played a major role in recruitment, so much so that I refer to this method of sampling as "avalanche" rather than the more commonly used phrase of "snowball" sampling. As evidence of this, my number of scheduled interviews more than doubled during one trip when intersexuals in that region spoke of my research on the Internet chat lists, sharing their personal experience in participating and encouraging others to participate in what was generally thought to be a "cathartic experience."[16] During this time, I received e-mail inquiries[17] or phone calls in my hotel rooms from people with whom I had no previous contact. I quote here my field notes about this experience:

> I also need to write about what's been happening on the intersex [chat lists] . . . Seems to be that I've been a rather hot topic of conversation on the list[s] with several posts about me, my research, my travels, . . . my style, etc. From what I hear, it was as though I would leave someone's home . . . and they would pop on the list and post immediately saying something like, "Well, she just left and this is what happened . . . Where's she going next?" As I was told by one person when I was asked "Where'd you just come from?" and I responded something like, "South" that despite my attempts at confidentiality, my movements were being well tracked across the country.

Once individuals expressed interest in participation by mailing a completed Research Reply Form or by contacting me via e-mail or phone, I conducted an initial telephone screening to be sure that person qualified for participation. In order to qualify, individuals had to be at least eighteen years of age and intersexed (that is, having ambiguous genitalia, sexual organs, or sex chromosomes).[18]

This discussion of screening brings me back to the issue of defining intersex—a topic of such major dispute that frequency estimates range from 1/2,000 to 4/100 live births.[19] Thirty-seven of the forty-one individuals I interviewed clearly met my working definition for intersex. Four, however, did not. Two were bearded women who were socially perceived and responded to as hermaphroditic in a far more visible way than many of the participants whose physical ambiguity was only apparent at the level of chromosomes or internal organs. I found their experiences very relevant to the issue of sex and gender nonconformity and stigma. For example, as I discussed in chapter 3, one of these women reported developing chronic injuries in her neck and forearms from plucking the hair from her face at her mother's insistence to "look like a girl."

The other two were male-to-female transsexuals[20] who were both born and reared as unequivocal males, but were certain that physiological intersexuality was the cause of their transsexuality and they were seeking to uncover the hidden truth of their intersexed bodies. Both told stories of experiencing puberty that was both feminizing and masculinizing at the same time. I decided to interview these four individuals because I found their "qualifying" stories to be theoretically rich in teasing apart the normative mandates for gender binarism and its deviations. I analyzed their stories with caution, and ultimately decided to exclude them from my analyses, noting that their experiences need to be treated separately or comparatively. Thus, throughout the book, except where noted, I report on findings from interviews with thirty-seven adult intersexuals.[21]

I traveled extensively throughout the United States and Canada while conducting the interviews, engaging in continent-wide research. Before taking to the road for much of the summers of 1997 and 1998, I developed very detailed and complex travel plans, attempting to complete most of the study's recruitment before doing such travel.[22] In this way, I maximized the possibility of meeting with participants in common regions or adjacent states. By doing so, I was able to minimize expenses considerably, conducting all of the interviews with only seven plane flights, averaging four interviews per trip. In total I interviewed thirty-seven individuals from nineteen different states or provinces. Ninety-two percent of these interviews were conducted during face-to-face meetings and 8 percent were conducted via telephone, due to lack of funding for travel to geographically disparate participants.[23] During my most intensive interview travel, I traversed eight states in ten days, after flying into one state and renting a car, conducting a total of eight interviews during that time period.[24]

The Research Setting

I conducted the interviews in a private, face-to-face format, primarily in participants' homes.[25] Privacy was essential for these meetings because the interview guide covered many private and sensitive topics. Face-to-face encounters were essential for this reason as well. In addition, building rapport was particularly significant given the sensitivity of the subject matter. Face-to-face meetings also provided ample contextual data and opportunities to glean more from people's lives than their spoken words provided. Finally, based on recurrent feedback I received from participants, meeting face to face allowed for a valuable interview experience.

Participants chose the location of our meeting in all of the face-to-face interviews. In addition to participants' homes, interviews took place in several locations. Other interview locations included participants' friends' homes, participants' offices, my hotel rooms,[26] my office, on the telephone, or in a public restaurant. After a brief greeting and settling-in period, I gave each participant a list of North American intersex support and advocacy organizations as a means of reciprocity for their participation and to further intersex networking and support.[27] I also informed participants that they would be offered a copy of their interview once it had been transcribed. Next, the participants and I each signed two copies of the research consent form, so that we could each keep a copy for our records. At this point, I asked whether or not it was okay to tape record the meeting. All participants were amenable to this request. Once the recording equipment was running, I provided a general outline for the interview meeting. Next, I asked participants to choose a pseudonym, if they cared to, for the purpose of confidentiality.[28]

Analysis

Interviews were tape recorded, using a clip-on microphone and two battery-operated hand-held tape recorders (one for back up), and ranged from one to four hours in duration, averaging two and a half hours each. Immediately following each interview, I dictated my field notes on tape at the end of each participant's story, recording impressions of key themes and methodological issues from each interview. I hired assistants to transcribe the interviews verbatim, which average fifty-one pages in length, single-spaced.[29] After they were typed, I cleaned each interview transcript by listening to the tapes while reading through the transcripts, making corrections where they were required. During this cleaning stage, I also constructed an initial coding schema, making note of similarities and differences throughout the more than 2,100 pages of interview data.

I used the Statistical Package for the Social Sciences (SPSS) to analyze the demographic portions of the instrument. I used quantitative measures for the sole purpose of providing descriptive measures of the sample. I used the gender identity map time line primarily to assist the participant and myself during the interview process in attaining a shared understanding and chronology of her/his experiences.

I employed content analysis as a means of systematically analyzing the interview and field note data, attempting to ascertain the major patterns and themes present in both. Content analysis of individuals' own experiences permits researchers to better hear individuals' "own voices."[30] A basic assumption of this type of analysis "is that there is a relationship between frequency of occurrence of a content theme and its relative importance."[31]

I coded interview transcripts and field notes by hand using a color coding system to identify the main categories present in the data from which I generated an index of primary codes. I generated these categories by reading through the data and noting patterns and frequency of content. "To make valid inferences from the text, it is important that the classification procedure be reliable in the sense of being consistent."[32] This task is difficult in a solo research endeavor because I employed no other coder to verify my thematic scheme. However, multiple efforts were taken to ensure both the reliability and validity of not only the data, but the analyses as well.

First, all interviews were conducted utilizing the same interview guide as a basis. Although each interview session differed somewhat in its content based on the experiences of the individual being interviewed, all questions were posed to each participant to generate reliable touchstones for each interview.

Second, multiple methods of data collection were incorporated to increase the strength and rigor of evaluating the phenomena at hand. Individual interviews provide an in-depth understanding of each individual's personal experiences with intersexuality. The demographic, quantitative sexual identity, and gender identity map data supplement the richness of the data gathered during the interviews, offering additional insight into the participants' experiences and stories.

Third, I engaged in multiple sessions of hand coding the interview transcripts to assure a saturation of data with the coding categories and themes.[33] Saturation was established when separate coding runs, using clean or unmarked text, resulted in the generation of identical coding frameworks. In addition to coding while cleaning the transcripts, I created a color-coding scheme by reading through each interview transcript three times and taking extensive notes on themes and patterns that occurred across interviews. After constructing the coding framework, I color coded each transcript twice to check for the accuracy, consistency, and exhaustiveness of my analysis. In total, I took notes four separate times on each interview and coded each interview by hand three times. I engaged in the same process for coding my field notes.

One Last Word

Throughout this project, I have heard and witnessed stories of powerlessness, violation, reclamation, and personal empowerment. Interview after interview, participants shared stories of feeling scrutinized and sexualized by medical professionals, of being treated as oddities and freaks, of lacking control over their own bodies, and of the resulting shame and secrecy. In turn, they spoke of arduous battles to gain information about their bodies and attempts to find other intersexuals—aiming to piece together a puzzle whose solution was sure to hold the key to identity.

I did not expect to resonate so personally and profoundly with these stories of exploitation and personal conquest, but I did, and I still do. Clearly my own ethics and personal history serve as one basis and motive for this research. But in an effort to conduct effective and ethical qualitative feminist research, I intentionally engage in what Michelle Fine and Virginia Vanderslice call "qualitative activist research," aiming to transform "inequitable social arrangements" through my work.[34]

Participants seemed to be aware of and drawn to the activist nature of my work. Following the interview, participants often thanked me for my research and its potential impact on clinical methods that might be disempowering. After receiving a copy of her interview transcript, Constance telephoned, stating that "reading it made her feel as though she 'counted,' that perhaps someday her experiences 'would make a difference' by participating in my research."[35] In addition, several participants emphasized the power of the researcher role as well as the trust with which they shared their life stories. For example, as Deborah and I parted at the end of our interview meeting, she said to me, "Do good things with my life." Her words concisely conveyed a theme that participants shared repeatedly: They were investing their trust and their life stories in my hands so that I could do it and them some justice.

Participants seemed dedicated to helping me in this effort, often giving me poems or free writing about their experiences with medicalization. Indeed, some participants presented me with sacred spiritual gifts such as a rock from a medicine bag that had been treasured for over twenty years by its owner, or other items meant to spiritually assist me in my work. After one interview I wrote the following in my field notes,

> It was another of those unusual experiences for me in which a person with whom I'm doing an interview bestows upon me an incredible amount of power, almost in a guru like sense. There was a big presentation of candles and feathers and such. These were accompanied by a card stating, "Dearest Sharon, Thank you for helping to light the way . . . and illuminate the darkness of untruths and misinformation!"

I found such displays of gratitude moving and reinforcing during all phases of the project.

In closing, I would like to thank all of you who shared your stories with me so courageously. Your willingness to do so not only made this book possible, but also may serve those who are not yet able to talk as freely as you did with me.

It is my strongest hope that this book encourages dialogue and promotes social change. I have written it for all of us who are engaged in this effort.

Notes

Chapter 1   *Beyond Pink and Blue*

1. West and Zimmerman 1987.
2. While there is tremendous cross-cultural variation in responding to physical sexual variation, I explore how North American intersexuals experience and cope with being labeled sexually ambiguous in a culture that demands sexual conformity.
3. Blackless et al. 2000.
4. Money 1989; Edgerton 1964; Fiedler 1978.
5. Dreger 1998b; Kessler 1998.
6. Hird 2000.
7. Blackless et al. 2000.
8. See Dreger 1998b:43; Desai 1997; and Roberts et al. 1998.
9. National Center for Health Statistics (2001). Note that others project an annual birthrate of 1,500–2,000 intersexed children in the United States (Beh and Diamond 2000).
10. Most research participants chose pseudonyms for themselves to be used in the study. Perhaps as evidence of their desire to overcome the secrecy and shame they associated with attempts to erase their intersexuality, 27 percent of those I interviewed chose to use their real names. I do not distinguish here or elsewhere between those who chose pseudonyms and those who did not.
11. I conducted the body of this research while I was a graduate student at the University of Minnesota. I transferred to Minnesota's Department of Sociology and Center for Advanced Feminist Studies in the fall of 1993.
12. Fausto-Sterling 1993.
13. Fausto-Sterling addresses some of these questions herself in her more recent article, "The Five Sexes, Revisited" (2000b). Scott 1993.
14. Burawoy 1991.
15. Goffman 1959, 1963, 1982.
16. Butler 1990, 1993; West and Zimmerman 1987.
17. Reinharz 1992:21.
18. I conducted three interviews over the phone.
19. Diamond and Sigmundson 1997b; Dreger 1998a; Kessler 1998.
20. Mills 1959:8.
21. Newman 2002; Becker 1963.
22. Herdt 1994, 1998.
23. Wilson and Reiner 1998; Kessler 1998; Diamond and Sigmundson 1997b.
24. Kessler and McKenna 1978.

25. Goffman 1959, 1963; Zerubavel 1991.
26. Goffman 1959, 1963, 1982.
27. Schwalbe and Mason-Schrock 1996.
28. Hewitt 1970, 1989.
29. Howard and Hollander 1997.
30. Thorne 1993; Sadker and Sadker 1994; Karraker 1995.
31. Kohlberg 1966.
32. Thorne 1993.
33. In Kessler and McKenna's (1978:113) words, "genitals are the essential sign of gender." This logic is readily apparent in sex-assignment decisions where phallic size is one of the primary criteria for assigning sex.
34. Adapted from Kessler and McKenna 1978:113–114. Note that in developing these tenets of gender binarism, Kessler and McKenna draw on Garfinkel's (1967) descriptive ethnomethodological study of a male-to-female transsexual known as Agnes.
35. See Money (1991b) for a related history of his coining the terms *gender identity* and *gender role* and Rosario's (1997) historical critique.
36. Butler 1990, 1993.
37. Butler 1990, 1993; Bockting 1995, 1997b; Bornstein 1994; Devor 1989, 1997a, 1997b; Feinberg 1996; MacKenzie 1994; Rothblatt 1995.
38. Voorhess 1982; Donohoe et al. 1991; Horowitz and Glassberg 1992; Meyers-Seifer and Charest 1992; Lee 1994; Kessler 1998; Hawkesworth 1997.
39. Garfinkel 1967.
40. Garfinkel 1967.
41. Becker 1963.
42. Goffman 1963.
43. Money 1968, 1991a; Money et al. 1995; Money and Ehrhardt 1972.
44. Cooley 1902; Mead 1934.
45. Cooley 1902; Parsons 1968; Charon 1992; Holstein and Gubrium 2000.
46. Cooley 1902:152.
47. Mead 1934:138.
48. Others have detailed the impact of oppression on the self-concept. See, for example, Paulo Freire's *Pedagogy of the Oppressed* (1970).
49. Hubbard 1990.
50. Whether medical sex assignment is successful in meeting its objective of preventing stigma remains open to question and is indeed a primary reason I initiated this research.

Chapter 2   *Medical Sex Assignment*

1. This is the common nomenclature used to signify that an individual has forty-six paired chromosomes, the twenty-third pair of which is typically XX (girl) or XY (boy).
2. Grumbach and Conte 1998; Horowitz and Glassberg 1992; Josso 1981; New 1992; Kupfer et al. 1992.
3. Grumbach and Conte 1998; Horowitz and Glassberg 1992; Josso 1981; New 1992; Kupfer et al. 1992.
4. Grumbach and Conte 1998; Horowitz and Glassberg 1992; Josso 1981; New 1992; Kupfer et al. 1992.
5. New 1992:301.
6. Klebs 1876. Although Klebs first introduced this taxonomy of hermaphroditism

in 1876, it was not widely adopted or discussed in the medical literature until the 1890s publications of Samuel Pozzi, Franz Neugebauer, George Blacker, and Thomas Lawrence (Dreger 1998b). Note that Klebs's initial classifications differed slightly from a contemporary version of the same taxonomy. Klebs's categories were feminine pseudohermaphroditism (rather than female pseudohermaphroditism), masculine pseudohermaphroditism (rather than male pseudohermaphroditism), and true hermaphroditism.

7. CAH may also be caused by the administration of exogenous androgens to the mother or a tumor on the mother's suprarenal gland, resulting in the absorption of excess androgens to the female fetus during pregnancy (Grumbach and Conte 1998). The imbalance in enzymes associated with CAH also appears in males, with less frequency.

8. A rare life-threatening form of CAH, known as salt-wasting, requires hormone therapy to balance the body's endocrine system (New 1992; Josso 1981). Grumbach and Conte 1998; Money and Ehrhardt 1972; Horowitz and Glassberg 1992; Josso 1981; New 1992; Glanze et al. 1996; Jost 1981; Baker 1981.

9. Quigley et al. 1995; Diamond and Sigmundson 1997b.

10. Grumbach and Conte 1998; Money and Ehrhardt 1972; Horowitz and Glassberg 1992; Kupfer et al. 1992; Josso 1981; Glanze et al. 1996; Baker 1981; Jost 1981.

11. Grumbach and Conte 1998; Money and Ehrhardt 1972; Horowitz and Glassberg 1992; Kupfer et al. 1992; Josso 1981; Glanze et al. 1996.

12. Grumbach and Conte 1998; Money 1968; Money and Ehrhardt 1972; Glanze et al. 1996.

13. A fetus with a 45,YO karyotype is not sustainable and will die (Grumbach and Conte 1998).

14. Grumbach and Conte 1998; Money 1968; Money and Ehrhardt 1972; Glanze et al. 1996.

15. I italicize words that interviewees emphasized during our conversations, in an effort to convey the character and tone of the interviews.

16. Nicholson 1997/1998; Martinez-Pineiro et al. 1998; Caldamone et al. 1998.

17. Foucault 1978, 1970, 1977; Weeks 1985; Conrad and Schneider 1992.

18. Moscucci 1991; Foucault 1980.

19. Conrad and Schneider 1992; Conrad 1992.

20. Friedson 1970; Turner 1987; Relman 1990; Conrad 1975.

21. Conrad and Schneider 1992.

22. Because the term *intersexuality* was not coined until the early twentieth century, I use the term *hermaphrodite* during this historical discussion (Hird and Germon 2001). Note that the theological and medical stages are more evident in the case of intersexuality. The second stage of criminalization seems to exist primarily as a punishment for theological or moral breaches.

23. Nederman and True 1996.

24. Dreger 1995b; Nederman and True 1996. Dreger (1998b) illustrates that late-nineteenth-century medical understanding was that hermaphrodite meant male and female, whereas early use of the word *intersex* means in between male and female (Dreger 1998b).

25. Note that there is evidence of substantial disagreement between Galenists and Aristotelians on the point of women's contribution to the formation of the embryo. According to Aristotle, females contributed no "seed" or "sperm" to their offspring; whereas, Galen purported females to actively give "seed" to their progeny (Cadden 1993).

26. Note that Aristotle valued "male" heat over "female" cold and viewed females' lack of heat as a sign of inferiority and even deformity (Cadden 1993).

27. Laqueur 1990.
28. Pare 1634. Laqueur (1990) seems to disagree with both Pare and Galen. He claims that Pare's theory is based on "reading" male anatomy onto female bodies, and that Galen viewed men as not only "hotter" than women, but also as superior to them.
29. Conrad and Schneider 1992.
30. Cadden 1993; Nederman and True 1996.
31. Nederman and True 1996; Jones and Stallybrass 1991; Moscucci 1991.
32. Azo 1610, quoted in Nederman and True 1996:512. It appears that although Azo wrote this text in the late 1100s, it was not published until early in the seventeenth century.
33. Nederman and True 1996.
34. Hird and Germon 2001.
35. Pagliassotti 1993.
36. Hekma 1994; Dreger 1995a.
37. Dreger 1998b; Hird and Germon 2001.
38. Quoted in Nederman and True 1996:510–511. The translation of Peter the Chanter used by Nederman and True is Boswell's (1980).
39. For evidence of historic tolerance of hermaphrodites, see Pare 1634; Nederman and True 1996; Jones and Stallybrass 1991; Epstein 1990; Pagliassotti 1993; Fausto-Sterling 1993, 1985; Laqueur 1990; Trumbach 1994.
40. Epstein 1990:124.
41. Pagliassotti 1993.
42. Nederman and True 1996.
43. Greenberg 1999; Hawley 1977; Ormrod 1972; Capron and D'Avino 1981.
44. Foucault 1978:37.
45. Ormrod 1972:85.
46. Greenberg 1999.
47. Lum 2002.
48. Lum 2002.
49. Dahir 2000.
50. Ormrod 1972; Hawley 1977.
51. Capron and D'Avino 1981.
52. Capron and D'Avino 1981:220.
53. Capron and D'Avino 1981:221.
54. Nederman and True 1996; Jones and Stallybrass 1991; Epstein 1990; Trumbach 1994.
55. Jones and Stallybrass 1991; Epstein 1990; Trumbach 1994.
56. Foucault 1978, 1980; Pagliassotti 1993; Epstein 1990; Dreger 1995b.
57. Dreger 1995a:57.
58. Goffman 1959, 1961, 1963, 1974, 1982.
59. See for example Chase 2002.
60. Kessler and McKenna 1978:22.
61. Herdt 1994; Imperato-McGinley et al. 1974, 1979.
62. In Papau New Guinea, kwolu-aatmwol is also known as "turnim-man" or "turning into a man" (Herdt 1994).
63. Imperato-McGinley et al. 1974, 1979.
64. Herdt 1994:429.
65. Nanda 1990:xv.
66. As gender is defined so closely with reproductive capacity in India, women who do not menstruate are also allowed to become hijras, although most hijras are impotent men (Nanda 1994).

67. This ritual includes penectomy and orchiectomy; that is, the removal of the penis and testicles (Nanda 1990, 1994).
68. Nanda 1990, 1994.
69. Similar to Western transsexual transitions that do not involve genital reconstruction, not all hijras undergo this emasculanization ritual of genital removal (Nanda 1990).
70. Butler 1993.
71. Nanda 1990.
72. Roscoe 1994; Williams 1986. For simplicity, I use the term *berdache*, which is a customary referent of Western anthropologists. The term, however, has pejorative overtones, as the French anthropologists who originated its use were seen as imperialistic in their studies. For that reason, some prefer to use the more indigenous term *two-spirit* (Jacobs et al. 1997). Indigenous names for two-spirits vary by tribe, such as the Navajo nadle ("one who is transformed"), the Crow bade ("not man, not woman"), and the Cree ayekkwew ("neither man nor woman" or "man and woman") (Williams 1986).
73. Williams 1986:2.
74. The majority of anthropological studies of berdaches have been on physiological males. There is a smaller body of research that discusses morphological female berdaches as well (Roscoe 1994; Williams 1986). I restrict my discussion here to natal "male" berdaches, for the sake of brevity.
75. Similar to estimates of intersex, rates of berdaches prevalence are variant and inconclusive.
76. Roscoe 1994; Williams 1986.
77. The Spanish Inquisition brought intense efforts to suppress sodomy and berdachism (Williams 1986). Despite these homophobic efforts beginning in the fourteenth century, berdaches' gender and sexual expressions continue to exist.
78. Roscoe 1994; Williams 1986.
79. Kessler and McKenna 1978:22.
80. Conrad and Schneider 1992; Freidson 1970; Turner 1987; Fox 1990; Relman 1990.
81. Conrad and Schneider 1992:9.
82. Conrad and Schneider 1992:10.
83. Conrad 1992:209.
84. Dreger 1999a.
85. *Chicago Hope*. 1996. Episode on Intersex. Columbia Broadcasting System, April 4.
86. Crawford 1980; Light 1989, 2000; Conrad and Schneider 1992.
87. Zola 1990.
88. Kessler 1997/1998.
89. For further discussion of the impact on language and perception, see Sapir 1929 and Whorf 1956.
90. Several linguists cite the Hungarian physician Karoly Maria Benkert, known as Kertbeny, to have first coined the term *homosexuality* in 1869.
91. Foucault 1978; Weeks 1985; Greenberg 1988; Conrad and Schneider 1992; Ned Katz 1996.
92. Conrad and Schneider 1992; Bockting 1995; Hekma 1994.
93. Findlay 1995; Lorber 1994; Kessler and McKenna 1978.
94. Lorber 1994:21.
95. Stone 1991.
96. Kessler and McKenna 1978:120.

97. See Relman 1990; Freidson 1970; and Turner 1987 for a discussion of the medi-
    cal industrial complex, and Martin 1987; Romalis 1981; Sumner and Phillips
    1981; Young 1982; Eastman and Loustaunau 1987; Mackey 1990; Leavitt 1989;
    Fox 1990; Rothman 1990; Ehrenreich and English 1990; Wertz and Wertz 1990
    for more on the medicalization of childbirth.
98. Martin 1987; Leavitt 1989.
99. Schwartz Cowan 1992.
100. Eastman and Loustaunau 1987; Leavitt 1989; Romalis 1981.
101. Wertz and Wertz 1990; Leavitt 1989.
102. Leavitt 1989.
103. Leavitt 1989.
104. Leavitt 1989:304.
105. Young 1982; Romalis 1981.
106. Leavitt 1989; Eastman and Loustaunau 1987.
107. Zola 1990.
108. Leavitt 1989.
109. Kessler 1990:2.
110. Romalis 1981.
111. Kessler 1998.
112. Schwartz Cowan 1992.
113. Donohoe et al. 1991:575.
114. Casper 1998.
115. New et al. 1994.
116. CARES Foundation web site: <http://www.caresfoundation.org/nbs.html>.
117. Fausto-Sterling 2000a.
118. Newman 2001.
119. MacKenzie 1994.
120. Jorgensen 2000.
121. MacKenzie 1994:44.
122. MacKenzie 1994; Fausto-Sterling 1993.
123. Coontz 1992.
124. Money et al. 1955.
125. Money 1952; Colapinto 2000.
126. Money et al. 1955; Money and Ehrhardt 1972; Colapinto 2000.
127. Money 1968, 1991a, 1994; Money and Ehrhardt 1972.
128. Money and Ehrhardt 1972.
129. It is important to note that although optimal gender theory aims to de-emphasize
    physical difference, medical practitioners pay significant attention to intersexuals'
    ambiguous anatomy during physical exams.
130. Meyer-Bahlburg 1993.
131. Money 1968:44.
132. Baker 1981.
133. Money 1968, 1991a, 1994; Money and Ehrhardt 1972.
134. Money 1968:33.
135. Money 1968:43.
136. Voorhess 1982; Kessler 1998; Donohoe et al. 1991; Meyers-Seifer and Charest
    1992; Horowitz and Glassberg 1992; Lee 1994.
137. Kessler 1998; Lee 1994.
138. Kessler 1998; Schwartz Cowan 1992.
139. Kessler 1998.
140. Lee 1994:17.
141. Ormrod 1972:83.

142. Natarajan 1996; Kemp et al. 1996; Wilson and Reiner 1998; Schober 1998b; Kessler 1990, 1998.
143. Lee 1994:17.
144. Money 1994, 1968; Kessler 1998; Foucault 1980; Butler 1990.
145. Meyers-Seifer and Charest 1992:336–337.
146. Kessler 1998, 1997/1998. It is interesting to note that newborn penile size charts were first published in the 1960s. In striking contrast, newborn clitoral size charts were not published until the late 1980s (Lee 1994).
147. Donohoe et al. 1991:537. See also Slaughenhoupt and Van Savage 1999.
148. This is what I call the "penis/no penis" logic of sex-assignment decision making.
149. Donohoe et al. 1991; Kessler 1998; Money 1985; Lee 1994.
150. Kessler 1998; Donohoe et al. 1991.
151. Hendricks 1993:15.
152. Kipnis and Diamond 1998:398.
153. Lee 1994.
154. Reilly and Woodhouse 1989; Van Seters and Slob 1988; Schober 1998a; Bin-Abbas et al. 1999.
155. Horowitz and Glassberg 1992; Dreger 1999b.
156. Kessler 1997/1998:35.
157. Schober 1998b:393.
158. Money 1991a, 1994, 1968; Diamond and Sigmundson 1997b; Meyer-Bahlburg 1998, 1993; Beh and Diamond 2000; Ford 2001.
159. Yronwode 1999:4.

Chapter 3   *Stigma, Secrecy, and Shame*

1. Anspach 1979; Barnard 1990; Hahn 1998; Sudsman 1994; Yoshida 1993.
2. Cass 1979, 1984; Coleman 1981–1982, 1987; Minton and McDonald 1984.
3. Stone 1991.
4. Bockting 1997a, 1995.
5. Cooley 1902.
6. Cooley 1902; Mead 1934; Goffman 1963; Becker 1963; Jones et al. 1984; Plummer 1975, 1995; Davis 1995, Hewitt 1989; Strauss and Corbin 1991; Holstein and Gubrium 2000.
7. Jones et al. 1984.
8. Mead 1934; Hewitt 1970.
9. Plummer 1975, 1995.
10. Goffman 1963; Jones et al. 1984.
11. Jones et al. 1984.
12. Fisher and Groce 1985.
13. This participant chose "J8" as her/his pseudonym. Rather than imposing my own name on participants for the sake of legibility, I honored their choices in naming themselves.
14. Goffman 1963.
15. Goffman 1963:16.
16. Plummer 1975.
17. Dreger 2000:162.
18. Jones et al. 1984.
19. Natarajan 1996.
20. Fisher and Groce 1985.
21. Flaubert 1887. Note that I draw this reference from Lennard Davis's (1995) insightful analysis of deaf culture in *Enforcing Normalcy: Disability, Deafness, and the Body.*

22. Butler 1990, 1993.
23. Snyder 1986.
24. Goffman 1959; West and Zimmerman 1987; Garfinkel 1967.
25. Anspach 1979; Barnard 1990; Hahn 1988; Sudsman 1994; Yoshida 1993; Becker 1981; Garfinkel 1967; Kessler and McKenna 1978.
26. Goffman 1959.
27. Goffman 1963; Jones et al. 1984.

Chapter 4 **Seeds of Change**

1. Johnson 1983.
2. Mills 1959.
3. Mona 1998.
4. Feinberg 1996:x (original emphasis).
5. Anspach 1979:765.
6. Bockting 1997a, 1997b, 1995.
7. Devor 1997a, 1997b; Bockting 1997a, 1995; Bolin 1994; Rothblatt, 1995; Bornstein, 1994; Garfinkel, 1967; Stone, 1991. According to Bolin (1994), Devor (1989, 1997a, 1997b), Bockting (1997a, 1995), and Stone (1991).
8. Goffman 1963.
9. Bem 1995, 1993.
10. Chase 1998b.
11. Preves 1998, 1999a, 2000; Dreger 1998a, 1998b, 1998c; Kessler 1998, 1997/1998, 1990; Diamond and Sigmundson 1997a, 1997b; Kipnis and Diamond 1998; Schober 1998a; Wilson and Reiner 1998; Glassberg 1999; Fausto-Sterling 1993, 2000a; Chase 1999, 1998a, 1998b, 1998c; Chase and Coventry 1997/1998; Groveman 1998; Elliot 1998.
12. Diamond 1999, 1997, 1996a, 1996b, 1995, 1993; Diamond and Sigmundson 1997a.
13. Kessler 1998, 1990, 1997/1998; Dreger 1998a, 1998b, 1998c; and Fausto-Sterling 1993, 2000a.
14. Kemp et al. 1996; Chase 1999, 1998a, 1998b, 1998c; Groveman 1998; Coventry 1998, 1997/1998; Moreno 1997/1998; Moreno and Goodwin 1998; Triea 1997/1998, 1997; Holmes 1998, 1997/1998, 1995, 1994; Walcutt 1997/1998; Nicholson 1997/1998; Beck 1997/1998; Derick 1997/1998; McClintock 1997/1998; Kaldera 1998.
15. Recall that some rare cases of intersexuality do require medical intervention. This is especially notable in salt-wasting forms of CAH or when infants have difficulty voiding urine or feces (Wilson and Reiner 1998; Kessler 1998; Diamond and Sigmundson 1997b).
16. Horowitz 1995.
17. Holmes 1994:29–30.
18. Chase 1998a:212.
19. Chase 1998a:212.
20. I take much of this history from Chase's GLQ article, "Hermaphrodites with Attitude: Mapping the Emergence of Intersex Political Activism" (1998b).
21. Recall that Turner's Syndrome is the most common form of "female" chromosomal variation where the typical karyotype is 45,XO, meaning that one sex chromosome is missing. (A fetus with a 45,YO karyotype is not sustainable and will die [Grumbach and Conte 1998].) Individuals with Turner's Syndrome typically develop unambiguous female genitalia, yet have underdeveloped breasts, uterus, and vagina. Some have testicular tissue and primitive gonadal "streak" tissue.

They commonly do not develop secondary sex characteristics and are very short. Some may have a webbed neck, "shield chest," and short fingers and toes. (Grumbach and Conte 1998; Money 1968; Money and Ehrhardt 1972; Glanze et al. 1996).

22. Recall that in androgen insensitivity syndrome (AIS), individuals have a male-typical 46, XY karyotype, but lack a key androgen (male hormone) receptor that facilitates the ability, fetally and onward, to respond to the androgens produced in normal amounts. This results in a feminization of the external genitalia and, typically, abdominal testicles. Some individuals with AIS are completely insensitive to androgen, and some only partially. Most individuals with AIS are sexed as female, unless virilization is only slightly affected by insensitivity to androgen, in which case male sex assignment would prevail (Quigley et al. 1995; Diamond and Sigmundson 1997b). At puberty, individuals with AIS respond to the normal levels of estrogen produced by their bodies and develop breasts. AIS individuals typically develop very little, if any, body hair, and are tall and lean. (It is indeed paradoxical that AIS "boys'" appearance is consistent with contemporary Western ideals of female beauty.) AIS individuals are sterile, but many do adopt children (Grumbach and Conte 1998; Money and Ehrhardt 1972; Horowitz and Glassberg 1992; Kupfer et al. 1992; Josso 1981; Glanze et al. 1996; Baker 1981; Jost 1981).
23. Personal communication with AISSG-US membership chair, May 23, 2002. International AIS Support Group Website: <http://www.medhelp.org/www/ais/>.
24. Recall that Klinefelter's Syndrome is a type of chromosomal variation in which a "male" child has a karyotype with more than one X chromosome, such as a 47,XXY (or 48,XXXY, or 49,XXXXY). Genital ambiguity is not present, but testes may be small and firm, and breast development (gynecomastia) is common. Secondary sex characteristic development is limited and these men are almost always sterile (Grumbach and Conte 1998; Money 1968; Money and Ehrhardt 1972; Glanze et al. 1996).
25. Chase 1993; Fausto-Sterling 1993.
26. Chase 1997, 1998b.
27. Kessler 1997/1998.
28. Chase 1997, 1998b; Harvey 1999.
29. Personal communication with Cheryl Chase, May 22, 2002.
30. Intersex Support Group International's website: <http://www.isgi.org>.
31. Turner 1999.
32. Colapinto 2000.
33. For further critical discussion on the medicalization of masculinity, see Fausto-Sterling (1996).
34. Colapinto 1997:62; Diamond and Sigmundson 1997a.
35. Money 1975; Money and Ehrhardt 1972.
36. Diamond and Sigmundson 1997a.
37. Colapinto 2000, 1997; Diamond and Sigmundson 1997a; Kipnis and Diamond 1998.
38. Diamond and Sigmundson 1997b; Kipnis and Diamond 1998; Diamond 1999.
39. Angier 1997a, 1997b, 1996; Cowley 1997; Colapinto 1997; Triea 1997; Coventry 1998; Hassibi 1998; d'Adesky 1996; Moreno and Goodwin 1998; *NBC Dateline* 1997; *Inside Edition* 1997; *Prime Time Live* 1997. Note that Diamond first reported Brenda's transition to David in the 1980s, in the *Archives of Sexual Behavior* (1982), as well as on a segment filmed by the British Broadcasting Company. In addition, he reported these findings at a sexology conference in 1995. Interestingly, there was little to no response to these earlier reports. I believe

that Diamond's prior reports were given little weight because there was very little mainstream social awareness or acceptance of gender nonconformity and sexual ambiguity before mid-to-late 1990s transgender visibility. In addition, his recent publications have been in clinical journals, whereas a largely theoretical audience read his 1982 article. Clinicians would surely find more practical application for these findings. Despite the significant reaction to Diamond's recent publications, I maintain that little is to be learned from this case about either social or biological influences on gender identity development and that the main benefit of Diamond's follow-up is its impact on intersex medicalization. Bruce Reimer received both unambiguous male social and genetic influences until he was eight months of age. Despite Money's theory of gender flexibility until eighteen to twenty-four months of age, I find it impossible to believe that no male gender salience had been created for this child in the first eight months of his life. Likewise, his internal physiology was entirely male. In addition, I suspect that David and his family had difficulty adjusting to the gender reassignment, which did not take place until he was twenty-two months of age. The biannual psychological and physical exams and other such scrutiny on the twins' development as well as hormone therapy for Brenda also called into question the feasibility of his gender reassignment. At the very least, generalizations regarding gender identity development, be they biological or sociological, should not be made using one case study, especially one where such conclusions are certain to be spurious.

40. Gecas and Schwalbe 1983; Cooley 1902.
41. Freire 1970.
42. Jones et al. 1984.
43. Jones et al. 1984.
44. Note that there are other potential strategies of exercising agency to develop a positive self-concept or to deflect a negative self-concept that I do not fully explore here.
45. Indeed it is possible that stigmatized persons mark one another as well.
46. Goffman 1963.
47. Goffman 1963:9.
48. Gecas and Schwalbe 1983; Jones et al. 1984; Cooley 1902.
49. Gecas and Schwalbe 1983:78.
50. Gecas 1991.
51. Gecas and Schwalbe 1983.
52. Gecas and Schwalbe 1983:81.
53. U.S. Department of Commerce 2000.
54. Jones et al. 1984.
55. Freire 1970.
56. Freire 1970.
57. Strauss and Corbin 1991.
58. Butler 1990.
59. Strauss and Corbin 1991.
60. Freire 1970:37.
61. This illustrates that gaining accurate information about oneself may indeed lead to feelings of stigma and shame that were not present before. In addition, the potential for developing feelings of stigma and shame extends far beyond the scope of medical intervention, and into the realm of routine daily social interaction.
62. Butler 1993, 1990; Kessler and McKenna 1978; Wilson 1998.
63. Jones et al. 1984.

64. In addition to interviewing thirty-seven intersexuals, I also interviewed two bearded women and two male-to-female transsexuals, both of whom claimed naturally occurring feminization at puberty and intersex as the underlying cause of their gender ambiguity. With the assistance of A. Evan Eyler, I explore transsexuals' belief in being born intersex in greater detail (Preves and Eyler 1999).
65. Kubler-Ross 1969.
66. Lee 1977.
67. Lee 1977:62 (original emphasis).
68. Mason-Schrock 1996.
69. Freire 1970.
70. Cass 1979, 1984; Coleman 1981–1982, 1987; Minton and McDonald 1984.
71. Gagne et al. 1997.
72. Jones et al. 1984:144.
73. Schwalbe and Mason-Schrock 1996:126.
74. Gagne et al. 1997.
75. Cass 1979.
76. Minton and McDonald 1984.
77. Schwalbe and Mason-Schrock 1996.
78. Zola 1987.
79. Seeman 1959; Gecas 1989.
80. Snyder 1986.

Chapter 5   Intersex Pride

1. Anspach 1979; Barnard 1990; Hahn 1988; Sudsman 1994; Yoshida 1993.
2. Jones et al. 1984; Freire 1970.
3. Cass 1979, 1984.
4. Coleman 1981–1982.
5. Jones et al. 1984; Freire 1970.
6. Grumbach and Conte 1998; Warne 1997; Kupfer et al. 1992; Writing Group from the Women's Health Initiative Investigators 2002. Note that the same is true in other medicalized conditions. For example, menopause is seen as a causal agent of both heart disease and osteoporosis (Preves 1995).
7. Davis 1995.
8. Namaste 1996.
9. Davis 1995:24.
10. Kuhn 1970.
11. Bell 1990.
12. Freire 1970.
13. See Schober, Wilson and Reiner, and others in the 1998 *Journal of Clinical Ethics* special issue on the efficacy of intersex medical protocol. (Also see *Intersex in the Age of Ethics*.)
14. Berkun 1986:381.
15. Jones et al. 1984:136.
16. Gamson 1992; Freeman 1999.
17. Klandermans 1992; Schwalbe and Mason-Schrock 1996.
18. Gagne et al. 1997.
19. Sandstrom 1990; Snow and Anderson 1987.
20. Klandermans 1992:78.
21. Dickson 1990:28.
22. Zola 1987.

23. Goffman 1959.
24. Suler 1984.
25. Back and Taylor 1976; Blumer 1969.
26. Back and Taylor 1976:301.
27. Zola 1987; Back and Taylor 1976.
28. Albrecht and Adelman 1987; Shumaker and Brownell 1984; Maguire 1983; Rosenberg 1984.
29. Davis 1989.
30. Martin 1987; Davis 1989:62.
31. Schwalbe and Mason-Schrock 1996:141.
32. Minton and McDonald 1984.
33. Sandstrom 1990; Gagne et al. 1997.
34. Jones et al. 1984:136.
35. Zola 1987.
36. Lee 1977:68.
37. Jones et al. 1984:201.
38. *Hermaphrodites with Attitude* is the title of the newsletter of the Intersex Society of North America and also the name the Intersex Society representatives use for their group when engaging in political protests at medical conferences and in other venues.
39. Beck 1997–1998.
40. Fifty-six percent of the sample who changed their names also chose to use their real names in the study.
41. Seidman 1995.
42. Several participants made media appearances in various print, radio, television, and film venues.
43. Kessler 1998.
44. Recall that in complete androgen insensitivity syndrome, individuals have XY, male typical, chromosomes and abdominal testicles, yet look externally female.
45. Cass 1979; Coleman 1981–1982.
46. The ability for intersexuals to integrate and synthesize their identities in this way signifies the value of longitudinal research with this and other marginal populations.
47. Vargo 1998:33.
48. Cass 1984; Jones et al. 1984.
49. Goffman 1959.
50. I am hesitant to draw conclusions about their ability to do so, for my instrument was not designed specifically with that intent. Future research could easily explore the question of overcoming stigma on a more complete scale.
51. Gamson 1992.

Chapter 6 **Implications of Intersex Mobilization**

1. Goffman 1963.
2. Chase 1998b, 1997; Harvey 1999. Note that, to a lesser degree, some intersex activists have made links to other types of surgery for which children do not provide informed consent themselves, such as male circumcision and cochlear implantation (see, for example, ISNA's web site).
3. Seidman 1995:135.
4. Namaste 1996:198–199.
5. Seidman 1995:135.
6. Davis 1995:78–79.

7. Historian Alice Dreger discussed this case during her talk on January 28, 2002 at the University of Minnesota's Center for Advanced Feminist Studies.
8. Loury 1996.
9. Zucker 2002.
10. ISNA News Release, February 2000.
11. NATFI is endorsed by the American Academy of Pediatrics, the American Urological Association, the American Academy of Child and Adolescent Psychiatry, the American College of Medical Genetics, the Lawson Wilkins Pediatric Endocrine Society, the Society for Pediatric Urology, the Society for Fetal Urology, and the Society of Genitourinary Reconstructive Surgeons. (NATFI web site: <http://www.natfi.org>.)
12. Fausto-Sterling 2000b.
13. American Academy of Pediatrics 2000:138.
14. Fausto-Sterling 2000a:18.
15. Personal communication with Cheryl Chase, May 2002.
16. Diamond and Sigmundson 1997b.
17. Dreger 1998b; Kessler 1998.
18. Wilson and Reiner 1998; Kessler 1998; Diamond and Sigmundson 1997b.
19. Gecas 1989, 1991.
20. Gecas 1989:300.
21. Freire 1970.
22. Recall UCSF Associate Professor of Urology and Pediatrics Laurence Baskin's statement, "I honestly feel sorry for those people who feel mutilated by their surgeries. They need counseling to get over their loss. Their surgeries were performed years ago, and the nerve supply wasn't understood. For [every] three [unhappy intersexuals], my guess is there are 97 who are happy. But they're not going to be out talking [about it]" (Yronwode 1999:4).
23. Kuhn 1962; Freire 1970.
24. Bockting et al. 1999; Freire 1970.
25. Wilson and Reiner 1998; Nussbaum 1999; Reinberg 1999; Reiner 1999.
26. Schober 1998; Wilson and Reiner 1998; Kipnis and Diamond 1998.
27. Garfinkel 1967, 1996.
28. Namaste 1996:203.
29. Namaste 1996:204.

Chapter 7 **Methodological Appendix**

1. Krieger 1991.
2. Glaser and Strauss 1967; Strauss and Corbin 1998.
3. Pierce 1995; Reinharz 1992; Thorne 1993; Longino 1990; Krieger 1991.
4. Krieger 1991:29–30.
5. I was aware of my research being emotionally disruptive in one case, when a participant became visibly upset while completing the gender identity time line. I quote here from my field notes about the interview, "With the gender identity map, she really had a hard time emotionally. She excused herself from the room...She left the gender identity map at the table and I heard her crying upstairs. I called up to her from the kitchen and said, 'You don't have to do this at all. This is completely voluntary and if it's troubling you, you don't need to do it at all.' She came back down and seemed very composed and apologized saying that this [instrument] just brought up flashbacks...that it just sent her right back to her experiences at [the hospital as a child]."

6. Money 1968, 1991a, 1994; Money et al. 1955; Money and Ehrhardt 1972.
7. Shively and De Cecco 1977; Coleman 1987; Bockting and Coleman 1992.
8. Note that similar methods are used to assess sexual identity in other populations, including transgenders (Bockting 1997; Bockting and Coleman 1992).
9. Butler 1993, 1990.
10. Shively and De Cecco 1977; Coleman 1987.
11. Volunteering their medical records perhaps indicates participants' desire to document and validate their intersexuality, as well as their history of researchers' interest in their clinical files.
12. Glaser and Strauss 1967.
13. Lebacqz 1997.
14. Below I provide additional information about the four persons whom I interviewed that were not intersexual.
15. I did not conduct interviews with the four persons who made remaining inquiries for several reasons. One potential participant moved off the continent, another moved and left no forwarding information, a third decided not to participate after scheduling an interview because she found discussion of these issues emotionally distressing, and by the time the fourth person contacted me, I had already finished interviewing participants.
16. The "cathartic experience" endorsement was communicated to me by a number of individuals who contacted me after seeing such postings on the private intersex chat lists.
17. I traveled with my laptop (and modem) for the purposes of correspondence with participants regarding interviewing logistics and to take field notes after each interview.
18. Surgical or hormonal intervention was not a requirement for participation.
19. Fausto-Sterling 2000a; Blackless et al. 2000; Money 1989; Fiedler 1978; Edgerton 1964.
20. One was preoperative and the other was nonoperative, meaning that she did not intend to undergo any genital surgery. Both were taking exogenous (external) female hormones.
21. Note that I have published reports that include all forty-one cases (Preves 1999b, 1998).
22. I scheduled some interviews as far as six months in advance.
23. My seven flights include two that I took for single interviews. I chose to fly to these individuals and not to the three I interviewed by phone in an effort to further theoretical sampling (Glaser and Strauss 1967). The stories I heard in both single-flight interviews were significantly different than others I had heard up to that point. In addition, my travel funds were less ample when I conducted the phone interviews.
24. Only six of these eight interviews were with intersexuals; the other two were with the bearded women that I ultimately excluded from my analyses. I include them here solely to illustrate my interview and travel schedule at its peak.
25. Three of the thirty-seven interviews were conducted by telephone.
26. Hotel rooms were potentially precarious as an interview setting due to their enclosed space and rather personal setting. When participants requested a hotel meeting, it was, to my knowledge, to avoid a lack of privacy in their own homes. To maximize the hotel rooms' formality, I met each participant in the lobby and walked up to the rooms with them. We sat at the rooms' table and chairs, which I always preset, typically located near a window.
27. Note that the University of Minnesota's Human Subjects Committee required that I provide a list of support resources for all participants. The committee re-

quired changes to this list, suggesting that in addition to intersex support groups, I list counseling resources as well.

28. As I mentioned previously, 27 percent of participants chose to use their real names rather than pseudonyms. These individuals signed a research consent form addendum, stating their preference to use their real first names in the research, including any published or presented works.

29. Interviews must be transcribed as consistently as possible to maximize the reliability of the data. I personally transcribed four interviews and then trained two transcriptionists to type the remainder; one transcribed eight interviews, the other transcribed the remaining twenty-nine. (Note that this calculation includes all forty-one interviews.)

30. Cross and Lovett 1994:190.

31. Cross and Lovett 1994:192.

32. Weber 1990:12.

33. Glaser and Strauss 1967.

34. Fine and Vanderslice 1992:199.

35. Excerpt from field notes.

Glossary

I have created this glossary from the compilation of many sources, too many of which to credit here. The purpose of the glossary is to clarify any confusion of my use of terms throughout the text. Others may disagree with my definitions. I offer the definitions of concepts that I have used throughout my research.

1. Note that in some cases of androgen insensitivity, there is a complete lack of response to androgens (complete AIS), while in other forms, there is a partial response to androgens (partial AIS). See Quigley et al. (1995) for a complete discussion of the various grades of AIS.

2. CAH may also be caused by the administration of exogenous androgens to the mother or a tumor on the mother's suprarenal gland, resulting in the absorption of excess androgens to the female fetus during pregnancy. CAH also occurs with less frequency in male children.

Glossary

5-alpha-reductase deficiency: A condition that causes chromosomal and gonadal males to appear externally female until puberty. Due to a lack of the enzyme 5-alpha-reductase, these children cannot convert their body's production of testosterone into dihydrotestosterone (DHT). At puberty, however, with the production of more testosterone, these children develop secondary sex characteristics standard for men including facial hair, muscularization of the body, and deepening of the voice, despite the continued low levels of DHT. Often, their testicles voluntarily descend and the phalloclit grows into a small penis.

androgen insensitivity syndrome (AIS; testicular feminization): A genetic condition in which chromosomal and gonadal males lack key androgen receptors and are unable to respond to testosterone from gestation onwards.[1] This results in a feminization of the external genitalia with, typically, abdominal testicles. At puberty, children who have AIS respond to the normal levels of estrogen produced by their bodies, normally overpowered by androgens, and develop breasts. They typically develop very little, if any, body hair, and are tall and lean, with round breasts. Individuals with AIS are sterile.

berdache(s): The anthropological term for Native American physiological males who do not fill a society's standard man's role, have a nonmasculine character, and may do work traditionally associated with women of a given tribe. These men are often esteemed economically and religiously and have a distinct third gender identity, role, and sexual orientation.

congenital adrenal hyperplasia (CAH): The most common type of female pseudohermaphroditism, where a child's endocrine system produces an excess amount of androgens due to an enlargement of the adrenal gland.[2]

CAH girls typically have an enlarged clitoris, with the possibility of nearly complete virilization (masculinization) of the external genitals. In contrast, the internal organs, such as the fallopian tubes, uterus, and upper vagina, develop in typical fashion and reproductive capacity is present.

female pseudohermaphrodite: A genetic female that presents as anatomically sex ambiguous or male at birth. Called "pseudo" by clinicians because the "true" chromosomal and gonadal sex are considered masked by outward ambiguity. The concept of pseudohermaphroditism emerged in Western Europe in the late nineteenth century and is still commonly used in clinical practice today. The most common type of female pseudohermaphroditism is congenital adrenal hyperplasia (CAH).

gender: The social attribution of femininity and masculinity, female and male.

gender identity: The self-attribution of being man, woman, or other.

gender role: The behavioral display or outward expression of socially defined gender.

guevedoche: The Dominican Republic term for boys with 5-alpha-reductase deficiency. This term translates as "balls at 12." These individuals are noted to have a gender which is distinct from either female or male.

hermaphrodite (ditic; tism): Those with genital, chromosomal, or gonadal characteristics that are not entirely female or male. (Synonymous with intersex.)

hijra(s): The third gender category in India, typically comprised of morphologically born men who surgically remove their penises and testicles and live outwardly as flamboyant women. Hijras are believed to possess supernatural powers and perform rituals at marriages and births to confer fertility upon normatively gendered Indians.

hypospadias: A variation in the positioning of the urethral opening on the penis where the opening is displaced from the tip of the penis somewhere along the underside or shaft of the organ.

intersex (ed; ual; uality): Those with genital, chromosomal, or gonadal characteristics that are not entirely female or male. (Synonymous with hermaphrodite.)

karyotype: The chromosomal pairing of an individual's body cell. The karyotype "shows the number, form, size, and arrangement of chromosomes within the nucleus" (Glanze et al. 1996:446).

Klinefelter's Syndrome: "Male" child has a karyotype with more than one X chromosome, such as a 47XXY (or 48XXXY, or 49XXXXY). Genital ambiguity is not present, but testes may be small and firm, and breast development is common. Secondary sex characteristic development is small and these men are almost always sterile.

kwolu-aatmwol: The Papua New Guinea term for 5-alpha-reductase deficiency "boys" which translates as "a female thing changing/transforming into a male thing." These individuals have a gender which is distinct from female or male.

male pseudohermaphrodite: A genetic male that presents as anatomically sex ambiguous or female at birth. Called "pseudo" by clinicians because the "true" chromosomal and gonadal sex are considered masked by outward ambiguity. The concept of pseudohermaphroditism emerged in Western Europe in the late nineteenth century and is still commonly used in clinical practice today. The most common types of male pseudohermaphroditism are AIS and 5-alpha-reductase deficiency.

sex: The primarily physiological traits which define a person as either female or male. Traditionally, these characteristics include genitals, reproductive organs, chromosomes, hormones, and secondary sex characteristics which typically develop during and after puberty.

transgender: Someone whose sex/gender/sexuality cannot be defined within a binary, two sex/gender system. Transgenders' sex/gender/sexual identity may be transient and fluid, covering a range on a continuum of possible sexes/genders/sexualities.

transsexual(s): A person whose gender identity is not congruent with her/his physiological sex.

transvestite(s): A cross-gender-dresser. One who receives pleasure in wearing the clothing of the gender "opposing" her/his physiological sex. (A desire to crossdress does not necessarily connote anything about a person's sexual orientation. Most crossdressers are heterosexual.)

true hermaphrodite: More commonly 46XX than 46XY, but may have either karyotype. Their distinctive feature is that they have both ovarian and testicular tissue. This simultaneous ownership of "female" and "male" tissue may be present in one gonad (e.g., one gonad with one-half testicular and one-half ovarian tissue) or may present itself separately in each gonad (e.g., one gonad is a testicle, the other is an ovary). The external genitalia of true hermaphrodites are ambiguous. This is the most rare form of hermaphroditism. Beginning in the nineteenth century, the conceptual acceptance of true hermaphroditism began to decline, and increasingly physicians and scientists categorized all presenting hermaphrodites as either pseudofemale or pseudomale, further enforcing sex/gender binarism.

true sex: A concept which is rooted in a physiologically ascertainable sex. This concept stems from the widely held Western belief that there is only one sex (which is discernable as either distinctly female or male) per body.

Turner's Syndrome: The most common form of female chromosomal variation where the typical karyotype is 45XO, meaning that one sex chromosome is missing. These girls will develop unambiguous female genitalia, yet will have underdeveloped breasts, uterus, and vagina. Some will have testicular tissue and primitive gonadal "streak" tissue. They commonly do not develop secondary sex characteristics, are very short, and may have a webbed neck, "shield chest," and short fingers and toes.

References

Albrecht, Terrance L., and Mara B. Adelman. 1987. *Communicating Social Support.* Newbury Park, Calif.: Sage Publications.

ALIAS. The biannual newsletter of the Androgen Insensitivity Syndrome support group. <http://www.medhelp.org/www/ais>.

American Academy of Pediatrics, Committee on Genetics. 2000. "Evaluation of the Newborn with Developmental Anomalies of the External Genitalia." *Pediatrics* 106(1):138–142.

Angier, Natalie. 1996. "Intersexual Healing: An Anomaly Finds a Group." *New York Times*, February 4:E14.

———. 1997a. "New Debate over Surgery on Genitals." *New York Times*, May 13:B7.

———. 1997b. "Sexual Identity Not Pliable After All, Report Says." *New York Times*, March 14:A1.

Anspach, Renee R. 1979. "From Stigma to Identity Politics: Political Activism among the Physically Disabled and Former Mental Patients." *Social Science and Medicine* 13A:765–773.

Azo, Portius. 1581. Summa Institutionum. Venice.

Back, Kurt W., and Rebecca C. Taylor. 1976. "Self-Help Groups: Tool or Symbol?" *Journal of Applied Behavioral Sciences* 12:295–309.

Baker, Susan W. 1981. "Psychological Management of Intersex Children." In *Pediatric and Adolescent Endocrinology: Special Issue, The Intersex Child*, 8:261–269.

Barnard, David. 1990. "Healing the Damaged Self: Identity, Intimacy, and Meaning in the Lives of the Chronically Ill." *Perspectives in Biology and Medicine* 33(4):535–546.

Beck, Max. 1997/1998. "Hermaphrodites with Attitude Take to the Streets." *Chrysalis: The Journal of Transgressive Gender Identities* 2(5)(Fall/Winter):45–46, 50.

Becker, Gaylene. 1981. "Coping with Stigma: Lifelong Adaptation of Deaf People." *Social Science and Medicine* 15B:21–24.

Becker, Howard. 1963. *The Outsiders*. New York: Free Press.

Beh, Glenn Hazel, and Milton Diamond. 2000. "An Emerging Ethical and Medical Dilemma: Should Physicians Perform Sex Assignment Surgery on Infants with Ambiguous Genitalia?" *Michigan Journal of Gender and Law* 7(1):1–63.

Bell, Susan. 1990. "Sociological Perspectives on the Medicalization of Menopause." *Annals of the New York Academy of Sciences* 592:173–178.

Bem, Sandra Lipsitz. 1993. *The Lenses of Gender: Transforming the Debate on Sexual Inequality.* New Haven, Conn.: Yale University Press.

———. 1995. "Dismantling Gender Polarization and Compulsory Heterosexuality: Should We Turn the Volume Down or Up?" *Journal of Sex Research* 32(4):329–334.

Berkun, Cleo S. 1986. "On Behalf of Women over 40: Understanding the Importance of the Menopause." *Social Work* 31(5):378–384.

Bin-Abbas, Bassam S., Felix A. Conte, Melvin M. Grumbach, and Selna L. Kaplan. 1999. "Congenital Hypogonadotropic Hypogonadism and Micropenis: Effect of Testosterone Treatment on Adult Penile Size—Why Sex Reversal Is Not Indicated." *Journal of Pediatrics* 134(5):579–583.

Blackless, Melanie, Anthony Charuvastra, Amanda Derryck, Anne Fausto-Sterling, Karl Lauzanne, and Ellen Lee. 2000. "How Sexually Dimorphic Are We?" *American Journal of Human Biology* 12(2):151–166.

Blumer, Herbert. 1969. "Social Movements." In *Studies in Social Movements: A Social Psychological Perspective*, ed. B. McLauglin. New York: Free Press.

Bockting, Walter O. 1995. "Transgender Coming Out: Gender Revolution?" Paper presented at the annual meeting of the Society for the Scientific Study of Sexuality, San Francisco, November 9–12.

———. 1997a. "The Assessment and Treatment of Gender Dysphoria." *Directions in Clinical and Counseling Psychology* 7(11):1–23.

———. 1997b. "Transgender Coming Out: Implications for the Clinical Management of Gender Dysphoria." In *Gender Blending*, ed. Bonnie Bullough, Vern Bullough, and James Elias, 48–52. Amherst, Mass.: Prometheus Books.

Bockting, Walter O., and Eli Coleman.1992. "A Comprehensive Approach to the Treatment of Gender Dysphoria." In *Gender Dysphoria: Interdisciplinary Approaches in Clinical Management*, ed. Walter O. Bockting and Eli Coleman, 131–155. Binghamton, N.Y.: Haworth Press.

Bockting, Walter O., Simon Rosser, and Eli Coleman. 1999. "Transgender HIV Prevention: Community Involvement and Empowerment." *International Journal of Transgenderism* 3(1+2), at <http:/www.symposium.com/ijt/hiv_risk/bockting.htm>.

Bolin, Anne. 1994. "Transcending and Transgendering: Male-to-Female Transsexuals, Dichotomy and Diversity." In *Third Sex, Third Gender: Beyond Sexual Dimorphism in Culture and History*, ed. Gilbert Herdt, 447–486. New York: Zone Books.

Bornstein, Kate. 1994. *Gender Outlaw: On Men, Women, and the Rest of Us*. New York: Routledge.

Boswell, John. 1980. *Christianity, Social Tolerance, and Homosexuality: Gay People in Western Europe from the Beginning of the Christian Era to the Fourteenth Century*. Chicago: University of Chicago Press.

Burawoy, Michael. 1991. "Reconstructing Social Theories." In *Ethnography Unbound: Power and Resistance in the Modern Metropolis*, ed. Michael Burawoy, Alice Burton, Ann Arnett Ferguson, Kathryn J. Fox, Joshua Gamson, Nadine Gartrell, Leslie Hurst, Charles Hurzman, Leslie Salzinger, Josepha Schiffman, and Shiri Ui, 8–27. Berkeley: University of California Press.

Butler, Judith. 1990. *Gender Trouble: Feminism and the Subversion of Identity*. New York: Routledge.

———. 1993. *Bodies That Matter: On the Discursive Limits of "Sex."* New York: Routledge.

Cadden, Joan. 1993. *Meanings of Sex Differences in the Middle Ages: Medicine, Science, and Culture*. New York: Cambridge University Press.

Caldamone, A. A., L. E. Edstrom, M. A. Koyle, R. Rabinowitz, and W. C. Hulbert. 1998. "Buccal Mucosal Grafts for Urethral Reconstruction." *Urology* 51(5A Suppl.):15–19.

Capron, Alexander Morgan, and Richard D'Avino. 1981. "Legal Implications of Intersexuality." In *Pediatric and Adolescent Endocrinology: Special Issue, The Intersex Child*, 8:218–227.

CARES Foundation web site: <http://www.caresfoundation.org/nbs.html>.

Casper, Monica J. 1998. *The Making of the Unborn Patient: A Social Anatomy of Fetal Surgery.* New Brunswick, N.J.: Rutgers University Press.

Cass, Vivienne C. 1979. "Homosexual Identity Formation: A Theoretical Model." *Journal of Homosexuality* 4:219–235.

———. 1984. "Homosexual Identity Formation: Testing a Theoretical Model." *Journal of Sex Research* 20:143–167.

Chanter, Peter the. *De Vitio Sodomitico.*

Chase, Cheryl. 1993. "Letters from Readers." *The Sciences* July/August, 3.

———. 1997. "Making Media: An Intersex Perspective." *Images* Fall:22–25.

———. 1998a. "Affronting Reason." In *Looking Queer: Body Image and Gay Identity in Lesbian, Bisexual, Gay, and Transgender Communities,* ed. Dawn Atkins, 205–219. New York: Harrington Park Press.

———. 1998b. "Hermaphrodites with Attitude: Mapping the Emergence of Intersex Political Activism." *GLQ: A Journal of Lesbian and Gay Studies* 4(2):189–211.

———. 1998c. "Surgical Progress Is Not the Answer to Intersexuality." *Journal of Clinical Ethics* 9(4):385–392.

———. 1999. "Rethinking Treatment for Ambiguous Genitalia." *Pediatric Nursing* 25(4):451–455.

———. 2002. "What Is the Agenda of the Intersex Patient Advocacy Movement." *Endocrinologist* 12:86.

Chase, Cheryl, and Martha Coventry, eds. 1997/1998. "Intersex Awakening" special issue of *Chrysalis: The Journal of Transgressive Gender Identities* 2(5)(Fall/Winter):1–56.

Chicago Hope. 1996. Episode on Intersex. Columbia Broadcasting System, April 4.

Colapinto, John. 1997. "The True Story of John/Joan." *Rolling Stone,* December 11: 54–73, 92–97.

———. 2000. *As Nature Made Him: The Boy Who Was Raised as a Girl.* New York: Harper Collins.

Coleman, Eli. 1981–1982. "Developmental Stages of the Coming Out Process." *Journal of Homosexuality* 7:31–43.

———. 1987. "Assessment of Sexual Orientation." *Journal of Homosexuality* 14(1/2):9–24.

Conrad, Peter. 1975. "The Discovery of Hyperkinesis: Notes on the Medicalization of Deviant Behavior." *Social Problems* 23:12–21.

———. 1992. "Medicalization and Social Control." *Annual Review of Sociology* 18:209–232.

Conrad, Peter, and Joseph W. Schneider. 1992. *Deviance and Medicalization: From Badness to Sickness.* 2d ed. Philadelphia: Temple University Press.

Cooley, Charles Horton. 1964 [1902]. *Human Nature and Social Order.* New York: Charles Scribner's Sons.

Coontz, Stephanie. 1992. *The Way We Never Were: American Families and the Nostalgia Trap.* New York: Basic Books.

Coventry, Martha. 1997/1998. "Finding the Words." *Chrysalis: The Journal of Transgressive Gender Identities* 2(5)(Fall/Winter):27–29.

———. 1998. "The Tyranny of the Esthetic: Surgery's Most Intimate Violation." *On the Issues: The Progressive Woman's Quarterly* 7(3)(Summer):16–20, 60–61.

Cowley, Geoffrey. 1997. "Gender Limbo." *Newsweek,* 19 May, 64–67.

Crawford, Robert. 1980. "Healthism and the Medicalization of Everyday Life." *International Journal of Health Services* 10(3):365–387.

Cross, Sandra K., and Joseph E. Lovett. 1994. "Women's Collective Meanings of Menopause: A Content Analysis." *Journal of Women and Aging* 6(1/2):187–212.

d'Adesky, Anne-Christine. 1996. "The Third Sex." *Out,* September, 104–108, 150.

Dahir, Mubarak. 2000. "Genetics vs. Love. (Same Sex Marriage)." *The Advocate (The National Gay and Lesbian Newsmagazine)* October 10.

Davis, Donna Lee. 1989. "The Newfoundland Change of Life: Insights into the Medicalization of Menopause." *Journal of Cross-Cultural Gerontology* 4(1):49–73.

Davis, Lennard J. 1995. *Enforcing Normalcy: Disability, Deafness, and the Body.* New York: Verso.

Derick. 1997/1998. "In Process." *Chrysalis: The Journal of Transgressive Gender Identities* 2(5):51–52.

Desai, Sindoor S. 1997. "Down Syndrome: A Review of the Literature." *Oral Surgery, Oral Medicine, Oral Pathology, Oral Radiology, and Endodontics.* September. 84(3):279–285.

Devor, Holly. 1989. *Gender Blending: Confronting the Limits of Duality.* Bloomington: Indiana University Press.

———. 1997a. *FTM: Female-to-Male Transsexuals in Society.* Bloomington: Indiana University Press.

———. 1997b. "More Than Manly Women: How Female-to-Male Transsexuals Reject Lesbian Identities." In *Gender Blending,* ed. Bonnie Bullough, Vern Bullough, and James Elias, 87–102. Amherst, Mass.: Prometheus Books.

Diamond, Milton. 1982. "Sexual Identity: Monozygotic Twins Reared in Discordant Sex Roles and a BBC Follow-Up." *Archives of Sexual Behavior* 11(2):181–185.

———. 1993. "Some Genetic Considerations in the Development of Sexual Orientation." In *The Development of Sex Differences and Similarities in Behavior,* ed. M. Haug, R. Whalen, C. Aron, and K. L. Olsen, 291–309. Dordrecht: Kluwer Academic Publishers.

———. 1995. "Sex Reassignment." Paper presented at the annual meeting of the Society for the Scientific Study of Sexuality, San Francisco, November 9–12.

———. 1996a. "Considerations for Sex Assignment—Response." *Journal of Sex and Marital Therapy* 22(3):61–74.

———. 1996b. "Prenatal Disposition and the Clinical Management of Some Pediatric Conditions." *Journal of Sex and Marital Therapy* 22(3):139–147.

———. 1997. "Sexual Identity and Sexual Orientation in Children with Traumatized or Ambiguous Genitalia." *Journal of Sex Research* 34(2):199–211.

———. 1999. "Pediatric Management of Ambiguous and Traumatized Genitalia." *Journal of Urology* 162(3(part 2)):1021–1028.

Diamond, Milton, and Keith Sigmundson. 1997a. "Sex Reassignment at Birth: Long-term Review and Clinical Implications." *Archives of Pediatric and Adolescent Medicine* 150(March):298–304.

———. 1997b. "Management of Intersexuality: Guidelines for Dealing with Persons with Ambiguous Genitalia." *Archives of Pediatric Adolescent Medicine* 151(October):1046–1050.

Dickson, Geri L. 1990. "A Feminist Poststructuralist Analysis of the Knowledge of Menopause." *Advances in Nursing Science* 12(3):15–31.

Donohoe, Patricia K., David M. Powell, and Mary M. Lee. 1991. "Clinical Management of Intersex Abnormalities." *Current Problems in Surgery* 28(8):513–579.

Dreger, Alice Domurat. 1995a. *Doubtful Sex: Cases and Concepts of Hermaphroditism in France and Britain, 1868–1915.* Ph.D. dissertation, Indiana University.

———. 1995b. "Doubtful Sex: The Fate of the Hermaphrodite in Victorian Medicine." *Victorian Studies* (Spring):335–370.

———. 1998a. "'Ambiguous Sex'—or Ambivalent Medicine? Ethical Issues in the Treatment of Intersexuality." *Hastings Center Report* 28(3):24–36.

———. 1998b. *Hermaphrodites and the Medical Invention of Sex.* Cambridge, Mass.: Harvard University Press.

————. 1998c. "A History of Intersexuality: From the Age of Gonads to the Age of Consent." *Journal of Clinical Ethics* 9(4):345–355.

————, ed. 1999a. *Intersex in the Age of Ethics*. Hagerstown, Md.: University Publishing Group.

————. 1999b. "When Medicine Goes Too Far in the Pursuit of Normality." *Health Ethics Today* 10(1) August.

————. 2000. "Jarring Bodies: Thoughts on the Display of Unusual Anatomies." *Perspectives in Biology and Medicine* 43(2):151–172.

————. 2002. "How Academic Feminism Delayed the Intersex Rights Movement . . . and How to Avoid This Kind of Problem in the Future." Guest lecture at the Center for Advanced Feminist Studies, University of Minnesota, January 28.

Eastman, Kathleen Sampson, and Martha O. Loustaunau. 1987. "Reacting to the Medical Bureaucracy: Lay Midwifery as a Birthing Alternative." *Marriage and Family Review* 11(3/4):23–37.

Edgerton, Robert. 1964. "Pokot Intersexuality: An East African Example of the Resolution of Sexual Incongruity." *American Anthropologist* 66(6):1288–1299.

Ehrenreich, Barbara, and Deirdre English. 1990. "The Sexual Politics of Sickness." In *The Sociology of Health and Illness: Critical Perspectives*, ed. Peter Conrad and Rochelle Kern, 270–284. New York: St. Martin's Press.

Elliot, Carl. 1998. "Why Can't We Go On as Three?" *Hastings Center Report* 28(3):36–39.

Epstein, Julia. 1990. "Either/Or—Neither/Both: Sexual Ambiguity and the Ideology of Gender." *Genders* 7(Spring):99–142.

Fausto-Sterling, Anne. 1985. *Myths of Gender*. New York: Basic Books.

————. 1993. "The Five Sexes: Why Male and Female Are Not Enough." *The Sciences* 33(2):20–25.

————. 1996. "How to Build a Man." In *Science and Homosexualities*, ed. Vernon A. Rosario, 219–225. New York: Routledge.

————. 2000a. *Sexing the Body: Gender Politics and the Construction of Sexuality*. New York: Basic Books.

————. 2000b. "The Five Sexes, Revisited." *The Sciences* 40(4):18–23.

Feinberg, Leslie. 1996. *Transgender Warriors: Making History from Joan of Arc to RuPaul*. Boston: Beacon Press.

Fiedler, Leslie. 1978. *Freaks: Myths and Images of the Secret Self*. New York: Anchor Books, Doubleday.

Findlay, Deborah. 1995. "Discovering Sex: Medical Science, Feminism, and Intersexuality." *Canadian Review of Sociology and Anthropology*, 32(1):25–52.

Fine, Michelle, and Virginia Vanderslice. 1992. "Qualitative Activist Research: Reflections on Methods and Politics." In *Methodological Issues in Applied Psychology*, ed. Fred B. Bryan, John Edwards, R. Scott Tindale, Emil J. Posavac, Linda Heath, Aaron Henderson, and Yolanda Suarez-Balcazar, 199–218. New York: Plenum Press.

Fisher, Sue, and Stephen B. Groce. 1985. "Doctor-Patient Negotiation of Cultural Assumptions." *Sociology of Health and Illness* 7(3):342–374.

Flaubert, Gustave. (1887) 1965. *Madame Bovary*. Trans. Paul de Man. New York: Norton.

Ford, Kishka-Kamari. 2001. "'First, Do No Harm'—The Fiction of Legal Parental Consent to Genital-Normalizing Surgery on Intersexed Infants." *Yale Law and Policy Review* 19:469–488.

Foucault, Michel. 1970. *The Order of Things: An Archaeology of the Human Sciences*. New York: Vintage Books.

————. 1972. *The Archaeology of Knowledge and the Discourse on Language*. Trans. A. M. Sheridan Smith. New York: Pantheon Books.

———. 1978. *The History of Sexuality*. Vol. 1. Trans. Robert Hurley. New York: Pantheon.

———. 1980. *Herculine Barbin: Being the Recently Discovered Memoirs of a Nineteenth-Century French Hermaphrodite*. New York: Pantheon.

Fox, Renee C. 1990. "The Medicalization and Demedicalization of American Society." In *The Sociology of Health and Illness: Critical Perspectives*, ed. Peter Conrad and Rochelle Kern, 409–413. New York: St. Martin's Press.

Freeman, Jo. 1999. "On the Origins of Social Movements." In *Waves of Protest: Social Movements since the Sixties, People, Passions, and Power*, ed. Jo Freeman and Victoria Johnson, 7–24. Lanham, Md.: Rowman and Littlefield Publishers.

Freidson, Elliot. 1970. *Profession of Medicine*. New York: Dodd, Mead.

Freire, Paulo. 1970. *Pedagogy of the Oppressed*. New York: Continuum.

Gagne, Patricia, Richard Tewksbury, and Deanna McGaughey. 1997. "Coming Out and Crossing Over: Identity Formation and Proclamation in a Transgender Community." *Gender and Society* 11(4):478–509.

Galen. [170 C.E.] 1916. *On the Natural Faculties*. Trans. Arthur John Brock. New York: Appleton and Company.

Gamson, William A. 1992. "The Social Psychology of Collective Action." In *Frontiers in Social Movement Theory*, ed. Aldon Morris and Carol McClurg Mueller, 53–76. New Haven, Conn.: Yale University Press.

Garfinkel, Harold. 1967. *Studies in Ethnomethodology*. Englewood Cliffs, N.J.: Prentice-Hall.

Gecas, Viktor. 1989. "The Social Psychology of Self-Efficacy." *Annual Review of Sociology* 15:291–316.

———. 1991. "The Self-Concept as a Basis for a Theory of Motivation." In *The Self-Society Dynamic*, ed. Judith A. Howard and Peter L. Callero, 171–185. Cambridge: Cambridge University Press.

Gecas, Viktor, and Michael L. Schwalbe. 1983. "Beyond the Looking-Glass Self: Social Structure and Self-Efficacy-Based Self-Esteem." *Social Psychology Quarterly* 46(2):77–88.

Glanze, Walter D., Kenneth N. Anderson, and Lois E. Anderson. 1996. *The Signet Mosby Medical Encyclopedia*. Rev. ed. New York: Signet.

Glaser, Barney G., and Anselm L. Strauss. 1967. *The Discovery of Grounded Theory: Strategies for Qualitative Research*. Chicago: Aldine Publishing Company.

Glassberg, Kenneth I. 1999. "Editorial: Gender Assignment and the Pediatric Urologist." *Journal of Urology* 161(April):1308–1310.

Goffman, Erving. 1959. *The Presentation of Self in Everyday Life*. New York: Anchor Press.

———. 1961. *Asylums: Essays on the Social Situation of Mental Patients and Other Inmates*. Garden City, N.J.: Anchor Press.

———. 1963. *Stigma: Notes on the Management of Spoiled Identity*. Englewood Cliffs, N.J.: Prentice-Hall.

———. 1974. *Frame Analysis: An Essay on the Organization of Experience*. Cambridge, Mass.: Harvard University Press.

———. 1982. *Interaction Ritual*. New York: Pantheon Books.

Greenberg, David F. 1988. *The Construction of Homosexuality*. Chicago: University of Chicago Press.

Greenberg, Julie A. 1999. "Defining Male and Female: Intersexuality and the Collision between Law and Biology." *Arizona Law Review* 41(2):265–328.

Groveman, Sherri A. 1998. "The Hanukkah Bush: Ethical Implications in the Clinical Management of Intersex." *Journal of Clinical Ethics* 9(4):356–359.

Grumbach, Melvin M., and Felix A. Conte. 1998. "Disorders of Sex Differentiation."

In *Williams Textbook of Endocrinology*, ed. Jean D. Wilson, Daniel W. Foster, Henry M. Kronenberg, and P. Reed Larsen, 1303–1425. Philadelphia: W. B. Saunders.

Hahn, Harlan. 1988. "Can Disability Be Beautiful?" *Social Policy* 18(3):26–32.

Harvey, Kay. 1999. "A Mother's Dilemma." *St. Paul Pioneer Press*, March 4:1F.

Hassibi, Mahin. 1998. "Designing Sex: Playing God, Have Doctors Gone Too Far?" *On the Issues: The Progressive Woman's Quarterly* Summer:13–15.

Hawkesworth, Mary. 1997. "Confounding Gender." *Signs: Journal of Women in Culture and Society* 22(3):649–685.

Hawley, Donna Lee. 1977. "The Legal Problems of Sex Determination." *Alberta Law Review* 15:122–141.

Hekma, Gert. 1994. "A Female Soul in a Male Body: Sexual Inversion as Gender Inversion in Nineteenth-Century Sexology." In *Third Sex, Third Gender: Beyond Sexual Dimorphism in Culture and History*, ed. Gilbert Herdt, 213–239. New York: Zone Books.

Hendricks, Melissa. 1993. "Is It a Boy or a Girl?" *Johns Hopkins Magazine*, November:10–16.

Herdt, Gilbert. 1994. "Mistaken Sex: Culture, Biology and the Third Sex in New Guinea." In *Third Sex, Third Gender: Beyond Sexual Dimorphism in Culture and History*, ed. Gilbert Herdt, 419–445. New York: Zone Books.

———. 1998. *Same Sex, Different Cultures: Exploring Gay and Lesbian Lives.* Boulder, Colo.: Westview Press.

Hermaphrodites with Attitude. The quarterly publication of the Intersex Society of North America. <http://www.isna.org>.

Hewitt, John P. 1970. *Social Stratification and Deviant Behavior.* New York: Random House.

———. 1989. *Dilemmas of the American Self.* Philadelphia: Temple University Press.

Hird, Myra J. 2000. "Gender's Nature: Intersexuality, Transsexualism and the 'Sex'/'Gender' Binary." *Feminist Theory* 1(3):347–364.

Hird, Myra J., and Jenz Germon. 2001. "The Intersexual Body and the Medical Regulation of Gender." In *Constructing Gendered Bodies*, ed. Kathryn Backett-Milburn and Linda McKie, 162–178. New York: Palgrave.

Holmes, Morgan M. 1994. *Medical Politics and Cultural Imperatives: Intersexual Identities beyond Pathology and Erasure.* Master's Thesis. York University.

———. 1995. "Queer Cut Bodies: Intersexuality and Homophobia in Medical Practice." Paper presented at the fifth annual National Lesbian, Gay and Bisexual Graduate Student Queer Frontiers Conference, March 23–26, University of Southern California.

———. 1997/1998. "Is Growing up in Silence Better Than Growing up Different?" *Chrysalis: The Journal of Transgressive Gender Identities* 2(5)(Fall/Winter):7–9.

———. 1998. "In(to) Visibility: Intersexuality in the Field of Queer." In *Looking Queer: Body Image and Gay Identity in Lesbian, Bisexual, Gay, and Transgender Communities*, ed. Dawn Atkins, 221–226. New York: Harrington Park Press.

Holstein, James A., and Jaber F. Gubrium. 2000. *The Self We Live By: Narrative Identity in a Postmodern World.* New York: Oxford University Press.

Horowitz, Mark, and Kenneth I. Glassberg. 1992. "Ambiguous Genitalia: Diagnosis, Evaluation, and Treatment." *Urologic Radiology* 14(4):306–318.

Horowitz, Sarah. 1995. "The Middle Sex." *San Francisco Weekly*, February 1, 11–13.

Howard, Judith A., and Jocelyn Hollander. 1997. *Gendered Situations, Gendered Selves.* Newbury Park, Calif.: Sage Publications.

Hubbard, Ruth. 1990. *The Politics of Women's Biology.* New Brunswick, N.J.: Rutgers University Press.

Imperato-McGinley, J., L. Guerro, T. Gautier, and R. E. Peterson. 1974. "Steroid 5-

alpha Reductase Deficiency in Man: An Inherited Form of Male Pseudohermaph-
    roditism." *Science* 186(4170):1213–1215.
Imperato-McGinley, J., R. E. Peterson, T. Gautier, and E. Sturla. 1979. "Androgens
    and the Evaluation of Male-Gender Identity among Male Pseudohermaphrodites
    with 5-alpha Reductase Deficiency." *New England Journal of Medicine*
    300(22):1233–1237.
Inside Edition. 1997. "Caught in the Middle." National Broadcasting Company, Sep-
    tember 11.
ISNA (Intersex Society of North America). The web site can be found at <http://
    www.isna.org>.
ISNA News Release. 2000. "North American task force on intersex formed, seeks broad
    interdisciplinary consensus on treatment." February 23.
Jacobs, Sue-Ellen, Wesley Thomas, and Sabine Lang, eds. 1997. "Introduction" to their
    Two-Spirit People: Native American Gender Identity, Sexuality, and Spirituality. Chi-
    cago: University of Illinois Press.
Johnson, Roberta Ann. 1983. "Mobilizing the Disabled." In *Social Movements of the
    Sixties and Seventies,* ed. Jo Freeman. New York: Longman.
Jones, Ann Rosalind, and Peter Stallybrass. 1991. "Fetishizing Gender: Constructing
    the Hermaphrodite in Renaissance Europe." In *Body Guards: The Cultural Politics
    of Gender Ambiguity,* ed. Julia Epstein and Kristina Straub, 80–111. New York:
    Routledge.
Jones, Edward E., Amerigo Farina, Albert H. Hastorf, Hazel Markus, Dale T. Miller,
    and Robert A. Scott. 1984. *Social Stigma: The Psychology of Marked Relationships.*
    New York: W. H. Freeman.
Jorgensen, Christine. [1967] 2000. *Christine Jorgensen: A Personal Autobiography.* San
    Francisco: Cleis Press.
Josso, Nathalie. 1981. "Physiology of Sex Differentiation: A Guide to the Understand-
    ing and Management of the Intersex Child." In *Pediatric and Adolescent Endocri-
    nology: Special Issue, The Intersex Child,* 8:1–13.
Jost, A. 1981. "Forward." In *Pediatric and Adolescent Endocrinology: Special Issue, The
    Intersex Child,* 8:vii–viii.
Kaldera, Raven. 1998. "Agdistis' Children: Living Bi-Gendered in a Single-Gendered
    World." In *Looking Queer: Body Image and Gay Identity in Lesbian, Bisexual, Gay,
    and Transgender Communities,* ed. Dawn Atkins, 227–232. New York: Harrington
    Park Press.
Karraker, Katherine Hildebrandt, Dena Ann Vogel, and Margaret Ann Lake. 1995.
    "Parents' Gender-Stereotyped Perceptions of Newborns: The Eye of the Beholder
    Revisited." *Sex Roles* 33:687–701.
Kemp, B. Diane, Sherri A. Groveman, Anonymous, H. Deni Tako, Karl M. Irwin,
    Anita Natarajan, and Patrick Sullivan. 1996. "Sex, Lies and Androgen Insensi-
    tivity Syndrome." *Canadian Medical Association Journal* 154(12):1829–1833.
Kessler, Suzanne J. 1990. "The Medical Construction of Gender: Case Management
    of Intersexed Infants." *Signs: Journal of Women in Culture and Society* 16(1):3–26.
————. 1997/1998. "Meanings of Genital Variability." *Chrysalis: The Journal of Trans-
    gressive Gender Identities* 2(4)(Fall/Winter):33–38.
————. 1998. *Lessons from the Intersexed.* New Brunswick, N.J.: Rutgers University Press.
Kessler, Suzanne J., and Wendy McKenna. 1978. *Gender: An Ethnomethodological Ap-
    proach.* Chicago: University of Chicago Press.
Kipnis, Kenneth, and Milton Diamond. 1998. "Pediatric Ethics and the Surgical As-
    signment of Sex." *Journal of Clinical Ethics* 9(4):398–410.
Klandermans, Bert. 1992. "The Social Construction of Protest and Multiorganizational
    Fields." In *Frontiers in Social Movement Theory,* ed. Aldon Morris and Carol
    McClurg Mueller, 77–103. New Haven, Conn.: Yale University Press.

Klebs, Theodore Albrecht Edwin. 1876. *Handbuch der pathologischen Anatomie [Handbook of Pathological Anatomy]*. Berlin: A. Hirschwald.

Kohlberg, Lawrence A. 1966. "A Cognitive-Developmental Analysis of Children's Sex-Role Concepts and Attitudes." In *The Development of Sex Differences*, ed. Eleanor Maccoby. Stanford, Calif.: Stanford University Press.

Krieger, Susan. 1991. *Social Science and the Self: Personal Essays on an Art Form*. New Brunswick, N.J.: Rutgers University Press.

Kubler-Ross, Elizabeth. 1969. *On Death and Dying*. New York: Macmillan.

Kuhn, Thomas S. 1962. *The Structure of Scientific Revolutions*. Chicago: University of Chicago Press.

Kupfer, Stuart R., Charmaine A. Quigley, and Frank S. French. 1992. "Male Pseudohermaphroditism." *Seminars in Perinatology* 16(5):319–331.

Laqueur, Thomas. 1990. *Making Sex: Body and Gender from the Greeks to Freud*. Cambridge, Mass.: Harvard University Press.

Leavitt, Judith W. 1989. "The Medicalization of Childbirth in the Twentieth Century." *Transactions and Studies of the College Physicians of Philadelphia Set 5*, 11(4):299–319.

Lebacqz, Karen. 1997. "Difference or Defect? Intersexuality and the Politics of Difference." *Annual of the Society of Christian Ethics*, 213–229.

Lee, Ellen Hyun-Ju. 1994. *Producing Sex: An Interdisciplinary Perspective of Sex Assignment Decisions for Intersexuals*. Senior thesis, Brown University.

Lee, John Alan. 1977. "Going Public: A Study in the Sociology of Homosexual Liberation." *Journal of Homosexuality* 3(1):49–78.

Light, Donald W. 1989. "Social Control and the American Health Care System." In *Handbook of Medical Sociology*, 4th ed., ed. Howard E. Freeman and Sol Levine, 456–474. Englewood Cliffs, N.J.: Prentice-Hall.

———. 2000. "The Medical Profession and Organizational Change: From Professional Dominance to Countervailing Power." In *Handbook of Medical Sociology*, 5th ed., ed. Chloe E. Bird, Peter Conrad, and Allen M. Fremont, 201–216. Englewood Cliffs, N.J.: Prentice-Hall.

Longino, Helen E. 1990. *Science as Social Knowledge: Values and Objectivity in Scientific Inquiry*. Princeton, N.J.: Princeton University Press.

Lorber, Judith. 1994. *Paradoxes of Gender*. New Haven, Conn.: Yale University Press.

Loury, Glenn C. 1996. "Address: Individualism before Multiculturalism." *Harvard Journal of Law and Public Policy* 19(3):723–731.

Lum, Matt. 2002. "'Slap in the Face': Christie Lee Littleton's Historic Texas Court Ruling Crosses State Lines to Deny Equality." *Texas Triangle*, March 22:20.

MacKenzie, Gordene Olga. 1994. *Transgender Nation*. Bowling Green, Ohio: Bowling Green State University Popular Press.

Mackey, Marlene C. 1990. "Women's Choice of Childbirth Setting." *Health Care for Women International* 11:175–189.

Maguire, Lambert. 1983. *Understanding Social Networks*. Beverly Hills, Calif.: Sage Publications.

Martin, Emily. 1987. *The Woman in the Body: A Cultural Analysis of Reproduction*. Boston: Beacon Press.

Martinez-Pineiro, J. A., L. Martinez-Pineiro, and A. Tabernero. 1998. "Substitution Urethroplasties with Free Graft Buccal Mucosa." *Archivos Espanoles de Urologia* 51(7):645–659.

Mason-Schrock, Doug. 1996. "Transsexuals' Narrative Construction of the 'True Self.'" *Social Psychology Quarterly* 59:176–192.

McClintock, Jeff. 1997/1998. "Growing up in the Surgical Maelstrom." *Chrysalis: The Journal of Transgressive Gender Identities* 2(5)(Fall/Winter):53–54.

Mead, George Herbert. 1934. *Mind, Self and Society*. Chicago: University of Chicago Press.

Meyer-Bahlburg, Heino. 1993. "Gender Identity Development in Intersex Patients." *Child and Adolescent Psychiatric Clinics of North America* 2(3):501–512.

———. 1998. "Gender Assignment in Intersexuality." *Journal of Psychology and Human Sexuality* 10:1–21.

Meyers-Seifer, Cynthia H., and Nancy J. Charest. 1992. "Diagnosis and Management of Patients with Ambiguous Genitalia." *Seminars in Perinatology* 16(5):332–339.

Mills, C. Wright. 1959. *The Sociological Imagination*. New York: Oxford University Press.

Minton, H. L., and G. J. McDonald. 1984. "Homosexual Identity Formation as a Developmental Process." *Journal of Homosexuality* 9:91–104.

Mona, Linda. 1998. "Cognitive Adaption Styles and Sexual Self-Esteem as Predictors of Sexual and Psychological Adjustment Following Spinal Cord Injury." Paper presented at the annual meeting of the Society for the Scientific Study of Sexuality, Los Angeles, November 11–15.

Money, John. 1952. "Hermaphroditism: An Inquiry into the Nature of a Human Paradox." Ph.D. dissertation, Harvard University.

———. 1968. *Sex Errors of the Body: Dilemmas, Education, Counseling*. Baltimore, Md.: Johns Hopkins University Press.

———. 1975. "Ablatio Penis: Normal Male Infant Sex-Reassignment as a Girl." *Archives of Sexual Behavior* 4(1):65–71.

———. 1985. "The Conceptual Neutering of Gender and the Criminalization of Sex." *Archives of Sexual Behavior* 14(3):279–290.

———. 1989. *The Geraldo Rivera Show*. "Hermaphrodites: The Sexually Unfinished." National Broadcasting Company, July 27.

———. 1991a. *Biographies of Gender and Hermaphroditism in Paired Comparisons*. Amsterdam: Elsevier Science Publishers.

———. 1991b. "Serendipities on the Sexological Pathway to Research in Gender Identity and Sex Research." *Journal of Psychology and Human Sexuality* 4(1):101–113.

———. 1994. *Sex Errors of the Body and Related Syndromes*. Baltimore, Md.: Paul H. Brookes.

———. 1995. *Gendermaps: Social Constructionism, Feminism, and Sexosophical History*. New York: Continuum.

Money, John, and Anke Ehrhardt. 1972. *Man and Woman Boy and Girl: The Differentiation and Dimorphism of Gender Identity from Conception to Maturity*. Baltimore, Md.: Johns Hopkins University Press.

Money, John, Joan G. Hampson, and John L. Hampson. 1955. "Hermaphroditism: Recommendations concerning Assignment of Sex, Change of Sex, and Psychologic Management." *Bulletin of the Johns Hopkins Hospital* 97(4):284–300.

Moreno, Angela. 1997/1998. "In Amerika They Call Us Hermaphrodites." *Chrysalis: The Journal of Transgressive Gender Identities* 2(5)(Fall/Winter):11–12.

Moreno, Angela, and Jan Goodwin. 1998. "Am I a Woman or a Man?" *Mademoiselle*, March, 178–181, 208.

Moscucci, Ornella. 1991. "Hermaphroditism and Sex Difference: The Construction of Gender in Victorian England." In *Science and Sensibility: Gender and Scientific Enquiry, 1780–1945*, ed. Marina Benjamin, 174–199. Williston, Fla.: Basil Blackwell.

Namaste, Ki. 1996. "The Politics of Inside/Out: Queer Theory, Poststructuralism, and a Sociological Approach to Sexuality." In *Queer Theory/Sociology*, ed. Steven Seidman, 194–212. Cambridge, Mass.: Blackwell Publishers.

Nanda, Serena. 1990. *Neither Man Nor Woman: The Hijras of India*. Belmont: Wadsworth Publishing Company.

———. 1994. "Hijras: An Alternative Sex and Gender Role in India." In *Third Sex, Third Gender: Beyond Sexual Dimorphism in Culture and History*, ed. Gilbert Herdt, 373–417. New York: Zone Books.

Natarajan, Anita. 1996. "Medical Ethics and Truth Telling in the Case of Androgen Insensitivity." *Canadian Medical Association Journal* 154(4):568–570.

NATFI (North American Task Force on Intersexuality) web site. <http://www.natfi.org>.

National Center for Health Statistics. 2001. "Births: Preliminary Data for 2000." NVSR 49, No. 5. 20 pp. (PHS) 2001–1120.

NBC Dateline. 1997. "Gender Limbo." National Broadcasting Company, June 17.

Nederman, Cary J., and Jacqui True. 1996. "The Third Sex: The Idea of the Hermaphrodite in Twelfth-Century Europe." *Journal of the History of Sexuality* 6(4):497–517.

Ned Katz, Jonathan. 1996. *The Invention of Heterosexuality.* New York: E. P. Dutton and Co.

New, Maria I. 1992. "Female Pseudohermaphroditism." *Seminars in Perinatology* 16(5):299–318.

New, Maria, A. B. Mercado, and R. C. Wilson. 1994. "Prenatal Hormonal Therapy Correcting Genital Ambiguity in Adrenal Steroid 21-Hydroxylase Deficient Genetic Females." In *New Trends in Neonatal Screening*, ed. N. Takasugi and H. Naruse, 111–116. Sapporo: Hokkaido Univeristy Press.

Newman, David. 2002. *Sociology: Exploring the Architecture of Everyday Life.* 4th ed. Thousand Oaks, Calif.: Pine Forge Press.

Newman, Judith. 2001. "How Sexism and Bad Science Have Teamed Up against Athletes." *SportsJones*, August 24.

Nicholson, Sven. 1997/1998. "Take Charge! A Guide to Home Catheterization." *Chrysalis: The Journal of Transgressive Gender Identities* 2(5)(Fall/Winter):39–42.

Nussbaum, Emily. 1999. "The Sex That Dare Not Speak Its Name." *Lingua Franca: The Review of Academic Life* 9(4):42–51.

———. 2000. "A Question of Gender." *Discover,* January: 92–99.

Ormrod, Roger. 1972. "The Medico-Legal Aspects of Sex Determination." *Medico-Legal Journal* 40(3):78–88.

Pagliassotti, Druann. 1993. "On the Discursive Construction of Sex and Gender." *Communication Research* 20(3):472–493.

Pare, Ambroise. (1634) 1968. *The Collected Works of Ambroise Pare.* Trans. Thomas Johnson. New York: Milford House.

Parsons, Talcott. 1968. "Cooley and the Problem of Internalization." In *Cooley and Sociological Analysis*, ed. Albert J. Reiss, 48–67. Ann Arbor: University of Michigan Press.

Pierce, Jennifer. 1995. *Gender Trials: Emotional Lives in Contemporary Law Firms.* Berkeley: University of California Press.

Plummer, Ken. 1975. *Sexual Stigma.* Boston: Routledge and Kegan Paul.

———. 1995. *Telling Sexual Stories: Power, Change and Social Worlds.* New York: Routledge.

Preves, Sharon E. 1995. "The Role of Social Support in Redefining Menopausal Transitions: An In-Depth Qualitative Exploration." Unpublished manuscript. University of Minnesota, Department of Sociology.

———. 1998. "For the Sake of the Children: Destigmatizing Intersexuality." *Journal of Clinical Ethics: Special Issue on Intersex* 9(4):411–420.

———. 1999a. "Sexing the Intersexed: Lived Experiences in Socio-Cultural Context." Ph.D. dissertation, University of Minnesota.

———. 1999b. "For the Sake of the Children: Destigmatizing Intersexuality." In

Intersex in the Age of Ethics, ed. Alice Dreger, 50–65. Hagerstown, Md.: University Publishing Group.

———. 2000. "Negotiating the Constraints of Gender Binarism: Intersexuals Challenge Gender Categorization." *Current Sociology* 48(3):27–50.

———. 2002. "Sexing the Intersexed: An Analysis of Socio-Cultural Responses to Intersexuality." *Signs: Journal of Women in Culture and Society* 27(2):523–556.

Preves, Sharon E., and A. Evan Eyler. 1999. "Belief in Having Been Born Intersexed as a Psychological Defense among 'Transphobic' Transsexuals: Report of Three Cases." Harry Benjamin International Gender Dysphoria Association. August; London, England.

Prime Time Live. 1997. "Boy or Girl?" American Broadcasting Company, September 3.

Quigley, Charmaine A., A. De Bellis, K. B. Merschke, M. K. El-Awady, E. M. Wilson, and Frank S. French. 1995. "Androgen Receptor Defects: Historical, Clinical and Molecular Perspectives." *Endocrine Review* 16(3):271–321.

Reilly, Justine M., and C. R. J. Woodhouse. 1989. "Small Penis and the Male Sexual Role." *Journal of Urology* 142(August):569–572.

Reinberg, Yuri. 1999. "Evaluation and Treatment of Children Born with Ambiguous Genitalia: Current Controversies in the Field of Sexual Reassignment." Grand Rounds Presentation, University of Minnesota Medical School; Minneapolis, January 27.

Reiner, William G. 1999. "Assignment of Sex in Neonates with Ambiguous Genitalia." *Current Opinion in Pediatrics* 11:363–365.

Reinharz, Shulamit. 1992. *Feminist Methods in Social Research*. New York: Oxford University Press.

Relman, Arnold S. 1990. "The New Medical-Industrial Complex." In *The Sociology of Health and Illness: Critical Perspectives*, ed. Peter Conrad and Rochelle Kern, 209–217. New York: St. Martin's Press.

Roberts, Helen E., Janet D. Cragan, Joanne Cono, Muin J. Khoury, Mark R. Weatherly, and Cynthia A. Moore. 1998. "Increased Frequency of Cystic Fibrosis among Infants with Jejunoileal Atresia." *American Journal of Medical Genetics* 78: 446–449.

Romalis, Shelly. 1981. *Childbirth: Alternatives to Medical Control*. Austin: University of Texas Press.

Rosario, Vernon A. 1997. "Review of Changing Sex: Transsexualism, Technology, and the Idea of Gender, by Bernice Hausman." *Configurations* 5:243–246.

Roscoe, Will. 1994. "How to Become a Berdache: Toward a Unified Analysis of Gender Diversity." In *Third Sex, Third Gender: Beyond Sexual Dimorphism in Culture and History*, ed. Gilbert Herdt, 329–372. New York: Zone Books.

Rosenberg, Pearl P. 1984. "Support Groups: A Special Therapeutic Entity." *Small Group Behavior* 15(2):173–186.

Rothblatt, Martine. 1995. *The Apartheid of Sex: A Manifesto on the Freedom of Gender*. New York: Crown Publishers.

Rothman, Barbara Katz. 1990. "Midwives in Transition: The Structure of a Clinical Revolution." In *The Sociology of Health and Illness: Critical Perspectives*, ed. Peter Conrad and Rochelle Kern, 339–347. New York: St. Martin's Press.

Sadker, Myra, and David Sadker. 1994. *Failing at Fairness: How America's Schools Cheat Girls*. New York: Charles Scribner's Sons.

Sandstrom, Kent L. 1990. "Confronting Deadly Disease: The Drama of Identity Construction among Gay Men with AIDS." *Journal of Contemporary Ethnography* 19(3):271–294.

Sapir, E. 1929. "The Status of Linguistics as a Science." *Language* 5:207–214.

Schober, Justine Murat. 1998a. "Feminizing Genitoplasty for Intersex." In *Pediatric Surgery and Urology: Long-Term Outcomes*, ed. M. D. Stringer, K. T. Oldham, P. D. E. Mouriquand, and E. R. Howard, 549–558. Philadelphia: W. B. Saunders.

———. 1998b. "A Surgeon's Response to the Intersex Controversy." *Journal of Clinical Ethics* 9(4):393–397.

Schwalbe, Michael L., and Douglas Mason-Schrock. 1996. "Identity Work as Group Process." *Advances in Group Processes* 13:113–147.

Schwartz Cowan, R. 1992. "Genetic Technology and Reproductive Choice: An Ethics for Autonomy." In *The Code of Codes: Scientific and Social Issues in the Human Genome Project*, ed. Daniel J. Kevles and Leroy Hood, 244–263. Cambridge, Mass.: Harvard University Press.

Scott, Joan W. 1993. "The Evidence of Experience." In *The Lesbian and Gay Studies Reader*, ed. Henry Abelove, Michele Aina Barale, and David M. Halperin, 397–415. New York: Routledge.

Seeman, M. 1959. "On the Meaning of Alienation." *American Sociological Review* 24:783–791.

Seidman, Steven. 1995. "Identity and Politics in a 'Postmodern' Gay Culture: Some Historical and Conceptual Notes." In *Fear of a Queer Planet: Queer Politics and Social Theory*, ed. Michael Warner, 105–142. Minneapolis: University of Minnesota Press.

Shively, Michael G., and John P. De Cecco. 1977. "Components of Sexual Identity." *Journal of Homosexuality* 3(1):41–49.

Shumaker, Sally A., and Arlene Brownell. 1984. "Toward a Theory of Social Support: Closing Conceptual Gaps." *Journal of Social Issues* 40(4):11–36.

Slaughenhoupt, Bruce L., and John G. Van Savage. 1999. "The Child with Ambiguous Genitalia." *Infectious Urology* 12(4):113–118.

Snow, David, and Leon Anderson. 1987. "Identity Work among the Homeless: The Verbal Construction and Avowal of Personal Identities." *American Journal of Sociology* 92:1336–1371.

Snyder, Mark. 1986. "On the Nature of Self-Monitoring: Matters of Assessment, Matters of Validity." *Journal of Personality and Social Psychology* 51:125–139.

Stone, Sandy. 1991. "The *Empire* Strikes Back." In *Body Guards: The Cultural Politics of Gender Ambiguity*, ed. Julia Epstein and Kristina Straub, 280–304. New York: Routledge.

Strauss, Anselm, and Juliet Corbin. 1991. "Experiencing Body Failure and a Disrupted Self-Image." In *Creating Sociological Awareness*, ed. Anselm Strauss, 341–359. New Brunswick, N.J.: Transaction Publishers.

Sudsman, Joan. 1994. "Disability, Stigma and Deviance." *Social Science and Medicine* 38(1):15–22.

Suler, John. 1984. "The Role of Ideology in Self-Help Groups." *Social Policy* Winter: 29–36.

Sumner, Phillip E., and Celeste R. Phillips. 1981. *Birthing Rooms: Concept and Reality*. St. Louis, Mo.: C. V. Mosby.

Thorne, Barrie. 1993. *Gender Play: Girls and Boys in School*. New Brunswick, N.J.: Rutgers University Press.

Triea, Kiira. 1997. "As a Former Intersexed Patient." Letter in *Time*, April 14:19.

———. 1997/1998. "Power, Orgasm and the Psychohormonal Research Unit." *Chrysalis: The Journal of Transgressive Gender Identities* 2(5)(Fall/Winter):23–24.

Trumbach, Randolph. 1994. "London's Sapphists: From Three Sexes to Four Genders in the Making of Modern Culture." In *Third Sex, Third Gender: Beyond Sexual Dimorphism in Culture and History*, ed. Gilbert Herdt, 111–136. New York: Zone Books.

Turner, Brian S. 1987. *Medical Power and Social Knowledge*. London: Sage Publications.

Turner, Stephanie S. 1999. "Intersex Identities: Locating New Intersections of Sex and Gender." *Gender and Society* 13(4):457–479.

U.S. Department of Commerce. 2000. Bureau of the Census *Current Population Survey*. Unpublished data, July.

Van Seters, A. P., and A. K. Slob. 1988. "Mutually Gratifying Heterosexual Relationship with Micropenis of Husband." *Journal of Sex and Marital Therapy* 14(2): 98–107.

Vargo, Marc E. 1998. *Acts of Disclosure: The Coming-Out Process of Contemporary Gay Men*. New York: Harrington Park Press.

Voorhess, Martin L. 1982. "Normal and Abnormal Sexual Development." In *Core Textbook of Pediatrics*, ed. Robert Kaye, Frank A. Oski, and Lewis A. Barness, 214–237. 2d ed. Philadelphia: J. B. Lippincott.

Walcutt, Heidi. 1997/1998. "Time for a Change." *Chrysalis: The Journal of Transgressive Gender Identities* 2(5)(Fall/Winter):25–26.

Warne, Garry L. 1997. *Complete Androgen Insensitivity Syndrome*. Victoria, Australia: Department of Endocrinology and Diabetes. Royal Children's Hospital.

Weber, Robert Phillip. 1990. *Basic Content Analysis*. 2d ed. Newbury Park, Calif.: Sage Publications.

Weeks, Jeffrey. 1985. *Sexuality and Its Discontents: Meanings, Myths and Modern Sexualities*. New York: Routledge.

Wertz, Richard W., and Dorothy C. Wertz. 1990. "Notes on the Decline of Midwives and the Rise of Medical Obstetricians." In *The Sociology of Health and Illness: Critical Perspectives*, ed. Peter Conrad and Rochelle Kern, 148–160. New York: St. Martin's Press.

West, Candace, and Don H. Zimmerman. 1987. "Doing Gender." *Gender and Society* 1(2):125–151.

Whorf, B. 1956. *Language, Thought and Reality*. Cambridge, Mass.: MIT Press.

Williams, Walter L. 1986. *The Spirit and the Flesh: Sexuality Diversity in American Indian Culture*. Boston: Beacon Press.

Wilson, Bruce E., and William G. Reiner. 1998. "Management of Intersex: A Shifting Paradigm." *Journal of Clinical Ethics* 9(4):360–369.

Wilson, Elizabeth A. 1998. *Neural Geographies: Feminism and the Microstructure of Cognition*. New York: Routledge.

Writing Group from the Women's Health Initiative Investigators. 2002. "Risks and Benefits of Estrogen Plus Progestin in Healthy Postmenopausal Women: Principle Results from the Women's Health Initiative Randomized Controlled Trial." *Journal of the American Medical Association* 288:321–333.

Yoshida, Karen K. 1993. "Reshaping the Self: A Pendular Reconstruction of Self and Identity among Adults with Traumatic Spinal Cord Injury." *Sociology of Health and Illness* 15(2):217–245.

Young, Diony. 1982. *Changing Childbirth: Family Birth in the Hospital*. Rochester, N.Y.: Childbirth Graphics Ltd.

Yronwode, Althaea. 1999. "Intersex Individuals Dispute Wisdom of Surgery on Infants." *Synapse* 43(22) (University of California, San Francisco), March 11:3–5.

Zerubavel, Eviatar. 1991. *The Fine Line: Making Distinctions in Everyday Life*. New York: Free Press.

Zola, Irving K. 1987. "The Politicization of the Self-Help Movement." *Social Policy* Fall:32–33.

———. 1990. "Medicine as an Institution of Social Control." In *The Sociology of Health and Illness: Critical Perspectives*, ed. Peter Conrad and Rochelle Kern, 398–408. New York: St. Martin's Press.

Zucker, Kenneth J. 2002. "Intersexuality and Gender Identity Differentiation." *Journal of Pediatric Adolescence and Gynecology* 15:3–13.

Index

About the Author

Sharon E. Preves is an assistant professor of sociology at Hamline University. She teaches and conducts research on gender, medicine, sexuality, ethics, and identity. Preves has published several articles based on her life history research with thirty-seven intersexed adults, in the *Journal of Clinical Ethics*, *Intersex in the Age of Ethics*, *Current Sociology*, and *Signs: Journal of Women in Culture and Society*. She has also published her research on international female genital cutting with Elizabeth Boyle in *Law and Society Review*. Preves lives in St. Paul, Minnesota, with her extraordinary spouse and four cats.